SLAVES IN RED COATS

Regimental Color, Fourth West India Regiment, 1795

SLAVES IN RED COATS

THE BRITISH WEST INDIA REGIMENTS, 1795–1815

ROGER NORMAN BUCKLEY

NEW HAVEN AND LONDON
YALE UNIVERSITY PRESS
1979

To

Wilhelmina Wagner Buckley

with

Love and Affection

Published with assistance from
the Louis Stern Memorial Fund.

Designed by Sally Harris
and set in IBM Journal Roman type.
Printed in the United States of America by
The Book Press, Inc., Brattleboro, Vermont.

Published in Great Britain, Europe, Africa,
and Asia (except Japan) by Yale University
Press, Ltd., London. Distributed in Aus-
tralia and New Zealand by Book & Film Ser-
vices, Artarmon, N.S.W., Australia; and in
Japan by Harper & Row, Publishers, Tokyo
Office.

Library of Congress Cataloging in Publication
Data

Buckley, Roger Norman, 1937–
    Slaves in red coats.

    Bibliography: p.
    Includes index.
    1. Slavery in the British West Indies.
2. Great Britain. Army—Colonial forces—
West Indies, British History. 3. Soldiers,
Black—West Indies, British—History. I. Title.
HT1091.B77   355.3'52   78–16830
ISBN 0–300–02216–6

CONTENTS

ILLUSTRATIONS AND TABLES

PREFACE

Warfare between European powers in the Caribbean was endemic for more than three centuries after Columbus's historic landfall. With the advent of African plantation slavery during the first half of the sixteenth century, the military potential of slaves was immediately recognized and quickly exploited by the rival nations. All over the Caribbean world blacks were employed as service troops and even as front-line soldiers. Indeed, with white immigration largely discouraged by the plantation system, expanding Negro slavery, and a deadly climate, the military use of slave labor rapidly became indispensable to West Indian warfare. To accommodate such a need, dramatic modifications of the slave order were instituted, such as the widespread manumission of slave soldiers. In the British West Indies during the tumultuous period of the French Revolution and the Napoleonic Wars, an unprecedented step was taken in the establishment, in 1795, of an entire large, standing slave army uniformed, armed, and trained along European lines.

In his *Fall of the Planter Class in the British Caribbean, 1763–1833*, Lowell J. Ragatz notes that the creation of imperial regiments of armed blacks to conserve the slave system marked the beginning of a new era in interracial relations. The measure dramatically underscored divergent imperial and colonial views on colonial government and defense and had a substantial effect on local race relations. During this period slaves were also being armed in unprecedented numbers all over the West Indies and throughout the North American mainland, North and South. Yet, with some notable exceptions, such as Professor Benjamin Quarles's investigations into the black role in the American Revolution and the Civil War, the broad question of war and slavery has elicited comparatively little response from historians. The large collection of important War Office, Colonial Office, Treasury, and Audit Office papers at the Public Record Office, London, remains virtually untouched. (The present study is, however, based for the most part on Public Record Office manuscript records.) The primary reasons for the lack of interest are threefold: (1) a traditional disinterest in the West Indies among British military historians, notwithstanding the vast treasure Britain lavished on the region, particularly during the seventeenth and eighteenth centuries; (2) the preoccupation of social scientists with the economic and social aspects of plantation slavery; and (3) a general disinterest in military history and the military as an institution among academic historians. The French, however, have not been so inattentive. De Poyen's *Les Guerres des Antilles de 1793 à 1815* was published in 1896; and Nemours, a Haitian, published his *Histoire militaire de la Guerre d'Indépendance de Saint-Domingue* between 1925 and 1928.

The present study, which is based on a doctoral dissertation submitted to McGill University in 1975, attempts to explore the effects of war on slavery by focusing on the British government's controversial decision of 1795 to defend its West Indian possessions with regiments of slaves—initially Creoles but subsequently and predominantly blacks born in Africa. The subject of the study then is the West India Regiments, Britain's prototype African army. Their development is examined in the context of the accelerating Africanization that was occurring in British West Indian society, an increasingly differentiated society in which more and more of the skilled functions were being filled by blacks, both slave and free. Revolutionary wars served as the catalyst for this enormous expansion of the black role.

The contextual framework of this study also includes the British Abolitionist movement, the French Revolution and Napoleonic Wars in the West Indies, and what might be termed the intermediate stage of British imperial expansion in West Africa. Finally, as a minor theme, I shall attempt to broaden our imperfect understanding of the impact of the British garrison in the West Indies, an important subject that has yet to attract the academic attention it deserves.

The focus of this study is a unique form of slavery—military slavery, the systematic preparation and employment of slaves as professional soldiers. In the informed opinion of Daniel Pipes, military slavery was the mainstay of Islamic armies for more than a thousand years, from the eighth to the nineteenth centuries. Pipes argues convincingly that as professional troops Islamic slave soldiers were unique, unlike the slaves that served a largely auxiliary role in the ancient armies of India, Greece, and Rome.*

The professionalism of the Islamic slaves does closely resemble that of Britain's West Indian soldiers, and it is reasonable to assume that it served as a model. Both systems, for example, stressed the importance of recruiting highly susceptible youths, although Muslim recruiters were apparently more successful at purchasing teenagers and even twelve-year-old boys. For the same reason, both systems placed a premium on alien recruits. For the Muslim recruiter, this meant a non-Muslim from *Dār al-Harb*—those areas of the world not under Islamic control—while the English recruiter preferred blacks born in Africa, who, ignorant of the language and customs of the country in which they were to serve, would be wholly dependent on their white officers and comrades-in-arms. In addition, each recruit was subjected to an intensive indoctrination designed to imbue loyalty and eradicate all vestiges of foreign loyalties, even primordial tribal links. As professional soldiers, both non-Muslim and African were forged into instruments with no competing interests; all skills and efforts were channeled toward year-round military service. The results were intensely loyal individuals who enjoyed the respect and power of soldiers. Although slaves, they bore arms and were visibly and indispensably part of the ruling elite.

Of course, there were profound differences between Islamic and British military slavery. Islamic military service, for instance, provided the intellectually promising slave with an education and the mobility to attain officer status and even governmental work. It is not surprising, therefore, to read that certain slave-soldiers became special envoys, top administrators, and even provincial governors. Some held high military command, while others climbed to the pinnacle of political

*I am indebted to Daniel Pipes for the following comments on Islamic military slavery. See his "Origins of Islamic Military Slavery" (Ph.D. diss., Harvard University, 1978).

power. Sometimes, when Islamic military slaves acquired too much power, which they did with startling frequency, they resorted to self-manumission. Their status as professional soldiers and their comrades in high government positions naturally facilitated such bold actions.

By contrast, the British military slave was both professionally and socially immobile. The rigidity of slave society in the British Caribbean, the unbridgeable social chasm between black and white (including metropolitan whites), and the lack of personal ties to individuals in political power prevented the black soldier from aspiring to any rank beyond that of senior noncommissioned officer. Nonetheless the African proved a loyal and disciplined professional soldier; no doubt the daily brutal reminders of an insular plantation-slave society made him constantly aware of the vastly superior status he enjoyed as a British soldier.

The special status of military slavery should further our understanding of slavery as a diversified institution. Typically, of course, the slave was oppressed, debased, and required to perform menial and despised tasks. Even so, slavery was not an undifferentiated or inflexible institution that condemned all to a wretched and servile existence; there were, for example, socioeconomic divisions among estate slaves in the Caribbean and a certain degree of mobility within this structure. Military enslavement was perhaps the most important variation, as it permitted comparatively large numbers of slaves to follow responsible careers, far removed from the horrors commonly associated with slavery, particularly chattel slavery as practiced in the New World.

As expected, there are many debts to be acknowledged in a work of this sort. Professor Hereward Senior of McGill University suggested the topic and provided advice and helpful criticism along the long way; Professor David Brion Davis, Yale University, took time from his very busy schedule to read a part of the manuscript and to give me vital leads to sources. The support of the Faculty of Graduate Studies and Research at McGill University, which supplied me on several occasions with the financial assistance necessary to complete research in Canada and the United Kingdom was invaluable, as was the assistance of Miss Hélène Bertrand of the McGill University Library who translated certain documents for me. My colleague at Vanier College,

Mary Alice Parsons, read the manuscript and recommended some important changes; and Captain D.C.M. Ormsby, First Battalion, Jamaica Regiment, provided certain hard-to-get records of the British garrison at Jamaica.

I owe a very special debt of gratitude to my wife, for her numerous contributions, but particularly for her assistance in the preparation of the tables and the several drafts of the manuscript and for her timely and incisive comments. Thanks are also owed to Professor Seymour Drescher, University of Pittsburgh, for his invaluable advice and encouragement, and, of course, to Daniel Pipes, who graciously provided me with excerpts from his research into Islamic military slavery.

I also acknowledge with thanks both the permission to use records in the following libraries and archives and the friendly assistance I received from officials in these institutions: McLennan Library and Inter-Library Loan, McGill University; Fraser-Hickson Library, Montreal; National Archives, Ottawa; William L. Clements Library, University of Michigan, Ann Arbor; Latin American Collection, University Libraries, University of Florida, Gainesville; Public Library, Port of Spain, Trinidad and Tobago; West India Reference Library and the Institute of Jamaica, Kingston; Scottish Record Office, Edinburgh; National Army Museum, the West India Committee Library, and the Royal Commission on Historical Manuscripts, London; and most important, the Public Record Office, London, which gave me permission to reprint the documents in Appendixes A, B, and C. The illustrations appear by the kind permission of the National Army Museum, London, and Gale and Polden Ltd., Aldershot.

Last but not least, I acknowledge my wonderful family, which I at times virtually abandoned during the six years I was engaged in researching, writing, and revising the original manuscript for publication. That they welcomed me back each and every time is a mark of their immense love, devotion, and understanding. I am a very grateful man.

Roger N. Buckley

Pointe Claire, Quebec
November 1977

ABBREVIATIONS

A.O.   Audit Office, Exchequer and Audit Department, Public Record Office, London.

C.O.   Colonial Office, Public Record Office, London.

H.O.   Home Office, Public Record Office, London.

P.M.G.   Paymaster General, Public Record Office, London.

T.   Treasury, Public Record Office, London.

W.O.   War Office, Public Record Office, London.

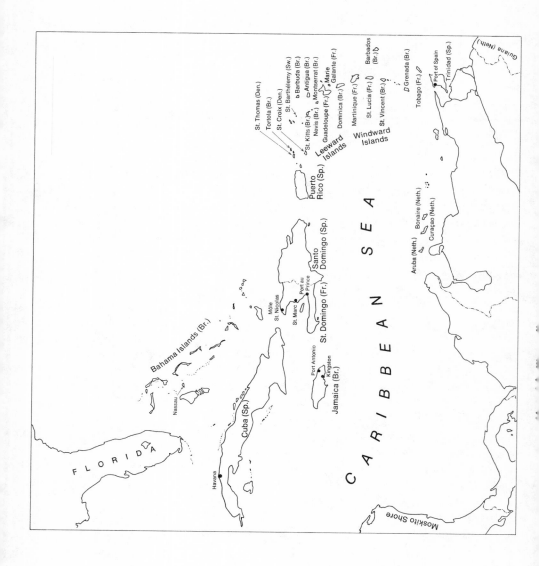

1

AFRICANS AND AFRICANIZATION

From the beginning of European colonial conquest in the New World, recruitment of non-European peoples for military service was common and necessary, not only during the initial conquest but for later protection and consolidation as well. American Indians were recruited as auxiliaries as early as 1519, when Hernando Cortés made decisive use of the Tlaxcalans in his war against the Aztec confederacy.[1] Later in the sixteenth century, as a result of the introduction of the plantation system and the subsequent failure of the policy of forced Indian labor in the Caribbean, African slave labor was utilized in various military projects. Early in the century, according to one source, slaves belonging to the king of Spain were employed to build fortifications on the island of Hispaniola.[2]

In 1635 the French enlisted a number of slaves at St. Kitts to fight against the English by promising them their liberty (which was never granted).[3] By the middle of the seventeenth century it was the universal practice in the West Indies to recruit slaves for a variety of military functions. Among the Portuguese and the Dutch it had also become customary to grant freedom to slaves used as soldiers, a practice that was later followed throughout the Caribbean.[4]

Although many European nations participated in the scramble for colonies, and although experience naturally varied from nation to nation and from region to region, some common factors encouraged the military employment of native Indians and, more successfully, African slaves. In addition to the size of the empires being forged, which required troops for their defense, a major factor was the scarcity of Europeans in the New World during the first two centuries of colonial settlement. Some regions of Latin America and the North American northeast Atlantic seaboard eventually attracted quite large white populations. Other areas—among them the British West Indies— did not. Largely as a result of the plantation-slave system (which quickly eliminated the small white farmer from the islands), an un- suitable climate for Europeans, and the nearly endemic yellow fever, the British islands never became an area favorable to European settle- ment. As a consequence, the African played a decisive military role there as well as serving his more familiar economic function in the development of the islands.

The conditions that led to British military use of African slaves were parallel to those experienced by other colonial nations.[5] A dwindling white population, coupled with the failure of the deficiency laws to maintain an acceptable black-white demographic ratio, made the induction of free blacks and coloreds into the colonial militia a practical necessity; by the middle of the eighteenth century the prac- tice had been adopted almost everywhere in the Caribbean.[6] The European wars of the late eighteenth century and the concomitant colonial struggles accelerated employment of blacks in both colonial and imperial military services in the British West Indies.

The recruitment of slaves, already considered indispensable to the success of military operations in the Caribbean by the close of the Seven Years' War,[7] resulted in what might be called Africanization of the entire British colonial military structure. The incorporation of blacks, both slave and free, into the British military in various capaci- ties was encouraged in 1662 by Charles II. To conciliate the good will of the troops in Jamaica and to urge them to cultivate the soil, he presented 300 slaves as a royal gift to the officers to be divided among them; some years later James II followed his brother's example. [8] The process was hastened by the limited size of the regular British army and the rigorous character of West Indian service.

Several crosscurrents adversely affected white recruitment during the eighteenth century. Economic restrictions on military spending, the absence of conscription, and the unpopularity of employing regu- lars to aid the civil power at home (as well as the unpopularity of lifetime service) prevented the maintenance of a British standing army large enough to satisfy expanding needs. Operationally, the use of soldiers as amphibious troops or as a corps of marines—particularly in the West Indies—further limited the number of men available for regular military duties. There was also successful competition for recruits from the metropolitan militia,[9] and many other potential soldiers were absorbed by the new factories established during these early years of the Industrial Revolution. Even debtor's prison, that traditional recruiting ground, ceased to be a supply depot by the 1770s.[10] In 1793 the entire regular British army numbered slightly fewer than 40,000 men.[11] Resorting to crimping and the payment of inflated bounties did little to swell the depleted ranks.

Moreover, West Indian service was in itself a deterrent to recruiting; it was rightly considered a death sentence by those destined to garrison the plantations. The need for troops in the Caribbean during the American Revolution, for example, became so desperate that recruiting teams scandalously plied their trade in Britain's jails. Felons, deserters, and even murderers were enlisted without inquiries into their crimes.[12] Once the Indies were reached, campaigning rapidly deteriorated into a life-and-death struggle against a debilitating climate, the usually fatal ravages of "yellow jack," and a shockingly inept central army administration. The latter alone added incalculably to the misery of the troops by producing a chaotic clothing system that sent out uniforms unsuited to the tropics and by permitting the issuance of new rum—a veritable poison. The situation was exacerbated by official acceptance of poor medical care and chaotically administered general hospitals whose systems of appointing surgeons and physicians were rife with abuses. The fate of thousands of British soldiers was sealed when the government unwisely sent newly raised regiments to the West Indies; they were composed largely of undisciplined men whose irregular habits frequently led to dissipation and death. Moreover, these unfortunate soldiers were often quartered in barracks constructed in low, swampy areas that were considered, even in the eighteenth century, to be unhealthy for Europeans.[13] West Indian expeditions, whether successful in achieving their objectives or not, were all characterized by the same grim feature: great loss of life, principally from disease.

Nor were reinforcements, which eventually included European mercenaries, the answer, for these "fresh troops" were similarly affected by climate and disease. Moreover, many soldiers sent from Britain never arrived in the Caribbean. One study shows that during the American Revolution, of the twelve regiments that embarked for the West Indies between October 1776 and February 1780—a total of 8,437 men—931 died in passage, an average 11 percent loss to each regiment.[14] Many of those who reached the West Indies were immediately sent back to Britain; either they were too young or were reluctantly rejected by commanders because of "extreme infirmities."[15]

Given the demographic character of West Indian society, it was logical that blacks be used to conserve the strength and thereby prolong the life—or so it was thought—of European soldiers. Early in the eighteenth century two slave "pioneers," military laborers, were attached permanently to each company of British infantry in the Jamaica garrison.[16] During the American Revolution, blacks hired out to the government by local planters built fortifications and were employed as porters to haul provisions.[17] The legislature of Antigua went so far as to agree to arm 1,000 of its slaves and to raise an additional corps of slave pioneers to perform fatigue duties for the regulars and the militia.[18] Efforts to recruit among the free black and colored population were periodically attempted, usually with poor results. Such men, who were successfully involved in a large number of trades and already liable for militia service as freemen, were naturally unwilling to accept the risk of enslavement if captured; most saw little personal advantage in imperial military service and were generally not recruitable.[19] Recruiting among free blacks in the North American colonies, however, was more successful. In 1779, in the colony of South Carolina, for example, the Black Carolina Corps was raised from among loyalists and free Negroes. After the British surrender at Yorktown this corps was distributed among several British islands; on the eve of the French Revolution, it numbered some 300 men, was quartered at Grenada, and consisted of pioneers, artificers, and a troop of dragoons.[20]

Thus, toward the close of the eighteenth century the use of blacks, both slave and free, as pioneers and artificers, infantrymen and cavalrymen was an established fact of colonial warfare in the West Indies. How then did Africanization of the British military fit into the larger pattern of development of West Indian society? The accelerating reliance on blacks, particularly slaves, can be viewed as an integral part of what Professor Elsa Goveia calls expanding Negro slavery: the heavy penetration of slaves into areas of economic activity other than estate-related labor that occurred near the end of the eighteenth century. Her study of the British Leeward Islands shows that nearly 50 percent of all fit adult slaves at Montserrat were employed as domestic servants or as tradesmen; the pattern held true for the British Caribbean as a whole.[21] A dwindling white population and the dislocations and demands of colonial wars were the generating forces behind increased mobility for the slave population. The dynamic slave system helped drive the poorer whites out of the mechanical trades, domestic services, fishing, huckstering, shopkeeping, and even the sedentary trades. As the century came to a close, slaves were increasingly in evidence in the towns, in the harbors, on board ships of the Royal Navy, in workshops, and in the military.

To be sure, the use of blacks in the lower grades of the British army produced measurable benefits to the service. Imperial troops were increasingly spared the drudgery and exhausting labors of fatigue work, although British sailors and artillerymen still shared with slave pioneers the arduous task of hauling and lifting heavy ordnance and stores in subtropical heat. Even so, British soldiers were frequently recorded as "sick in quarters," an appellation indicating incapacitated troops not judged ill enough to warrant the facilities of regimental or garrison hospitals. Nonetheless, returns continued to show appalling casualties among the Europeans.[22] Clearly the principle of Africanization of the British army had not yet been fully extended; the missing and essential ingredient was a standing black army. The corps of slave laborers and, particularly, the occasional contingent of free blacks were largely auxiliaries whose nonprofessional services could be used only for fixed periods of somewhat limited duration. There was a permanent need for such units, for the army's responsibilities were both civil and military, the latter continued almost unabated during peacetime. But even this solution would have failed to provide a panacea for the army's medical woes; only full Africanization was a significant remedy to a seemingly insoluble problem, and it was recognized as such by many officials at the time.[23] The real question

to be resolved then was how this indispensable feature of Africanization could be executed within a rigid slave society inextricably bound
by commerical imperatives and accompanying local defense needs.

In a period marked by the widespread practice of raising regiments
for rank, a practice motivated largely by the pecuniary and proprietary
rewards it bestowed on successful recruiters, it was not uncommon
for the War Office to receive proposals to raise nonwhite corps in the
West Indies. One such plan, received in 1788 from a regular army
officer, represented an approach to the problem of West Indian
defense. The regiment Captain John Gosling proposed to raise would
not only consist of free blacks and coloreds, but, most significantly,
it would be a permanent force. During peacetime it could either be
maintained as an infantry corps or converted into a labor battalion.[24]
Although his scheme was never adopted, Gosling's model was apparently not forgotten. The future West India Regiments were patterned
after the dual features of Gosling's proposed corps: they were permanent regiments, *and* they served concurrently as service corps.

Other models underscored vividly the value of a locally recruited
and permanent military force. The Black Carolina Corps was a nearby
reminder. The importance of this contingent, which was under the
command of regular army officers, was recognized all over the West
Indies; the governor of Antigua, for example, requested that fifty or
sixty black soldiers from this corps be attached to the garrison there.[25]
A much more distant example was the British East India Company's
Indian or sepoy regiments. Locally recruited sepoy troops even outnumbered the combined strength of European soldiers serving in both
imperial and Company regiments.

The creation of a standing indigenous army in the West Indies was
supported by other strong arguments. As mentioned above, the
regular British army was simply inadequate in numbers and in health
to meet the demands of West Indian defense toward the end of the
eighteenth century. There was, of course, the possibility that colonial
militias, West Indian and even North American, could take up the
slack created by the deficiencies of the regular army. In fact, the
precedent of using volunteer militiamen for overseas service had
already been established, with varying degrees of success. Barbadians

had, for instance, relieved Nevis and St. Kitts in 1666 and 1667, respectively. From the end of the seventeenth century through the period of King George's War (1740–1748), militiamen, albeit chiefly North American colonials, had taken part in expeditions to Nova Scotia, Quebec, Cape Breton, Florida, Havana, and Carthagena. They were encouraged to volunteer by the attractions of bounty money, land grants, high pay, prize money, and even plunder. With American independence in 1783, however, the principal reservoir of manpower dried up. West Indian militias, on the other hand, were no longer as adventuresome nor as cooperative in matters of imperial defense.[26] Dictated by a steadily declining white population, whose interests were essentially commercial and insular, West Indian militias adhered to a purely defensive role. Furthermore, because of poor training, numerous exemptions from service, and the light punishments meted out to offenders, West Indian militias were undisciplined and generally inefficient.[27]

One of the weightier arguments in favor of a black army was the apparent fact that blacks were not susceptible to the ravages of yellow fever, which was the curse of Europeans—at least those who had only recently arrived in the islands. As a result, early in the 1790s a degree of consensus emerged on the subject of Negro immunity to the disease. Prompted by a traditionally high death rate among British soldiers in the West Indies and an epidemic of yellow fever that reached as far as Philadelphia in 1793, assertions were made about the biological distinctiveness of the Negro. One physician suggested that blacks native to the Americas were susceptible to yellow fever, although at a lower rate than whites, and he called attention to a recent study by an English doctor, Robert Jackson. Jackson, who had been a doctor's assistant at Savanna la Mar, Jamaica, from 1774 to 1780, and who was to serve as a surgeon with the British army in St. Domingo in 1796, indicated that blacks born in Africa, as well as Creole blacks who had lived constantly in the West Indies, were not subject to the disease. Jackson's opinions must certainly have been known at the War Office, and they undoubtedly influenced the British government's later decision to raise permanent black regiments for service in the West Indies. In addition to his publications on yellow fever, Jackson may have been known at the War Office because of his promotion to the rank of army physician in 1794—the result of the personal intercession of the Duke of York who, in 1795, became the commander in chief of the British army.[28]

It is interesting that physicians, at a time when the principles of immunology were unknown, had in fact groped their way towards a reasonably accurate conclusion on racial differences in immunity. With yellow fever endemic in West Africa and nearly so in the West Indies, and with large proportions of both populations contracting it during childhood, survivors did acquire prolonged immunity or at least high resistance.[29] Of course, blacks did contract the disease, but the idea of their immunity faded from the minds of whites very slowly.

The egalitarian principles of the French Revolution did much to establish the character of the early phase of the war that broke out between Britain and France in February 1793. The revolutionary assumptions and the confusion in the French government created political division among the French planters in the Caribbean. The ideals and principles of revolution also made a deep and lasting impression on the mulattoes or coloreds and the vast slave population of the West Indies. Moreover, the vacillating behavior of the National Assembly in Paris, which several times granted and then withdrew full political equality for coloreds, aggravated the unstable situation on the French islands. A horrific three-sided civil war ensued, characterized by confusion, atrocities, and a kaleidoscope of changing alignments as Jacobin commissioners, and French, Spanish, and eventually British troops became enmeshed in the bitter struggle.

Violence in French-held St. Domingo (Haiti), only one day's sail from Jamaica, and similar disorders in Martinique, Guadeloupe, and St. Lucia, spread alarm throughout the British West Indies. Britain too had a large slave population and believed it necessary to increase its military forces in the Caribbean. Thus, before war had actually been declared by France, no fewer than nineteen British battalions—out of a total strength of eighty-one—were in the Caribbean or en route.[30] The volatile situation in the West Indies even induced the usually parsimonious Jamaica assembly to request an increase in its military establishment and to pay for these additional troops out of its own treasury.[31]

Even before France's declaration of war, Home Secretary Henry Dundas had entered into agreement with a number of French proprietors from St. Domingo. He agreed that during any war between Britain and France, St. Domingo, perhaps the most prized colonial possession in the world, would receive the protection of Britain. By the end of February 1793, Dundas had committed Britain's meager forces not only to an interventionist role in the rebellion in St. Domingo but to the conquest of French possessions to windward.

Early British operations in those areas produced indecisive results. A small force from Barbados, the seat of the Leeward and Windward Islands Command, captured tiny Tobago in April. However, a larger force of some 1,100 troops, including the Black Carolina Corps, failed to take Martinique in June. To the north, the Jamaica Command, which was responsible for the defense of the Bahamas, Bermuda, and the territory of British Honduras, on 9 September sent a ludicrously small contingent—about 700 men—against St. Domingo. Surprisingly, this force captured the town of Jeremie on 19 September and soon after took St. Nicolas and Cape Tiburon.[32] It is significant that, prior to the departure of this unit, news was received that Jacobin emissaries had been dispatched from France to infiltrate the British slave islands and to sow discord among the slaves by bringing to them the message and the meaning of the revolution. Moreover, the Jacobin commissioner at Cape Francois, St. Domingo, had on 29 August 1793, proclaimed the abolition of slavery. In February 1794, slavery was abolished in all French possessions.[33] Thus, despite British successes in December 1793, and in the spring of 1794, the initiative in the war had passed to revolutionary France. British troops sailed into St. Domingo waters and into those of other French Caribbean islands as the red-coated enforcers of the old slave order.

Nonetheless, efforts to make decisive gains moved apace. The defeat at Martinique prompted Dundas to prepare a major offensive against the French Leeward and Windward Islands in early August 1793. General Charles Grey, the commander of the expedition, sailed from Barbados in Februray 1794, with a force nearly 7,000 strong. The brilliantly combined naval and military campaigns resulted in rapid and stunning victories. By June of the same year the French West Indian empire was virtually liquidated.

Although British amphibious operations were standard, new dimensions had been added to Caribbean warfare. For one, the heaviest demands for slave labor were placed by both Britain and France. Military commanders and colonial governors were instructed from London of the urgency of raising a huge corps of slave laborers to act in conjunction with the army. Certain officers were even given plenipotentiary authority empowering them to buy as many slaves as they considered necessary. General Sir John Vaughan, who replaced Grey toward the end of 1794, was notified in unequivocal terms that the establishment of this slave corps was one of the most important tasks of his command.[34] Subsequent War Office regulations intensified the need for black laborers. Operating on the false, yet historic, assumption that continuous exertions in the West Indies invariably resulted in illness and death for Europeans, commissioned officers who embarked on service in the West Indies were ordered not to employ white soldiers on fatigues or as batmen. Instead, "fatigue negroes" or "fort negroes" were to be used. The number of servants used by each officer, for which he was allowed a monthly sum, was determined by rank: a field officer was entitled to three blacks; a captain two; and a subaltern one.[35] French officers too employed large numbers of blacks and mulattoes. The garrison that surrendered Martinique to Grey's army in March 1794 included a mulatto corps under the command of a mulatto general. And, according to British intelligence, the enemy force at Cayenne, French Guiana, was said to be comprised of about 1,000 European regulars and some 4,000 blacks and mulattoes.[36]

Another new feature of West Indian warfare occurred first on St. Domingo. Here the substantive involvement of the slave population not only transferred much of the fighting into the little-known interior of the colony, but it also transformed the struggle into a protracted and extensive guerrilla war. The small British invading force quickly found itself fighting a "war of posts" for which it was totally unprepared. Scattered, under-strength, and unsupported British detachments dressed in scarlet tunics, quickly proved no match for a numerous, intrepid, and inspired foe with the advantage of personal knowledge of the terrain. An identical war was soon to engulf several British possessions in the Caribbean.

Grey's speedy triumphs just as rapidly evolved into a continuous nightmare as he attempted to garrison the conquered colonies, particularly Martinique, Guadeloupe, and St. Lucia. With a force now numbering around 5,200 men, Grey was responsible for guarding all the British Leeward and Windward Islands, as well as for policing the hostile and unhealthful conquered territories.[37] He was also expected to support British operations in St. Domingo with troop reinforcements, which he somehow managed to do. But by mid-June, Grey was warning his superiors that unless he received reinforcements, the French conquests were in danger of being lost. In July, he reported that the situation had become critical, and that a force of no fewer than 11,500 troops was required to defend the islands under his charge.[38]

What were the causes of Grey's urgent demand for more soldiers? First, his army, which was rapidly dying out, was not being replaced. Because there was no conscription policy in Britain, many men who might have joined the regular army were being siphoned off by Britain's separate armies—the militia, Fencibles, and volunteers. As in earlier West Indian wars, many of the recruits sent were unfit for service. They arrived in exceedingly poor health and, wrote Grey, "only serve to fill the Hospitals and are sweeped [sic] away by the climate."[39] By the end of the first week in September he forwarded the startling news that in less than four weeks, his army had been reduced by another 1,359 men. Desperately he embodied the militias on the conquered islands. Even corps of resident British merchants and their employees were formed. A similar grim situation prevailed inside the British garrison at St. Domingo, and was accompanied by serious military reverses.[40]

A second cause for urgency was the continued warfare in the so-called conquered colonies. Although French garrisons had surrendered Martinique, St. Lucia, and Guadeloupe, segments of the slave populations in these islands continued to fight from bases within the interior. Like those in St. Domingo, these blacks were inspired by the revolutionary doctrine of French republicanism. Grey wrote dejectedly in September that all three islands were infested with what he derisively termed "brigands";[41] Guadeloupe, for instance, was estimated to have a considerable force of some 4,000 to 5,000 blacks under arms.[42] However, before Grey was able to carry through with his threat to bolster Britain's sagging position in the West Indies by whatever means available, he resigned his command in October 1794 and returned to England to answer charges of extorting property taken from captured French islands. He was replaced by Sir John Vaughan.

Vaughan, a veteran of the campaigns in the West Indies during the American Revolution, was convinced that only the establishment of regular and permanent regiments of blacks and coloreds could end the string of such British defeats as the loss of Guadeloupe in December 1794, which resulted in the capture of hundreds of Britain's best troops.[43] Toward the end of December, he began a sustained effort to raise permanent black regiments. On 22 December 1794, he wrote of his plan to the Duke of Portland, the new Home Secretary, in somewhat general terms:

> I am of the opinion that a corps of one thousand Men, composed of blacks and Mulattoes, and commanded by British Officers would render more essential service in the Country, than treble the number of Europeans who are unaccustomed to the Climate. And as the Enemy have adopted this Measure to recruit their Armies, I think we should pursue a similar plan to meet them on equal terms.[44]

In a later dispatch, Vaughan provided a more detailed description of his proposal. For a start, the initial corps he proposed to raise would be in every respect patterned after British line regiments. It would be divided into ten companies of one hundred men each, with the usual complement of officers and noncommissioned officers. The drafts for the regiment would be slaves, "the ablest and most Robust Negroes." They would be given to the British government as "Grants or Gifts" by all the British Leeward and Windward colonies, including recently captured Tobago, under quotas established for each island. If, somehow, the required number of slaves could not be obtained, the corps would be completed by enlisting free blacks "at a modest Bounty." Failing even this alternative, there was a contingency plan that, significantly, called for purchasing blacks from slave ships recently arrived from Africa. To leave no doubt as to the permanency of this corps, Vaughan insisted that "whether the War should continue, or Peace take Place, the Benefit to be derived from this Regiment . . . remain equally strong."[45] Vaughan reminded Dundas that what he was proposing already had a precedent in India; namely, the sepoy regiments. Dundas was also informed that Britain's critical position in the West Indies was the result of the military imbalance created by France's militarization of large numbers of blacks and coloreds. To correct this situation Britain had no alternative but to arm its own slaves. The war in the West Indies, Vaughan warned, could be waged only by "opposing Blacks to Blacks." He closed the dispatch on an ominous note:

> I am convinced that unless we can establish and procure the full Effects of such a Body of Men, to strengthen our own Troops, and to save them in a thousand situations, from Service, which in this Country will always destroy them, that the Army of Great Britain is inadequate to supply a sufficient Force to defend these Colonies.[46]

At the time Vaughan began to press for permission to raise the black regiment, which he offered to command personally, there were already prototypes in existence in the West Indies. Some were under immediate colonial control and others under the direct jurisdiction of the British army; but they were all, for one reason or another, of limited strategic value to the British army. Various slave-recruited ranger regiments were under the jurisdiction of the local assemblies. According to historian Thomas Coke—a close associate of John Wesley and considered the father of the Methodist missions in the West Indies—these corps were first raised on the island of Tortola soon after the start of the war. Because no regular force on this island was adequate to its defense, the governor of Tortola requested the Methodist missionaries on the island and the other Virgin Islands to arm their trustworthy slave parishioners and to place themselves in command. Impressed with the loyalty of these troops, the governor general of the Leeward Islands soon after directed the missionaries to prepare lists of all slaves attached to their stations who could be trusted to carry arms. Although Coke does not mention how many slaves were embodied, he does state that most of them eventually saw service in the Leeward Islands.[47]

By April 1795, nearly all the British islands had similar corps.[48] Antigua, for instance, reportedly had embodied 1,000 slaves by August 1795. St. Christopher raised 1,100, and the number eventually armed by this island exceeded the size of the militia.[49] Trained in the principles of light infantry tactics—hence the designation "ranger"—these troops were paid when mobilized, as in the example provided by Antigua's slave contingent. Bondsmen on this island earned one pence local currency per diem and their owners were paid an additional two pence local currency per slave each day.[50]

Although many of these units reached a high degree of proficiency, they were of limited military value to the British army because their use was confined to defense of their home islands. Ranger corps could not be removed from these colonies except by mutual agreement of both metropolitan and colonial governments.

One such occasion is worthy of special mention, not only because it illustrates the military importance of the ranger corps to the British army, but also because it provides a glimpse of an unusual aspect of British West Indian slavery. Early in 1797, Sir Ralph Abercromby, then British commander in the West Indies, wished to incorporate the Tobago Rangers into his expeditionary army, which was preparing for an attack on Puerto Rico. In a dispatch from the Committee of Correspondence of Tobago to the island's agent in London, the Tobago Assembly agreed to Abercromby's request; it could not, however, simply order these men off the island, for they had been embodied and armed "for the sole defence of the Colony, and under promise to be returned to their families at the expiration of the War." Nor could the slave soldiers simply be coerced into leaving. Instead

> The Corps were drawn up, and . . . it was explained to them the Nature of the Service they were to go upon, and the reason that induced their Masters to wish them to go on it; they all said they were not afraid to fight, and if they were killed they could not help it, but that they did not want to be sold, or to be King's Negroes, and that was the only objection they had to going; on being solemnly assured they were not, nor would not be sold, and

would return at the end of the Campaign, they gave three cheers, and all said they would cheerfully go & fight the french, except one Man rather advanced in Years, who said he did not wish to go, as he had four Children & did not like to leave them; he was excused and his Master was directed to furnish another in his place.[51]

It would appear that at least some military slaves had considerable influence, if not control, over their fates.

Ranger corps were also raised on the conquered French islands of Martinique and Guadeloupe in April 1794. Although later drafts were principally slaves, apparently most of the early recruits were free or emancipated blacks and coloreds. Many of the officers were French, and the pay of the troops was the same as British regulars and was drawn from Army Extraordinaries.[52] These units included Gaudin de Soter's Royal Island Rangers and Malcolm's Royal Rangers, which were raised in Martinique, and Drualt's Guadeloupe Rangers. Although they were imperial regiments, none of these units appeared on any British *Army List*, nor were their appointments and promotions cited in the official *London Gazette.* But the French ranger corps, like those from the British colonies, could not satisfy the Army's strategic requirements. They were raised as "provincial troops," and, while they could be used on expeditions to other islands, their home islands had first claim on their services, particularly in times of emergency. Moreover, these battalions were temporary establishments, corps raised only for the duration of the war.

Prototype units under the immediate command of the British army were the Black Carolina Corps and a number of black and colored provincial corps raised in St. Domingo during the early months of 1794. The latter contingents, "Corps de Chasseurs," were commanded not only by British officers, Creole whites, and adventurers from France, but were even led, in a few cases, by mulattoes and blacks. One of the black commanders was Jean Kina, who led a corps of 300 slaves.[53] By October of 1794, 3,600 blacks and mulattoes were embodied in British colonial legions as infantrymen, cavalrymen, and artillerymen.[54] Within a year, the number of blacks alone had risen to 2,630. Because the French had emancipated *their* slaves and armed them, Sir Adam Williamson, Governor of Jamaica (1791–1795), considered it "prudent to hold out something like it" to the growing number of slaves in British service on St. Domingo. As a result, slaves were enlisted for a fixed period of five years, at the expiration of which they were to be given their freedom. Slaves as well as brigands were enlisted under these conditions as early as September 1794. Although Dundas disagreed with the terms offered, Williamson assured him that at the end of the period of service few blacks would "be alive to partake of the terms now offered them."[55]

Yet again, even though the usefulness of these black and mulatto provincial corps was indisputable—because among other things, of their ability to undertake successful operations in the mountainous interior of the colony against the insurgents—there were certain restrictions on their deployment. As provincial corps, they could not be removed from the colony, and the five-year enlistment meant that these units were only a temporary establishment. In addition, the latent fear of British commanders in St. Domingo that their French blacks might desert was probably well justified, for blacks in French service had already been declared free, whereas those in British service had to wait five years. There was also the disquieting intelligence that French agents were already busy inciting Britain's black soldiers to desert.[56]

The year 1794 had begun with impressive victories. However, as it came to a close Britain was on the defensive in the West Indies and, in order to maintain her presence in the conquered territories, had been forced to bring into imperial service a number of black and mulatto provincial or irregular corps. Although of great value, these corps were of limited operational use. As Vaughan had prescribed in December, regiments of blacks established "in all Respects upon the same Footing as the marching Regiments," were needed by the British army.[57] The West Indian proprietors, however, who feared the strengthening of imperial, as opposed to colonial, sovereignty, that was inherent in Vaughan's scheme—and who also doubted the loyalty of these troops—used their great influence and leverage in Parliament to dissuade the government from sanctioning the plan.[58] Vaughan, in the meantime, had actually begun to augment Malcolm's and Soter's Rangers, which he intended, apparently, as the nucleus of his new black regiment. The new recruits were slaves obtained from planters in Martinique, and the cost was met by levying a tax on the entire colony.[59] But before Vaughan received Dundas's rejection of his plan, as well as an order to cease enlarging the two ranger corps, the disaster that had crippled the army in the conquered territories overtook British forces in their own islands.

What Fortescue described, somewhat fancifully, as a "Negro Revolt" broke out simultaneously in two British islands in March 1795. At Grenada on the evening of March 2 the slaves rose, captured the governor and some other whites, and massacred every white man at Grenville. The following month it was reported that there were large-scale defections among the plantation slaves and that the runaways were being trained and armed. By July, nearly all of the island's plantations had been destroyed by rampaging slaves.[60] At St. Vincent as well, during the early part of March, the Carib Indians in the northern part of the island had risen and were in the process of putting the torch to that area. In July, even Jamaica experienced a serious rebellion of the Trelawney Maroons that necessitated, among other measures, the raising of two companies of slaves to assist in crushing the rebellion.[61]

Nor was this the extent of the disaster. In addition to effectively exploiting the good will of their slave population by freeing them, the French landed a force of some 6,000 reinforcements at Guadeloupe in early January 1795. Small parties of these troops and their supplies managed to evade British cruisers and land on the coast of St. Lucia. Greatly assisted by rebelling slaves and some sympathetic whites, this motley force confined British units to just two posts by April; by June they had forced the total evacuation of the island.

To these defeats was added the continued diminution of British forces, in spite of reinforcements from England. All five of the regiments that arrived in April, for example, were unfit for active service and were of no practical value to the army. One of these regiments, the Forty-fifth, was composed of boys too weak even to bear arms; Vaughan dismissed it abruptly as unfit for service "in any climate." Indignantly, he considered it an injustice to be expected to produce military success with such soldiers, and he demanded instead reinforcements of veteran troops.[62]

The black rebellion in the British islands had resulted from abolition of slavery in the French islands, French military support, and the activities of both white and black Jacobins among the British slaves. In September 1794, before he resigned his command, Grey had warned London of this French activity.[63] It was William Wilberforce's belief that a British act abolishing only the slave trade in early 1795 would have countered successfully the effects of the French abolition decree of 1794. He argued, unreasonably I believe, that this action would have dissuaded many blacks in Guadeloupe, Grenada, and St. Vincent from joining what amounted to an anti-British or anti-slavery crusade.[64] This tack seems rather doubtful at best, for the abolition of the slave trade would not have changed the status of thousands of blacks already in bondage. Nevertheless, in what must have been a singularly embarrassing episode, the British army was forced to conduct operations against large numbers of rebellious slaves in the rugged, and largely unknown interiors of their own islands.[65] This revolution in West Indian warfare, which paralleled British military operations and experiences in the conquered French territories (and to Dutch military activities against the "Bush Negroes" in Guiana), posed acute problems for the British army.[66] Many years after the defeat of the slaves and the Carib Indians in the Windward Islands and the defeat of their own Maroons, Jamaica was still fearful of the possibility of an enemy occupying the vulnerable interior.[67]

The landing of the large French reinforcement in early January 1795, prompted Vaughan, on January 26, to renew his effort to obtain official sanction to raise a black or colored regiment. While he personally considered the arming of slaves a desperate measure, he continued his efforts to convince London of the urgent necessity to adopt his plan. When Dundas rejected his proposal in mid-April, Vaughan openly deplored a situation in which merchants and planters, rather than the military, influenced government policy and determined official decisions.[68] However, news of the deteriorating situation in St. Lucia and the extent of the insurrection in Grenada and St. Vincent reached London some time in early April and eventually convinced the government of the emergency in the West Indies and the necessity of raising black regiments. On April 17, faced with the imminent loss of several British islands, Dundas reluctantly authorized

Vaughan to raise two black regiments.[69] On the same day a dispatch was sent to Sir Adam Williamson in St. Domingo, informing him of Vaughan's instructions and empowering Williamson to raise a similar corps in St. Domingo—if the situation warranted it.[70] Vaughan received the directive only a few days before the British evacuation of St. Lucia on 19 June 1795. His efforts, nonetheless, appear to have been crowned with success: regular British regiments recruited with blacks were to be raised. They would be borne on Britain's military establishment and added to its *Army Lists*. The government's plan, however, was not in keeping with Vaughan's proposal, although Vaughan never lived to witness the difficulties that would surround the establishment of the future West India Regiments. Like countless thousands of Europeans, particularly British soldiers, he was claimed by the climate in July 1795. He was succeeded by General Paulus Irving.

2

PLANS, ACTIONS, AND REACTIONS

On 16 April 1795, the day before he wrote authorizing Vaughan and Williamson to raise regular corps of blacks and mulattoes in the West Indies, Dundas notified the Duke of York of the decision. As Commander in Chief of the British army–a post to which he was appointed in February and in which he was to prove himself a most able administrator, the Duke was requested to transmit the decision to the King and to obtain royal approval, a mere formality. Dundas admitted the usefulness of black troops in hot climates, where they could withstand the heat and military fatigues better than Europeans, and he noted their adeptness at pursuing insurgents. But, as he made clear on this occasion, the King's confidential servants considered the raising of these corps a politic but unprincipled action.[1] The emergency in the West Indies had impelled them to sanction a measure that under other circumstances would have never received their endorsement. Later, when colonial opposition sought to destroy the units, this official aversion proved significant.

Nonetheless, letters of service were issued authorizing the raising of two black regiments, and Major General John Whyte and Brigadier General William Myers were appointed their commanders.[2] The two regiments were placed on the British Establishment from the date of the appointment of these officers as colonels, and their commissions were gazetted on 2 May 1795:

A Regiment of Foot, Major-General John Whyte, from the 6th Foot to be Colonel

A Regiment of Foot, Brigadier William Myers, from the 15th Foot, to be Colonel[3]

The most important consideration in the selection of these officers was their West Indian service: "the knowledge they . . . possess of the habits and dispositions of the Negroes and Mulattoes, and of the nature of the operations for which they are destined."[4] So with this ordinary, terse military pronouncement that imperial regiments of blacks and mulattoes would help garrison Britain's precious sugar islands, the West India Regiments quietly came into existence.

As the seriousness of Britain's position in the West Indies continued to unfold in London with each succeeding dispatch, the British government was goaded into further action. In May, Dundas sanctioned the raising of four additional black regiments. A few months later, in September, two more "Corps of People of Colour & Negroes" were ordered, bringing the total number to eight. Following British practice, these corps were named after their commanding officers: Whyte's, Myers's, Howe's, Nicolls's, Keppel's, Whitelocke's, Lewes's and Skerrett's. In the *Army List* of March 1796, they were listed and indexed under the heading "Regiments raised to serve in the West Indies."[5]

What type of force did the War Office create as reflected by the establishment, recruitment, and conditions of service of this embryonic army? In accordance with Vaughan's plan, the black corps would be regular British regiments, commanded chiefly by British officers. Gazetted officers would have permanent rank in the British army and would receive half-pay upon reduction. Toward the end of 1798, a number of French émigrés from Guadeloupe, Martinique, and St. Domingo received temporary commissions in the Ninth, Tenth, Eleventh, and Twelfth West India Regiments,[6] which were former ranger corps.

At first thought, the policy of commissioning only Europeans is not unexpected; yet, the absence of black officers in the West India Regiments and the government's failure to enlist blacks as officers, was in fact a departure from current British practice in the islands (or at least in St. Domingo). Beginning in 1794, several black corps raised in the former French colony had black officers; some blacks, like Jean

Kina, even commanded their own regiments. These blacks and mulattoes were all regularly commissioned officers who received the usual army pay commensurate with their rank.[7]

Surely the reason for an all-white officer corps was not the paucity of experienced black soldiers in the British West Indies in 1795; for there were, on the contrary, quite a number of black veterans of the American Revolution in the Caribbean at the time. Many of these soldiers were members of the Black Carolina Corps and by 1795 most of them had more than fifteen years of military service. A case in point was Richard Durant, the only black recruited into the Fourth West India Regiment in 1795 and the first enlistment entry for that year in the regimental *Description and Succession Book.* At the time of his enlistment, 25 June 1795, at Martinique, the thirty-eight-year-old Durant, whose place of birth was listed as "America," had had sixteen years of military service. Because of this experience, he was appointed a sergeant in the Fourth.[8]

Several reasons have been suggested for this policy of exclusion. One was that free blacks, English- or French-speaking, were not interested in an uncertain career in imperial military service. Historically, as we have seen, the free black and colored population had good reasons for resisting recruitment. Moreover, few of them, even if willing to serve, could afford the purchase price of a commission in the British army.[9] In 1776, the cost of an ensign's commission in a line regiment, the lowest commissioned rank, was already £400 sterling.[10] A far more formidable obstacle, however, was the slave society in which these regiments were raised. Britain had already alarmed and antagonized its West Indian colonials by deciding to conserve and protect them by training and arming thousands of blacks. To local whites it was distressing enough that these corps were to be put on an equal footing with European regiments. (A group of whites at Jamaica, witnessing a detachment of black troops leading several pinioned white deserters, considered it a "revolting sight.")[11] But to commission blacks in the regular British regiments that were to garrison British islands would be bestowing on them a dignity and social elevation that was the guarded preserve of upper-class whites. Even Britons in Britain believed blacks did not possess the gifts needed for military leadership: namely, English manners, education, and the "way of thinking of gentlemen."

In the minds of Creole whites, blacks were at worst slaves and at best free men who should still suffer economic, social, and political restrictions. Not even the imperial government was willing to offer such an affront to its West Indian colonists. Only in the present century did blacks finally receive commissions in West India regiments.

The original establishment of the West India Regiments was fixed at ten battalion companies, each with a rank-and-file strength of ninety-five privates. In addition to the officer cadre, there was the usual regimental staff: a quartermaster, an adjutant, a surgeon and his assistant, and a chaplain.[12] The presence of the latter in a black corps is of particular interest, even though a chaplain, an Anglican clergyman, was attached to every English regiment. Yet the Church of England in the West Indies was a white man's church and remained so long after emancipation. This meant that although large numbers of slaves were baptized, they were given no instruction. Besides, the religious education of slaves was in fact looked upon with mistrust and fear in the colonies and was usually proscribed.[13]

It is not known if the British government had assessed the local situation and determined whether the chaplains of black regiments should carry out their duties perfunctorily, in conformity to local dictates, or should offer genuine instruction to black soldiers. (The attitudes of the Church hierarchy in Britain and of the Anglican clergy in the West Indies are also unknown). Nonetheless, the blacks in question were under the legal control and immediate supervision of the British army; and if the army's later efforts to ameliorate the condition of its black soldiers are indicative, then almost certainly the local ban on religious teaching for slaves was ignored and instruction was provided.[14]

Further examination of the organization of the black regiments reveals that they did not conform exactly to the organization of British line regiments. At the time these corps were raised in 1795, a typical line regiment consisted of eight battalion companies and two flank companies.[15] Flank companies were the specially trained and elite grenadier and light-infantry companies that were posted on the right and left sides, respectively, of a battalion drawn up in line. Line regiments were trained principally to fight in close order, and they were mainly effective in open and unrestricted terrain. The absence of flank companies from the original establishment of the West India Regiments suggests that these corps were light-infantry troops to be used in the mountainous and heavily wooded interiors of the islands.

Also included in the initial establishment were two troops of light dragoons or mounted infantry;[16] this unusual addition was recommended by General Whyte,[17] a colonel of one of the corps and a veteran of St. Domingo. The desire to add versatility and mobility to the black regiments was the result of the lessons gleaned from the war against the "brigands." Jamaica's war against the Maroons from 1795 to 1796 underscored the value of light dragoons in guerrilla warfare. This combination furthermore suggests a plan to form each of the black regiments into a kind of modern mini-division. This scheme, if it did exist, was never realized, for the proposed augmentation miscarried. In 1797, with the insurgent phase of the war nearly at an end, the troops of dragoons were dropped from the establishment of the West India Regiments.

Before passing on to the crucial recruiting plans, a brief comment on the significance of the overall size of this black force is in order. In 1795, excluding the white officers, an army of nearly 9,000 black soldiers was to be trained and equipped along European lines. Measured against the traditional size of white garrisons in the West Indies, this was an enormous force. It was about 2,000 short of the number Grey considered necessary to the defense of all the British Leeward and Windward Islands, including the conquered French colonies.[18] A force of this size, even if distributed among all British garrisons, would place a relatively large black contingent in each island. Such a large force was not permanently established, much to the untold misery of European troops dispatched to the Caribbean as a result. A black force of the projected size actually would have made the presence of a white garrison redundant; the only European presence needed would have been a token force of administrators and field officers. For incontrovertible reasons of health, humanitarian considerations, economy, and military efficiency, this was the only viable solution to West Indian service.

Yet, such a force never existed. Local whites and absentee proprietors nervously and angrily considered the clear implications of the

creation of a standing, slave, professional army in the West Indies.
Just the sheer size of the force was enough to arouse determined colonial resistance. Britain's difficulties in recruiting the black regiments
would quickly demonstrate how remote was the hope of ever over-
coming it.

By the end of the summer of 1795, War Office recruiting plans,
which were almost immediately modified to meet local conditions,
called for four black regiments to be raised in British West Indian
islands and four in St. Domingo.[19] Probably anticipating the serious
problem that would arise over the legal status of black soldiers,
Vaughan had reconsidered his original proposal of recruiting slaves
and recommended unsuccessfully that free blacks and coloreds be
enlisted instead.[20]

In the British Caribbean, slave recruits were to be procured by
inducing the islands to contribute a proportionate quota of their
slaves.[21] Governors of the islands were instructed to bring the entire
measure of raising black regiments before the attention of their
respective legislatures and to recommend "earnestly" the recruiting
plan decided on by London.[22] If the desired number of slaves were
not "granted" in this way, Vaughan was authorized to complete, at
his own discretion, the establishment of those regiments under his
command—either by purchasing slaves or by enlisting free blacks.[23] In
St. Domingo, Sir Adam Williamson was instructed to recruit his regiments along similar lines. According to Williamson's subsequent "l'Ordonnance de création des Corps Nègres du 26 Juin 1795," the
owners of slaves were to provide one slave for every fifteen they
owned. Other provisions would be arranged at a later date for proprietors who had fewer than the requisite number. Recruits were to be
selected by their owners, and only those who were too old or too
weak to bear arms could be refused. Unlike their counterparts in the
British islands, proprietors in St. Domingo were to be reimbursed.
The method of reimbursement established was as follows: one-third
of the appraised value of each slave at the time of enlistment; one-
third six months later; and the final third a year later. This method of
indemnification was the same used to recruit the black colonial legions,
the "Corps de Chasseurs," in St. Domingo in 1794.[24]

The conditions of service for the new recruits, however, were greatly inferior to those of the various "Corps de Chasseurs," alongside whom West India soldiers were expected to serve. The slaves taken into British service in St. Domingo earlier were enlisted for a fixed period of five years, after which they were to be "ipso facto enfranchised." The new recruits would be enlisted for an indefinite period; according to the Duke of Portland, it would be left to "His Majesty to discharge them when it should be judged proper."[25] Although it was the universal practice in West Indian warfare to reward slaves who had won military distinctions by granting them freedom, and even though Britain had followed this practice on a relatively large scale in St. Domingo, Dundas was inflexible in refusing to remunerate West India soldiers in this fashion. He underscored this point in a dispatch to Vaughan:

> But I cannot help intimating to you the absolute necessity of avoiding forming any eventual engagements with Persons who have not previously acquired their liberty, which might lead them to an expectation of future Emancipation, as a Reward for their Military Services:[26]

The explanation for this departure from practice, according to Dundas, was that

> any ill timed encouragement of this nature, and more especially, if it terminated in a disappointment, would give rise to the most serious evils, and, independently of the great alarm which it would excite among the Planters, might be considered by the Negroes themselves, as a concession made by necessity, in imitation of the French, and as the first step towards those dangerous expedients to which the Enemy have had recourse in order to encrease their Forces in that quarter of the World.[27]

Instead of emancipation, Dundas said, the fidelity of these troops would be ensured by promises of pecuniary rewards or small grants of land in the conquered islands at the end of the war.

In stating these reasons, Dundas had omitted two other more important reasons for the government's refusal to enfranchise (at this point) its black soldiers. A large number of slaves had already been enlisted into British military service on this condition; 2,000 to 3,000 men were, as we have seen, under arms as rangers in St. Domingo. Recruiting the West India Regiments on a similar basis would yield a force of almost 12,000 blacks, about 4,500 of them from the British islands. A large number of former slaves would therefore have to be reabsorbed into the slave islands, British as well as French, as freedmen. Moreover, these blacks would have had military training and experience. It is certain that Dundas was referring to this dreaded outcome when he warned Vaughan of the alarm and excitement the emancipation of thousands of black soldiers would cause among the proprietors.

Williamson, in spite of Dundas's instructions, proceeded to raise his corps by enlisting recruits for a period of five years, with the promise of freedom on completion of the term.[28] As blacks formerly in French service had enlisted as freedmen beginning around 1794 and as slaves already in British service in St. Domingo had at least the promise of freedom at the end of a fixed period, Williamson had no other alternative. The French declaration of emancipation in 1794, the confused situation in St. Domingo, and Britain's tenuous military presence there had resulted in a situation in which coercion as a recruiting device was not possible.

Nonetheless, Dundas was insistent. His attitude, which accurately reflected the wishes of the British planters, had not changed since 1794, when Williamson began recruiting slaves on this basis.[29] Even Portland complained that official recruitment instructions had not been followed.[30] Williamson's subsequent recall and replacement by General Forbes was almost certainly in large measure due to Dundas's reaction to Williamson's ordinance. It would appear that the later suspension of recruitment for Howe's and Keppel's regiments in St. Domingo and the ordering of these corps to Jamaica to complete their establishments with slaves granted by the Assembly,[31] was also the result of Dundas's opposition. Forbes, however, pointing to the other black regiments still in the colony, advised Dundas that it would be unwise and perhaps dangerous to alter Williamson's recruiting measures. He warned that the inducements were the only means of maintaining Britain's position, which was already "extremely critical" because of the French Convention's abolition decree, of which every black in the colony was aware.[32] Dundas apparently heeded Forbes's caution and permitted the remaining two regiments to recruit under the same conditions as before.

Vaughan's idea of a West India regiment was a regular British regiment established on a permanent footing for garrison service in the West Indies. Such units should be a combination of general service regiments, for they were to be permanent corps, and fencible regiments—that is, they were to be raised specifically for service in the West Indies.[33] The Twentieth or Jamaica Light Dragoons, which consisted of a headquarters detachment and four troops about 140 strong, arrived at Jamaica in June 1792, and it may well have served as Vaughan's model and inspiration. The Twentieth was a permanent corps recruited in Britain especially for service in Jamaica; it was borne completely on the Jamaica Establishment.[34] The black corps, however, according to War Office dispatches, were initially seen as strictly fencible units, temporary corps "formed for Service in the West Indies."[35] Evidence on this point is inconclusive, but it appears that the West India Regiments were not considered permanent troops of the type envisioned by Vaughan until early in 1797.[36] As late as November 1796, for example, the Duke of York was still recommending to the King that a number of permanent black regiments should be kept in British service.[37]

The origins of British fencible regiments can be traced to first such corps, raised in Scotland in 1759 during the Seven Years' War. At the time, Scotland had no militia, and a large part of the regular army was required for service abroad. Between 1759 and 1802 some 109 fencible regiments, infantry and cavalry, were embodied throughout the British Isles.[38] In 1789 the principle was extended to the colonies. That year a small corps of approximately 300 troops was raised for the protection of a penal settlement recently established at Port Jackson, New South Wales. Two years later a similar corps was formed for service in Upper Canada, and during 1794 a single independent company was raised for service in West Africa. The following year, when the West India Regiments were being raised, a fencible regiment of infantry was recruited for service in Newfoundland and North America.[39]

Although all the black regiments were originally established as fencible infantry, some of them were raised for localized service, which meant that they would be attached to the garrisons of particular islands for the war's duration. Others were general service regiments, units that could be employed on operations anywhere in the Caribbean. The corps originally raised in St. Domingo fit the former description, as stated in Article III of "l'Ordonnance de création des corps Nègres":

> Ces Corps de Nègres seront attachés à la Colonie, & ne pourront jamais en être distraits pour être employés ailleurs: Ils pourront seulement, d'après nos ordres, se porter dans toutes les parties de l'Isle où le bien du service l'exigera.[40]

As a result of Dundas's disagreement with Williamson, two of these regiments were ordered to Jamaica. General Forbes and Earl Balcarres, who became governor of Jamaica in 1795, were now instructed that unless it was necessary to attach one of them to Jamaica's garrison for the remainder of the war, both of the black regiments were to be free to serve anywhere in the West Indies.[41] The regiments of Myers, Whyte, and Skerrett were initially general service corps,[42] but two months after Skerrett's appointment, his corps was reassigned to service at St. Vincent.[43] A great deal of uncertainty surrounds Whitelocke's Regiment. Because it was recruited in Jamaica and later at British Honduras, it is thought that this corps too was originally intended for general service.

The major consideration determining the type of service to which the black regiments were assigned in 1795 was the state of military operations in the embattled colonies. Originally the government deployed four regiments at St. Domingo, partly because of the value of the colony and its proximity to Jamaica. The critical situation on St. Vincent lay behind the attachment of Skerrett's Regiment to that garrison. The other regiments, according to military jargon then in use, were to act as a "disposable force" or, in conjunction with European troops, as an expeditionary force.

Other important issues concerned the size of this black West India army and its proportional distribution among the various British garrisons. It is surprising, in view of the controversy surrounding the decision to raise regular slave regiments to guard the sugar islands, that no clear policy on these matters was formulated until almost four years after their establishment. As late as November 1796, the Duke of York wrote to George III, indicating that "it is wished" that 5,000 black troops could be under arms in the Leeward Islands, Jamaica, and St. Domingo.[44] Official regulations, however, were not forthcoming until January 1799, when it was decided that one-third of the total British force in the West Indies would consist of black soldiers. In each garrison where blacks would be quartered, the ratio of one-third black to two-thirds white was to apply.[45]

The black regiments were given several designations before the title "West India Regiments" was universally adopted. Collectively they were often officially referred to as "Corps" or "Regiments of People of Colour and Negroes."[46] Individual regiments were identified frequently by the name of the commanding officer; the latter designation appears in the *Army Lists* of 1796, 1797, and 1798, and in the *London Gazette.* In the West Indies itself they were immediately styled "West India Regiments," and muster-roll records and other War Office papers make use of this title.[47] In 1798, other designations were finally discontinued;[48] the *Army List* of 1799 indexes these corps under "West India Regiments." The semi-official numbering system in use in 1795 was based on the date of each commanding officer's appointment:[49]

First West India Regiment of Foot—Colonel John Whyte 24 April 1795

Second West India Regiment of Foot—Colonel William Myers 24 April 1795

Third West India Regiment of Foot—Colonel William Keppel 20 May 1795

Fourth West India Regiment of Foot—Colonel Oliver Nicolls 20 May 1795

Fifth West India Regiment of Foot—Colonel Stephen Howe 20 May 1795

Sixth West India Regiment of Foot—Colonel John Whitelocke 1 September 1795

Seventh West India Regiment of Foot—Lieutenant-Colonel John Lewes 15 September 1795

Eighth West India Regiment of Foot—Lieutenant-Colonel John
   Skerrett   15 September 1795

Alterations of the original War Office recruiting plans produced no
significant changes. It was decided that only two West India Regiments,
the Fourth and the Seventh, were to be raised in St. Domingo. The
rest were to be recruited in the British Caribbean, but not necessarily,
as it turned out, from among "English blacks" or even Creole blacks.
Jamaica was to supply the rank-and-file for the Third and the Fifth,
while the Leeward and Windward Islands were responsible for raising
the First, Second, Sixth, and Eighth West India Regiments.

A major source of information on the recruiting of the West India
Regiments are the regimental *Description and Succession Books.*
These records—one of a number of regimental, company, quartermaster, and paymaster books kept by every British regiment—provide
biographical data on the officers, noncommissioned officers, and the
rank-and-file. When completed according to regulation, they contained the name, physical description, age, place of birth, trade, and
enlistment and service-record information of every soldier and officer
who served with the regiment. Unfortunately, not one of these price-
less documents is complete for the period under study.[50]

The surviving books, nonetheless, show that the nucleus of each
West India Regiment was a group of European sergeants, corporals,
and drummers. Even a few of the rank-and-file were Europeans.[51] Of
the first fifty-two enlistees recorded in the *Description and Succession
Book* of the Fourth West India Regiment, fifty-one were Europeans.
Enlistment information for only three of these men is missing. The
majority were Irish who came chiefly from Cork, Dublin, Tipperary,
Galway, and Waterford. Many had at least one year of military service,
while older sergeants had anywhere from eighteen to twenty-nine
years of experience.[52]

The officers who purchased commissions in the West India Regiments in 1795 were Europeans, and nearly all of them were taken on
the establishment of their respective corps in the British Isles. At
least half of the officers of the Fourth were born in Scotland and
Ireland. A few were Creole whites. Where information is furnished, as
in the case of the Fourth, they came mainly from Barbados.[53]

In attempting to complete the officer establishment of the West India Regiments to their prescribed strength, the army in the West Indies was confronted with a serious problem that plagued the entire British army at that time: officer absenteeism was common in the West India Regiments and remained so for the duration of the war against France. An early indication is seen in the raising of the First and Fourth regiments. Near the end of December 1795 a total of fifty-nine officers had received commissions in the First.[54] Although most of these commissions date from 1 July 1795,[55] only twelve of these men were present with their corps by the end of the year. Of the remaining forty-seven, the Colonel, Major General John Whyte, was in St. Domingo; eleven were listed as not having joined the regiment since their appointments; and nineteen others had been either reappointed to other regiments, sent back to former regiments, or had resigned. Ten men were apparently drowned on passage to the West Indies, had died or been killed, or were sick in quarters. The remaining seven were on official leave-of-absence.[56]

The Fourth West India Regiment was in a similar predicament. Although letters of service authorizing the raising of the regiment were issued in May 1795, a return dated November 11 lists only eleven commissioned officers as present. Twenty-five commissioned officers were listed as "on Board Transport at Cove [Ireland]," but ten others had not reported since being appointed. One of these, a captain, was "supposed" to be in the West Indies, while another captain was listed as incarcerated in an English jail.[57]

One of the principal reasons for absenteeism was the widespread practice of exchanging commissions. An officer might wish to exchange his commission for one in a different regiment because his own corps was ordered to an unhealthy or unpopular station such as the West Indies. Exchanging commissions was also an established means of gaining entrance to distinguished regiments. An officer in a West India Regiment might, for example, offer money to a prospective officer of equal rank who needed cash so badly he was willing to serve in a less-prominent regiment in an inhospitable tropical garrison. But even these officers, to judge from the unremitting efforts of the British command in the West Indies to persuade recalcitrant officers to join their regiments, were frequently a long time in coming or simply never appeared at all; in the latter case, they lost their commissions. Charles Oman, the historian of the Peninsular War, confirms that the system of exchange often involved commissions in West India Regiments. Accounting for the absenteeism of officers who had originally purchased commissions in the West India Regiments with the hope of exchanging them later, Oman states that it was possible for an officer to get established in a new regiment "without ever really having quitted home, or served in the corps into and out of which he had rapidly come or gone—on paper only."[58]

An aversion among officers to the measure of raising imperial regiments of blacks also contributed to absenteeism in the West India Regiments, even though senior officers were almost unanimous in their support of the plan. General William Dyott went so far as to recommend boldly an all-black garrison for the Caribbean.[59] But Dyott's views on West Indian defense were not shared by others, particularly, it seems, junior officers.[60] One veteran officer informed William Windham, then Secretary at War in Pitt's first administration, that he personally knew many officers who loathed service in the West India Regiments.[61] Similar contempt was reported by other officers.[62] The author of the popular and contemporary *Universal Military Dictionary in English and French* probably voiced the sentiments of many brother officers when he libeled these corps "dangerous battalions" and recommended that they be disbanded and the men distributed among white regiments as pioneers.[63] Perhaps Dr. George Pinckard, a regimental surgeon, was representative of many prospective and commissioned absentee officers who were not as opposed to the measure as that author but who did seriously question the wisdom of arming slaves and refused to participate in the experiment. At Barbados in December 1796, Pinckard, who was unalterably opposed to slavery, expressed his misgivings:

It is a measure which unquestionably provides a strong defence for the present exigency—but it admits of a question whether it may not be employing a temporary convenience to establish what may be found a future evil. May it not teach the slaves a fact which will not readily be forgotten: may they not learn that they are not only the most numerous, but also, the strongest party: in

short—may it not instruct them that they are men—and that a
single step might ensure to them the rights of their common
nature! Compared to slavery the restrictions of military discipline
are as exquisite freedom; and the negro who has once tasted it
cannot be expected to return quietly to the yoke, and again
expose his back to the whip.

Should the slaves once feel sensible of their power, the effect of
this assurance will not be retarded by an religious or moral consideration.[64]

Thus, for many reasons, and contrary to the conclusions of one
authority,[65] absenteeism remained a problem in black as well as white
regiments in the West Indies for the duration of the war.[66]

Yet officer absenteeism, serious as it was in itself, also reflected a
larger problem in the British army. The demands of the war for more
and more troops led to the creation of many new regiments. The
resulting proliferation of commissions enabled many men with little
genuine enthusiasm and few qualifications to attain military leadership, and the consequences for the British army were serious. The
negative effects were perhaps felt most acutely by the army in the
West Indies, where Britain was militarily preoccupied from about
1794 to 1797. This leadership crisis was described in rather blunt and
unequivocating language by Major General John Moore, the future and
famous Sir John Moore.

Moore arrived at Barbados in April 1796, as part of Sir Ralph
Abercromby's relief expedition. He served as the military governor of
St. Lucia from June 1796 to the time of his departure for England in
May 1797. Later, in 1798, he also became the colonel of the Ninth
West India Regiment.[67] Moore took up his post at St. Lucia soon after
Britain's reinvasion of the island in April 1796. Before long he was
openly and harshly criticizing the officers under his command. In a
letter to Abercromby written in September, Moore noted the low
morale of the officers and its consequences. He also mentions the
dubious means by which many of the undesirable ones had obtained
their commissions.

The Officers and men are dispirited, the former thinking only of getting home and framing excuses—in many instances the most shameful—to bring it about.

I fear the same fate (should the War continue) will attend whatever troops are sent out unless serious attention is paid to get proper Officers to put at the head of Regiments—who will reestablish discipline, and inspire those under them with some of that zeal and ardor, which I am not too young to have seen—but which you must recollect so much better to have existed in the Service. Such Officers, I am sure, still exist in the British Army, tho they are not to be found exclusively amongst those who have much money or most political interest.[68]

Soon Moore was writing again on the same subject. He complained of the "blockheads at the heads of Regiments," the "bad composition of the Officers," and the "degenerated" state of the army. In October 1796, he wrote dejectedly to his father that "most of the officers commanding the British Regiments, which fell to my lot, are the most indolent, ignorant and negligent men that ever were placed at the head of Corps."[69]

Moore was specifically concerned about the types of men obtaining commissions in the West India Regiments. His concern centered on the fact that the only soldiers under his command able to carry the war successfully to the insurgents in the interior of St. Lucia were the black troops.[70] In his letter to the military secretary of the Duke of York he gave his high assessment of these troops; but he also sent along a sharp warning and reminder:

[These] Corps should not be given to General Officers to make jobs of, but clothed by Government and given to Lt.-Colonels and Majors, who are to command and serve with them. These Officers must be chosen and possess certain qualities which render them peculiarly fit for such an Office.[71]

A month before his death Vaughan had recommended to Dundas that the officers as well as the rank-and-file of Soter's Corps and Malcolm's Rangers and the fit men of the Black Carolina Corps be drafted into the West India Regiments. Vaughan believed that these changes would hasten the discipline of the rangers and would also be an inducement for others to enlist.[72] His proposal received official approval, and Malcolm's Rangers and the Black Carolina Corps were both drafted into the First West India Regiment. Later, in 1798, Soter's Island Rangers was drafted as a body and became the Tenth West India Regiment, with Gaudin de Soter as its lieutenant-colonel. It took about three years to complete these transfers,[73] which established the precedent whereby other ranger corps, British and French, were similarly drafted.

In the process, it was disclosed that some of the soldiers in Soter's and Malcolm's Rangers were slaves belonging to proprietors on Martinique. Learning that the two ranger corps were being taken directly into imperial service as British regiments, the owners demanded that the government either pay the value of these slaves or return them. The governor of Martinique notified Portland that the amount owed was £8,600.[74] The manner in which this problem was settled illustrates clearly the considerable influence the colonial party exercised over the raising of the West India Regiments. The slaves in question would not be purchased outright; instead, they would continue to be hired out to the British government, under terms of service determined jointly by the army and the owners.[75] This arrangement, however, was unworkable, for the military needs of the colonies and the army, and the strategies that would satisfy each, were diametrically opposed. Two short years would confirm the futility of this venture.[76]

Not surprisingly, overall recruiting efforts were dismally unsuccessful. Although the drafts of rangers did permit the First and Second West India Regiments to take on some semblance of military formation, both were considerably understrength.[77] The other corps, with the notable exception of the Seventh, existed only on paper.[78] The Third only began recruiting at Jamaica around May 1796, and by December 1797, it had recorded just two drummers.[79] The *Description and Succession Book* of the Fifth West India Regiment shows ten enlistments before 1798: eight Europeans and two black Creoles.[80] The only bright spot was the Seventh: a total of 395 men were recruited in December 1795, at Barbados.[81]

While the British army was failing in its attempt to raise the West

India Regiments, the British cabinet, at a meeting in August 1795, was requesting more troops for West Indian service. Those in attendance, among them Pitt, Dundas, and Portland, requested no fewer than 27,000 "effective infantry" to undertake offensive operations in the Leeward Islands and St. Domingo; the famous Guard regiments were to provide 3,000 of these troops. The King agreed with Dundas's troop projections for the joint campaign but was adamant in his refusal to permit the Guards to perish in the West Indies. "The truth," the King rebuked Dundas, "is we attempt too many objects at the same time, and we forget for them that we must keep some force at home."[82] George III was correct in his criticism of the direction of Britain's war effort. The limited strength of the regular army was being diffused among several simultaneous campaigns, a counterproductive yet traditional policy that stemmed from the muddled and fragmented military administration.

"The West India Regiments . . . no way succeeded under the proposed Plan, not a Man having been given by any one of the Islands toward completing them."[83] Thus did the officer responsible for recruiting in the Windward and Leeward Islands describe, somewhat exaggeratedly, the recruiting fiasco to Dundas. Why, in view of imminent military disaster, did the British colonies so immediately, effectively, and nearly unanimously defeat the measure?

There were a number of peripheral reasons. The slowness of communication between England and the West Indies was partly responsible for the delay in implementing the plan in 1795. Governor Stanley of the Leeward Islands reported that he did not receive Portland's April 18 circular letter about the plan until 28 June 1795. By the middle of July he still had not received the details of the project. The governor of Tobago complained of an even longer delay.[84] These delays account to some extent for the poor recruiting results in 1795, but they do not explain the situation the following year, when all governors had been fully informed.

More important was the internal opposition to the scheme, which appears to have come from a small number of senior British officers directly involved in recruiting. Lieutenant General Henry Bowyer, future Commander in Chief of British forces in the West Indies, opposed the measure strongly. He thought the difficulties of raising the regiments could be removed and the recruits made serviceable by disbanding the black corps and attaching the men to white regiments. This modification was eminently acceptable to the colonial party. Nevertheless, Bowyer was quickly admonished by Dundas and told to get on with the job,[85] which he did, it seems, without further complaint. Opposition within the army ceased after this brief and candid exchange.

How important a motive was fear? Professor Goveia cites the terror conjured up in the minds of proprietors in the Leeward Islands by the scheme.[86] Similar fears were voiced by planters on Barbados and Tobago,[87] where recent experiences with the rangers had shown that arming slaves with muskets provided them with a knowledge and dignity inappropriate to field slaves. A British military governor expressed this alarm when he wrote that "A Negro is never of any use in the plantation after they [sic] have carried arms."[88] The army, which had initiated its own program of indoctrinating West India soldiers into the habit of self-esteem, naturally concurred.[89] Some, like the proprietors who anticipated a St. Domingo–style insurrection of soldiers and slaves in common cause, were genuinely anxious.[90]

This fear, however, was not always consistent with colonial practice. Brigadier General Thomas Hislop, colonel of the subsequently raised Eleventh West India Regiment and lieutenant governor of Trinidad, noted this inconsistency. He found it ironic that some of the most vociferous spokesmen representing the regiments as a threat to the security of the colonies—and even as contemptible in the eyes of the French—had only recently relied on the fidelity and expertness of slave rangers,[91] many of whom were now becoming West India soldiers. The French, moreover, far from holding black troops in disdain, had often strategically relied on black soldiers. The war measures taken by St. Kitts are illustrative of inconsistent colonial behavior. Some 1,168 slaves, including, remarkably, a small artillery contingent, were raised by this tiny Leeward island between 1795 and 1798.[92]

Regardless of the merits of these arguments, colonial opposition to recruitment had other, more important reasons. Chief among them was the intrinsic economic value of slaves, particularly healthy and robust males (those most desired by the army), to estate productivity. Slaves were a form of capital investment, they were multipurpose equipment; recruiting slaves constituted a forced liquidation of the planters' most flexible capital machinery. Other conditions increased the scarcity, and thus the worth, of slaves. Several thousand slaves had already been procured by the quartermaster general of the army as laborers,[93] and the insurrections of 1795–1796 and ensuing damages to plantations and losses among the slave population made proprietors exceedingly reluctant to part with their remaining bondsmen. Hiring out slaves to other planters was an important means by which Grenadian planters hoped to recover their losses. Wartime fluctuations of markets and prices and the additional burden of inflated customs duties on colonial produce entering Britain made the slaves essential to estate operations.[94] Little wonder then that Tobago, for example, went so far as to estimate the labor cost that would be lost annually to the island if its quota of slaves were met at £8,000.[95] The British Home Secretary was also warned that any slaves given up by the proprietors would make poor soldiers, since only the "refuse" would be offered to the army. The price of a healthy male slave at Tobago in 1795 was reputed to start at £80.[96]

The impact of this economic imperative on local war efforts meant a colonial affinity for slave units raised by local assemblies. This permitted the colonies to continue to employ soldier-slaves on the plantations until such time as they were needed for local defense; immediately afterward they could be re-employed in commercial activities. Permitting the government to use slaves in its regiments, on the other hand, would result in a corresponding decrease in the number of slaves available for planting, harvesting, and defense of plantations. Furthermore, it would be impossible to guarantee the return of these slaves once they had been taken off an island as part of an expeditionary force. Campaigns and garrison duties might combine to keep a corps away for a period of many months, even years. Major General Moore confirms the colonial preference for troops who could satisfy this dual role; on his return to England, he made the following entry in his diary on 8 June 1797, having observed two slave corps in St. Kitts:

> In St. Kitts besides the militia there are two corps of 500 each of Negroes embodied—composed of the trustiest and best slaves. . . . These corps are only called upon occasionally—at other times they work upon the habitations. The officers are the different proprietors. [97]

The question of the West Indian defense mirrored another, far larger issue that was beginning to divide Britain and its Caribbean colonies. More gradual and subtle than the confrontation over the black regiments—perhaps even unintended—was the government's initial effort to assert greater control over the colonial governments. At the end of the eighteenth century the initiative in everything related to the internal affairs of the islands resided with the local assemblies, and in Britain colonial governments were understood to function in this way. Nonetheless, the formal institutions within the colonies were designed to ensure that the real direction and regulation of colonial government lay with the representatives of the metropolitan government—the governors and the garrison commanders.

The weakness of the metropolitan government during this period was caused by at least two factors. First, the shock of the American Revolution had forced politicians in Britain to adopt a policy of caution and nonlegislative interference with its West Indian possessions. Parliament simply avoided passing laws that might offend the colonists' sensibilities. Second, although the governors were the direct representatives of the British government and were expected to support and promote actions originating in Britain, they had in fact become more the instruments of the colonial legislatures than of the imperial Parliament. This situation stemmed in large measure from the fact that by the end of the century, the majority of West Indian governors had themselves become the owners of estates, and as proprietors they shared a common dependence on West Indian merchants, which resulted in a community of outlook between themselves and the colonists. Moreover, the power of the governors was severely limited since the considerable powers given in their *Commission and Instructions* were not designed for continuous exercise but for use in cases of emergency only.

As the century came to an end, the roles of the British government and the colonies in colonial government slowly started to reverse. The initiative in colonial government gradually began to shift from the legislatures in the islands to Parliament. According to Dr. D. J. Murray, this reversal was the result of the pressure of the antislavery movement. He cites, for instance, the introduction of Crown Colony government into the newly conquered colonies, the creation of the Colonial Office in 1801, the reconstruction of government in the old British West Indian islands during the Napoleonic Wars, the abolition of the slave trade in 1807, and the emancipation of the slaves in 1833 as evidences that the initiative had passed to the government.[98] Although it is not mentioned by Dr. Murray, the government's decision to garrison the plantations with black regiments was an important episode in the contest for supremacy, and as such it was vigorously opposed by the colonies throughout the war.

Although the decision in 1795 to raise the West India Regiments produced no legislation to which the colonies could take exception, it did eventually lead to an act that has been all but overlooked by historians and that, along with those actions cited by Dr. Murray, underscores the British government's resolve to assume greater direction in colonial government. In 1807, twenty-six years before the emancipation of the slaves in the British West Indies, an act of Parliament declared the soldier-slaves of the West India Regiments to be freedmen.[99] Not only was the act in direct opposition to colonial efforts to bring black soldiers under the jurisdiction of the local slave laws, but, when the British government had considered this maneuver in 1801, even the law officers of the Crown had questioned its legality and inquired whether it "would not be an interference with the internal Legislation of the Colonies, which Parliament has of late not been disposed to exercise."[100]

In accordance with that late-eighteenth-century practice of non-interference in colonial governments, the imperial government had sought initially to create and maintain the West India Regiments with the assistance of the colonies. Nonetheless, the initiative to create the local black army came from Britain; and, when the colonies continued to refuse their assistance in raising this force, Britain unilaterally recruited the West India Regiments and distributed a considerable portion of the black troops to all the garrisons of the Caribbean.

Opponents of the government's growing assertiveness in colonial affairs could point to the establishment of the West India Regiments as a clear example of imperial meddling. The imperial plan to defend the West Indies with regiments of locally procured slaves did indeed strike deep at the basic economic, military, and political self-interests of the colonies. The colonists' reaction to the measure crippled the army's initial recruiting attempts, but, ironically, their successful obstruction guaranteed the eventual formation of truly effective West India Regiments.

3

THE JAMAICAN EXPERIENCE
AND THE POLICY OF PURCHASE

During 1797 and 1798, Jamaican planters successfully impeded the formation of the Sixth West India Regiment on the island. The story of how they did so provides a case study of the racial attitudes of a plantation slave society and illustrates some of the reasons for the escalating conflict between imperial and colonial influences.

In November of 1795, before the attempt to recruit the Sixth in Jamaica, Governor Balcarres, a professional soldier who learned his trade leading American Indian auxiliaries during the American Revolution, notified Dundas that the principal people on the island had rejected the British government's original request that a number of slaves be enlisted into one of the West India Regiments that were then recruiting in St. Domingo.[1] The reasons given for the refusal were Jamaica's contribution of slaves to the corps of pioneers, the Maroon War, and the expense of furnishing the slaves.[2] The news surprised no one in London, for Williamson had warned Portland in early July 1795 that Jamaica would refuse to raise any black corps "to be sent out of the Island." Williamson added that the government should not hope to enlist either slaves or free blacks there; if slaves were to be furnished by the planters, they would have to be purchased at exorbitant prices. Free blacks were unavailable because they were supposed to be serving in the militia.[3]

Nor was Balcarres's alternative recruiting plan well received. His suggestion to raise two regiments of 1,000 blacks each was rejected by both the government and the Jamaicans. Britain spurned the project because the proposed corps would be fencible regiments and therefore tied to the Jamaica garrison. The planters' objection probably rested on the fact that the slaves recruited would be rewarded with their freedom at the conclusion of their service.[4]

The failure to raise the Third and Fifth at Jamaica during 1796[5] did not discourage London from making a second attempt to raise a black regiment, this one to be composed of free blacks, free coloreds, and slaves. In December 1796, therefore, it was decided to station the Sixth West India Regiment at Jamaica, and the following month Balcarres was instructed to raise the Sixth as quickly as possible on a basis of "strictest economy."[6] Serious recruiting efforts did not get under way until April 1797, and they produced immediate opposition. At the end of the first week Balcarres reported that the Assembly was still opposed to the measure of raising a regiment on the island.[7] Toward the end of the month, on April 23, Brigadier General White-locke, the colonel of the Sixth, noted that Jamaicans were opposed to arming not only slaves but even emancipated blacks.[8] Exactly one month later Balcarres related a slightly different story to Portland; he claimed the colonists were even more opposed to arming free coloreds (as distinct from free blacks): "People of colour with Arms in their hands, are a more dangerous body than purchased Slaves. People of colour, they say, look up to Rights and Privileges; a Negro rather looks to indolence and a Red Feather."[9]

It was not surprising that the colonists were alarmed at the plan to arm free coloreds, for the latter were in direct economic, social, legal, and political competition with the white ruling class. Free men of color were free in the limited sense that they were not slaves; but they did not enjoy equality with whites. Not until 1830 were free coloreds declared equal with whites in civil and political rights. Before then, the legal and educational rights of free men of color were rigidly circumscribed, their political and civil rights were limited, and they were barred both legally and socially from the white community.[10] Alarmists at Jamaica pointed to the turmoil in the French islands and claimed that their social structures had been destroyed by the end of the free coloreds' subservient status. As Professor Goveia points out in discussing the Leeward Islands, the political and social subordination of free persons of color was considered a necessary bulwark of the slave system.[11] Writing to Portland, Balcarres acknowledged this belief: "the Policy of the Country very properly prevents People of colour from attaining too much power or property." Nonetheless, Balcarres's plan for the Sixth called for each company to be composed of twenty free coloreds or free blacks, twenty Creole slaves, and twenty "Ship Negroes."[12]

Local reaction was swift and hostile. In a report to the Speaker of the Assembly at the end of July, a committee of inquiry looking into the scheme to raise the Sixth noted, among other points, that the plan to integrate free coloreds, free blacks, and slaves was contrary to the policy of the island. The committee found that:

> The Distinction and Subordination of Ranks, by which the Peace, Good Order and Safety of this Island have hitherto in a great Measure been preserved, will be destroyed by the Adoption of this Plan.

Further,

> The Inhabitants of this Colony consist of Four Classes: Whites, Free People of Color having special Priviledges granted by Private Acts, Free People of Color not possessing such Priviledges, and Slaves. Hitherto all these Classes when employed in the Public Service have as far as it has been practicable been kept separate. We have in the Militia distinct Companies composed of Whites, of Browns, and of Blacks. Slaves are only employed as Pioneers or as Partymen. The Regiment of Color under Brigadier General Whitelocke is to be form'd as it appears to your Committee on a Footing of Equality, and on a System contrary to this Practice.[13]

As an alternate but unsuccessful solution aimed at conciliating the planters and ensuring the islands' subsistence payments, Whitelocke recommended that the Sixth be recruited principally from among Musquito Indians, with the addition of fifty or sixty "London Blacks."[14]

On 1 May 1797, the Commissioners of Public Account, an administrative body that supervised the financial administration of the island, resolved that because the rank-and-file of the Sixth were "not European Troops sent here for the protection of this Island, for whom alone this Board are of the opinion they are authorized to provide," the Assembly should not furnish subsistence or rations.[15] The commissioners, most of whom were assemblymen, were attempting to make a distinction between the Sixth West India Regiment and the white regiments of the island. They narrowly interpreted the phrase "His Majesty's Troops" and similar phrases contained in the title of the Jamaica Act, which regulated the British government's and Jamaica's mutual commitment to the defense of the island.[16] The commissioners, who were empowered to contract for the victualling of British troops quartered on the island, ordered the resolution inserted for one month in *the Royal Gazette, the St. Jago Gazette,* and *the Cornwall Chronicle.*[17]

"Subsistence" was the annual grant the Jamaica Assembly made toward the costs of imperial defense of the island; continuous friction between the government and the colonists had developed over the use of the money. By threatening to withhold the grant, the colonists hoped to coerce London into rescinding the measure, but Portland made it clear in his reply to Balcarres that the West India Regiments were indeed included in the Jamaica Act:

> All His Majesty's Troops are raised by virtue of the same Prerogative and are all subject to the same Laws and Regulations and that the West India Regiments are to all intents and purposes as much a part of the King's army as any other Regiment in His Majesty's Service.[18]

While this issue was being argued throughout May, June, and July, opposition was mounting. Portland was told that the entire island was aroused and that resolutions and remonstrances were being prepared everywhere. On May 29 the freeholders of St. John's Parish formally resolved that the raising of the Sixth was unconstitutional unless it gained local legislative approval. Three days later the grand jurors of the county of Middlesex, at a meeting held in Spanish Town, issued a public protest in which they predicted darkly that "the most calamitous events" would engulf the island if the government persisted in its efforts to raise the Sixth. The jurors called for "steady, vigorous, and united opposition" to the plan on the part of their representatives in the Assembly.[19]

While the colonists were marshalling their forces to prevent the raising of the Sixth, Balcarres was, ironically, complaining that he had an inadequate number of troops with which to defend the island. On June 20 he lamented that not only was he unable to furnish British regulars to guard Spanish prisoners-of-war at the Bath prison, but also that "not a Soldier" was available to protect the island windward of Kingston. "That very interesting part of the Island," he mused, "is left defenceless."[20] But in spite of this shortage of troops, Balcarres ordered the Sixth—which by then had a total rank-and-file of 108—to stop recruiting until the attorney general of the island had advised him about the legal details of purchasing slaves.[21]

In July the legal battle widened when the committee of inquiry, which had been looking into the constitutionality of arming slaves on the island, rendered the opinion that to do so was contrary to the island's annual Gunpowder Act.[22] According to this act, the giving, selling, or lending of gunpowder or firearms to slaves, with malicious design or "even without any evil intent," was prohibited. Both Balcarres and Portland, however, believed that the proviso to Section 5 of the act—which allowed a slave to be armed in the presence of the owner or an overseer, or "under the direction of such proprietor" —provided a legal basis on which slaves could be armed.[23] Although the proviso had been intended to preserve the traditional right of the planter in the British West Indies to arm his slaves as he saw fit, the clause permitted the British government several options.

First, by taking title to a slave through purchase from the current proprietor, the government, as the new owner, could legally arm the slave. This is precisely what Balcarres had been doing, and he reported that because of the intense opposition to the measure he had to be "uncommonly nice & correct as to obtaining the Title of the Slave."

Second, an unpurchased slave could be armed with the owner's permission or, as stipulated in the act, "under the direction of such proprietor." This precedent had already been established on other islands when slaves were hired out to the British army and armed as rangers. The attorney general of the island, however, found the restrictions of Section 5 "so comprehensive" that he could find no legal basis for the army to arm slaves on Jamaica. He also warned Balcarres that it would be "dangerous" for the government to attempt to employ the proviso.

Finally, the government could obtain title to a slave by purchasing him directly from a Guinea ship; and as the proprietor, the government could legally arm him. Resorting to this last method would, in effect, involve the government even more directly in the increasingly objectionable and controversial trade in human beings. Yet to London there were powerful arguments for doing exactly that. Direct purchase would save the delay and the costs involved with taking title from local proprietors; moreover, a seasoned Creole slave was more expensive than a comparable "Ship Negro." Of course, as Balcarres put it, the latter came off the ship "with only a Rag around him."[24]

Apparently Portland and other ministers also contemplated the manumission of prospective slave recruits before arming them as a means of circumventing the restrictions of the Gunpowder Act.[25] Balcarres, who personally disliked radical solutions to problems, forwarded to Portland a copy of the preamble of the Jamaica Act, which regulated the manumission of slaves on the island. According to the act, a slave could not be enfranchised until a "sufficient" portion of the money required to support him for the rest of his life was deposited with the church wardens of his owner's parish. The annual cost of providing for a freed slave was set at £5 local currency.[26] This maneuver was obviously not feasible and was never resorted to by the government. The cost of recruiting in this manner would have been not only exorbitant but wasteful as well; in addition to the purchase price, there would be the subsistence charges related to manumission, plus the normal military expenses of training, clothing, and paying the slave as a soldier.

However, in early June 1797, an effort was already underway to end the mounting tension and strained relations between the Jamaica Assembly and the British government. On June 6 Balcarres proposed to Portland that the 3,000 British soldiers the island was pledged to subsidize should all be white. In return, a considerable proportion of these troops would be completely maintained by Jamaica, without any expense to the British government. This plan, Balcarres continued, could take effect in 1799, by which time the island would be free from debt.[27] By the end of November, Balcarres's plan had widespread local support and had been fully developed. According to the resolutions passed by the Assembly on November 28, which appeared in *The Diary and Kingston Daily Advertiser* of 5 December 1797,

2,000 of the 3,000 white men in the British garrison were to be wholly subsidized by the island. If these troops could not be raised in the British Isles or in North America, they could be recruited from among "foreign European Protestants."[28] Many foreigners were already in British service in the several battalions of the Sixtieth Regiment and in certain emigrant regiments, notably German and Swiss corps, that were first taken into British pay in 1794.[29]

These 2,000 troops were to be permanently attached to Jamaica's garrison. At the conclusion of their service they were to remain on the island and be provided with small plots of land in the interior.[30] This last condition was an obvious attempt by local whites to solve two serious problems: their declining numbers, which was reflected in the militia, and protection of the vulnerable interior of the island from would-be invaders, runaways, and rebelling slaves. London's eventual acceptance of the plan in early May and the removal of the Sixth West India Regiment to Honduras by October 1798[31] marked a momentary but ignominious government retreat on the issue of racially mixed garrisons. The decision came not a day too soon, for after the British evacuation of St. Domingo near the end of the year, hundreds of St. Domingo slaves, some of them soldiers in the colonial legions of the island, flooded into Jamaica, much to the expressed horror of white Jamaicans.

The British government, by its April 1795 decision to raise West India Regiments, had finally recognized how invaluable was the service of black soldiers. No further delays could be permitted, for only these troops could successfully conduct certain critical operations. They were to save the lives of many Europeans by reducing drastically the need for white troops in the West Indies. Portland himself restated this argument to Balcarres with seemingly irreversible conviction in August 1797, after news had reached London of Jamaica's continuing refusal to cooperate in the raising of the Sixth:

> I . . . particularly feel myself called upon, to press this observation upon you, from the evident advantages which the Publick Service in general, and our West India Islands in particular, are at this moment deriving from the measure in question, which you may be well assured was not adopted on slight grounds, or with

confined or temporary views, but on a full consideration of what our West India Possessions may require hereafter as well as at present of what may be the probable extent and nature of the European Force, which can be applied to that Service and of the necessity of endeavouring to render that Force adequate to its various objects by the assistance of the West India Regiments now raising. In forming a Plan of general arrangement for this purpose it is not possible to appropriate a Force composed exclusively of Europeans to any particular Island because such a procedure would Militate against the very principle of the Plan itself, which by mixing Troops composed of Negroes and Men of Colour with our European Forces, is intended to give strength and efficacy to both, not merely in proportion to their numbers respectively but by a judicious combination of their Force which it is conceived when so composed must be infinitely superior to the same number of Europeans acting alone as heretofore and exposed for any length of time to the severity of that Climate, the Ravages of which have been too fatally experienced not to call upon Government to try every means to avoid or prevent the Troops from being exposed to in the future. His Majesty's Confidential Servants, therefore, cannot but feel that they should ill discharge the trust reposed in them if in deference to the respectable authorities by whom opinions are given and apprehensions are entertained which appear to them on the fullest investigation and consideration to be not well founded they were to abandon a measure, which unites the two most important objects that can come under their contemplation, namely, the preservation of the Health and Strength of His Majesty's Forces in the West Indies, and the Defence and Security of our Possessions in that Quarter of the World.[32]

Even though it was "not possible to appropriate a Force composed exclusively of Europeans to any particular Island," the following month Portland abruptly instructed Balcarres to accept any proposal from the inhabitants to raise and subsidize an all-European force for Jamaica's exclusive use![33] Moreover, when the British government found itself unable to raise the 2,000 men from Dutch and German troops, the Fourth and First Battalions of the Sixtieth Regiment were committed to the defense of one of the most unsalubrious garrisons in the Caribbean.[34] The principle of a racially mixed garrison was to be abandoned only in Jamaica,[35] but the British government was prepared to send hundreds of its soldiers to certain death to save money and to appease the sensibilities of the colonists. Such was the blind intransigence of the white Jamaicans that they too seemed little concerned that their insistence on an all-white garrison meant a gruesome death for many of these troops. Even bearing the total cost of these troops—according to one authority, an act unprecedented in British imperial history[36] —was not too high a price to pay.

The Fourth Battalion of the Sixtieth was already on the island when the Assembly agreed to accept it as part of its exclusive force in March 1799, and by October both battalions were in garrison. Their combined strength was 1,321, almost 700 men short of their prescribed establishment.[37] The departure of the Sixth West India Regiment, and the subsequent arrival and speedy removal of the Fifth West India Regiment—which had been reordered to Jamaica from St. Domingo[38] —eliminated for the moment the controversy over subsistence, arming, and manumission of slaves. The return for May 1799 is the last one showing black troops on the island.[39]

But Jamaica's victory was short lived. The Assembly soon began to haggle with London over the support of the two battalions. Balcarres, in a sudden lapse of memory, went so far as to argue that the plan to pay and subsidize an all-white force had originated with the British government rather than with the Assembly.[40] There were also fears of a slave insurrection and the imminent danger of an invasion from St. Domingo, with the result that both the colonists and the government agreed that there were too few imperial troops on the island. It was therefore decided in London that reinforcements, including a West India Regiment, should be sent to Jamaica, and the agreement of the Assembly to support its own force of 2,000 European troops was dissolved.[41] The Second West India Regiment came ashore amidst a renewed storm of verbal assaults and petitions from proprietors in Jamaica and London.[42] Balcarres, in an odd gesture of defeat (he was, after all, the representative of the imperial government), ruefully acknowledged that the principle of employing black soldiers to defend

Jamaica had become fixed. He speculated that blacks might also be used to man gunboats as a further and necessary means of defending the island.[43]

In the midst of the conflict, until its removal to Honduras, the Sixth West India Regiment was slowly being raised, although it remained under strength for a long period. The records for 1798 show the Sixth with a strength of about 200 men.[44]

Nevertheless, concession was still in the air. The government remained willing to appease Jamaicans by making an exception to its commitment to integrated garrisons, and it was quite content to reduce its own military expenditures, even at the certain expense of increased casualties. In early April 1802, Lord Hobart, the secretary of war in Addington's administration, instructed General Sir George Nugent, who had replaced Balcarres as governor, that black troops would remain on the island unless the Assembly agreed to support an all-white force. This time, however, the size of the force to be completely subsidized was to number 5,000 men, or whatever proportion thereof the government deemed necessary for the island's defense.[45] This suggestion—or, rather, threat—fell on deaf ears, for Jamaicans and other West Indian colonists were just then busily engaged in legal efforts to rid the Caribbean of the black regiments permanently.

In this entire episode there is a distinct hint of blackmail: the government would add black troops to the Jamaica garrison unless the local Assembly voted additional military funds. Clearly, London was using the threat of armed blacks to get what it could from the colonists, and it is hardly surprising that Jamaican acceptance of the radical plan of racially mixed imperial garrisons was painfully slow in coming. The dogged resistance to the scheme by Jamaica and the other islands was in no small way influenced by this counterproductive policy of imperial extortion, and the anger and hatred of the colonists would be lavished on those most visibly associated with the whole affair--the black soldiers.

Failure to raise the West India Regiments in 1795 spurred activity the following year. Beginning early in 1796, a number of resident blacks, unemployed lascars, and even several Portuguese were enlisted in Britain and shipped to the West Indies. However, as blacks in

Britain were also likely to shun military service, and as the recruitment of East Indian sailors ran afoul of the directors of the East India Company (whose vessels employed them), the effort provided few recruits.[46] In April, several hundred black pioneers in imperial service in the Caribbean were armed, in direct contravention of their conditions of service.[47]

More important was the British government's controversial alternative recruiting plan of October 1796 (and subsequent modifications of this scheme), which became the established method of raising and maintaining the West India Regiments until 1807. Henceforth recruits would be purchased slaves. This feature is explicit in Dundas's instructions to Abercromby of 28 October 1796:

> As it appears impossible to procure Negroes for these ... Corps except by purchasing them for Government, I am to signify to you His Majesty's pleasure that you are to authorize the officer commanding His Majesty's Forces in the Leeward Islands to procure in this manner the number that may be necessary for this purpose.[48]

Although the initial preference was for "old English Negroes," even as early as 1798 most of the men recruited were African-born slaves obtained through the efforts of specially commissioned merchants. The accessibility of this seemingly inexhaustible reservoir of manpower, as well as the lower purchase cost of "raw" as opposed to Creole blacks, encouraged this mode of recruitment. Also, buying African-born slaves had the distinct advantage of eliminating dependence on uncooperative and obstructive proprietors; and the efforts to avoid enlisting French-speaking blacks influenced by Jacobin ideas also fostered the purchase of slaves newly imported from Africa.

According to the historian of the British army, many British activities during the war in the West Indies were shrouded in secrecy, making a complete understanding of Britain's wartime operations very difficult.[49] Certainly London chose to keep certain of its more dubious transactions under wraps and therefore away from public examination—particularly hostile political scrutiny. Nurturing the odious slave trade with large purchases of Africans at a time of swelling abolitionist feeling would have been embarrassing, to say the least.[50] But the problem Fortescue refers to stems equally, if not more, from a traditional disinterest in the West Indies among British military historians who, to use their own lexicon, were more engrossed in mapping the battles of the "big battalions" elsewhere—this despite the attention and expense that Britain lavished on the region. Even Fortescue's study of the war in the Caribbean terminates mysteriously in 1798, although the struggle continued almost without interruption until 1815. The records of British operations were available, but no one, quite obviously, was concerned.

There are, for example, several surviving contracts between the army and slave merchants which shed much light on the policy of purchase. Suppliers were engaged to provide a specific number of slaves, preferably "those of the Gold Coast, Coromantie, or Congo Nations," by a given date. Initially the number varied from several thousand slaves to only a few hundred. Very soon after the inauguration of this plan, the number of slaves supplied by each contractor was limited to 200 to 400. This stipulation did not come about through accident but rather by design. In January 1798, in a purported effort to keep slave prices down (and, it is thought, to save the government future embarrassment), Dundas ordered the officer in charge to buy slaves in small numbers, taking every precaution to conceal the fact that the government was the purchaser.[51] Failure of the merchant to satisfy these and any other terms of an agreement meant forfeiture of a security. The title to every slave had to be properly warranted to the British government.

Prospective recruits furnished under these arrangements were marshalled in long, silent rows in an open space adjacent to the West Indian port where, only hours before, the slaver had disgorged its cargo. In a scene repeated many times during the war, each slave awaited in quiet but anxious ignorance a minute and roughly administered medical examination to determine if he was, in the stilted legal prose of one contract, of "sound Body, and in all points able to carry Arms." Each also had to satisfy the minimum age (usually sixteen) and height (five feet three inches) requirements. Finally, if the slave was not "incumbered with Family or Follower," he was tagged around the neck with a white card bearing his new name, to which the now-recruited African was abruptly introduced by the repeated shouts of a splendidly uniformed black noncommissioned officer.[52] Still silent and, perhaps, still ignorant of his new vocation, he was marched off in a manner conspicuous for its unmilitary cadence to a West India regimental depot where he would be adorned with a dazzling scarlet tunic and begin immediately to earn the King's shilling. All this for his troubles in coming across the ocean![53]

How many slaves were purchased and what was the cost to the imperial treasury? Available records, some diligently prepared, provide a clear picture of the dimensions of this operation. From 1795 to 1808, the British government bought an estimated 13,400 slaves for its West India Regiments at the considerable cost of about £925,000.[54] (See table 1.) The cost of these purchases was buried in

Table 1. Slaves Purchased by the Windward and Leeward Islands Command, 1795–1808

Year	Number of slaves	Average price (in £)	Total Cost (in £)
1795–1797	1,366	56	76,496
1798	1,053	63	66,443
1799	810	58	47,720
1800	763	74	57,049
1801	407	77	31,689
1802	19	54	1,042
1803	—	—	—
1804	914	71	64,929
1805	1,238	75	91,821
1806	1,554	75	115,887
1807–1808	800	75	60,000
Totals	8,924	69	613,076

Sources: See pertinent returns in W.O. 1/82, 634, 645, 769; W.O. 25/662, 653; C.O. 101/35; C.O. 285/4; and C.O. 318/30; and, particularly, C.O. 318/31, Bowyer to Windham, no. 31, 18 April 1807 and enclosures.

Note: Purchases are included up to 1 March 1808, the final date ships leaving England by 1 May 1807 were permitted to arrive in the West Indies under the Abolition Act. The significant reduction in purchases beginning in 1801 and leading to the discontinuation of purchases in 1803 was apparently linked with the negotiations of 1801 that eventually culminated in the Peace of Amiens (March 1802–May 1803).

the unaudited and much-abused account of Army Extraordinaries. Based on Professor Curtin's calculations, and using 15,000 as the average annual number of slaves imported into the British Caribbean at this time, total British slave imports reached about 195,000.[55] The army's purchases represented about 7 percent of this sum. Recent studies into the volume of Britain's slave trade, most notably those of Roger Anstey, Seymour Drescher, and J. E. Inikori, indicate that Curtin's census figures require some upward revision.[56] This would necessitate an increase in total British imports and a corresponding decrease in the proportion of this revised estimate siphoned off to maintain the black regiments. Nonetheless, the British government was itself, perhaps, the largest individual buyer of slaves and, consequently, one of the major promoters of the wretched trade.

Finally, and most importantly, what were the consequences of the policy of purchase? There can be little doubt that the British government's demand for slaves multiplied, at least proportionately, all the horrors associated with the trade. In this respect we have the words of a troubled William Wilberforce, who communicated his fears to Prime Minister William Pitt in September 1804, after receiving information about the army's dependence on the slave trade to maintain the West India Regiments. Referring to this activity as a "vicious principle," Wilberforce skirted the evident hypocrisy of Pitt, who had publicly advocated abolition but was privately working against it. Instead, he confronted his friend with the somewhat limited ramifications of his actions.

> That their situation as soldiers would be beyond comparison preferable to that of plantation slaves cannot be doubted; but how can we justify buying slaves for that desirable and even humane purpose, when we reflect that the increased demand will produce a proportionately increased supply, and consequently as many more marauding expeditions, acts of individual rapine, injustice, and condemnations, etc. are necessary for obtaining the requisite number of negroes.[57]

This letter is of interest for what it states explicitly. It is also important for what it implies. Clearly deducible is the puzzling and even startling realization that Wilberforce had never before heard of the army's African recruitment policy—which had been in operation for almost ten years by 1804.[58] Bewilderment is replaced by disbelief when it is remembered that despite subsequent efforts to cloak recruiting operations in secrecy, the decision to raise the West India Regiments in 1795 was greeted immediately by a virtually unending storm of protest from the colonies as well as from the West Indian faction and its political backers in Britain. To this general awareness of the measure must be added the publicized events surrounding the alleged mutiny of the Fourth West India Regiment at St. Kitts in 1797, the actual mutiny of the Eighth West India Regiment at Dominica in 1802, and a longstanding dispute over the legal status of the black soldier in the Caribbean between government ministers and the army on one side and the colonies on the other. Efforts to solve the question of whether the West India soldier was subject to military law or to colonial police regulations produced no fewer than three opinions by the law officers of the Crown between 1799 and 1801.[59] Also strikingly absent from Wilberforce's letter is any awareness of the serious implications of this recruiting policy for the cause of abolition. Such inattentiveness—if such it was—was highly uncharacteristic of the man.

Looking at the record, it is only too clear that an ominous silence surrounded the abolitionists vis-à-vis Pitt's policy of using the trade to maintain the black regiments. Other than Wilberforce's one incredulous statement of 14 September 1804, no written or spoken word came from the abolitionist camp to demand explanation or, in conformity with their often repeated public avowal regarding the trade, termination. It was left to the enemies of abolition to publicly confront and humiliate Pitt, who had chosen expediency over principle.[60] Since the reputed talents of a friendly Pitt were deemed vital to the success of the abolitionists, the situation suggests collusion. It is made all the more reprehensible by the identity of the participating parties and the humanitarian principles they momentarily subverted.

The policy of purchasing slaves as soldiers influenced in no small way the efforts to end the slave trade. Between 1796 and 1807, it was an important reason for delaying abolition; it also helps explain Pitt's puzzling behavior.[61] We might first ask, however, what conclusions historians have come to on the issue of delay. Three arguments, only partially explanatory, have been adduced: (1) the unpopular linkage of abolition with Jacobinism and the influence of the latter in causing the revolution in St. Domingo; (2) the threat of a St. Domingo–style slave insurrection if British slavery were similarly altered; and (3) the necessity to continue the trade in order to harvest St. Domingo's valuable sugar crop after that colony had been taken over by Britain.[62]

The evident connection between abolition and Jacobinism did prove temporarily detrimental to efforts to end the trade. At one point, toward the end of 1792, the most vehement champions of abolition were usually radical political groups.[63] But from about 1800 on, the revolutionary excitement on the Continent waned and with it the antidemocratic spirit in Britain.[64] As for the lesson imputed to the upheaval in St. Domingo and similar slave societies elsewhere in the Caribbean, these events genuinely frightened the proprietor class, as indeed they should have. In this climate of fear, many waxed eloquent on the imagined dangers that would befall British islands in the wake of abolition. As we have seen in the case of Jamaica and the Sixth West India Regiment, a variation on this theme was employed to prevent the raising of the corps. However, it was reassuring that modification of the slave system in the Danish West Indies in 1803[65] failed noticeably to unleash the anticipated violence. Moreover, largely because of British military successes from 1796 to 1798, a pronounced tranquillity characterized the once-turbulent sugar islands as the century came to an end; much of the fear that was so pervasive during the early years of the war was dissipated. Dundas took evident pride in observing this change.[66]

The final argument, that the trade had to continue in order to maintain St. Domingo's sugar plantations, is a plausible explanation of events up to 1798. At the end of that year, faced with mounting expenditures and enormous casualties in a losing cause, Britain grudgingly abandoned its dream of extended empire and evacuated the stricken island. As a result of the Peace of Amiens of 1802, Britain returned all West Indies possessions taken from France.[67]

More recent scholarship comes closer to the mark. As reasons for the delay of abolition until 1807, it stresses royal hostility, the tardy use of the argument that abolition would advance rather than hinder traditional imperial and national interests, limitations of then-current constitutional conventions, opposition in the House of Lords to reform measures, and the absence of cabinet agreement (which resulted in free voting on the issue).[68] Yet there are still gaps in the knowledge represented by these arguments, and in developing several of these explanations further Pitt's policy of purchase sheds some additional light on the controversy. How is this so?

I would contend that obstacles to making abolition a government measure were not limited to conventions of the Constitution, nor to the presence of powerful anti-abolitionists in successive cabinets, particularly those headed by Pitt. Looking at the question of cabinet unanimity from a different angle, it is clear that an agreement had in fact been reached: not an official or public avowal but a privately reached consensus; not one to support abolition, obviously, but concord to oppose it! The chief abolitionists in the cabinet—Pitt, Grenville, and Windham—and the leading opponents of abolition—Portland and Dundas—had reached accord, probably as early as the end of 1795, to use the slave trade to recruit the West India Regiments. [69] The decision satisfied the immediate interests of all concerned: for those opposed to abolition, it permitted the trade to continue; and to both abolitionists and anti-abolitionists with responsibilities for directing the war, [70] it afforded an opportunity to prosecute the war successfully in the West Indies and soon in other theaters of operations. Numerous official dispatches, many of which have already been cited in this study, confirm the participation of Portland, Dundas, and Windham in all stages of the development and implementation of the policy of purchase. As head of government, Pitt is compromised: it is inconceivable that a decision such as this could have been reached and implemented without his cognizance and approval.

The actions and priorities of the abolitionists in the cabinet deserve special attention since they conflicted with those of the cause of abolition and thereby doomed it to a slow and agonizing birth.

Windham, who had a long and close association with abolition and its leaders, [71] bolted from the movement soon after agreeing to serve under Pitt as secretary at war, a post he held from 1794 to 1801. [72] As the executive head of military administration at the War Office and answerable to Parliament on matters of military expenditure, Windham assumed much of the responsibility for the inner workings and success of Pitt's recruiting policy. Later, as secretary for war and colonies from 1806 to 1807, one of Windham's chief concerns was to provide the soldiers, white and black, necessary for the war effort. From the start of the war in 1793, the manpower needs of the regular army severely taxed the talents and energies of successive secretaries. [73] Given the limitations imposed by these imperatives, how could

Windham simultaneously fulfill the duties of his offices and champion the death of the trade that provided the African soldiery so necessary to the protection of the empire in both the West and the East Indies?

Thus, in 1806, on the eve of abolition, the trade was squeezed dry in an effort to procure the required number of slaves. London apparently felt justified in exploiting the trade this last time since the Commander in Chief of the army informed Windham that no fewer than 22,000 troops were needed for West Indian defense;[74] about a third of these would be black. Several revealing dispatches in Colonial and War Office records attest to frantic attempts to obtain more Africans before the trade expired.[75] One in particular, from Lieutenant Colonel Willoughby Gordon, Military Secretary to the Commander in Chief, to Pudsey Dawson, of the Liverpool slave-trading firm of the same name,[76] describes the cooperative, urgent, and confidential nature of the government's efforts to enter into a contract for, as Gordon candidly puts it, "2 to 4,000 slaves of the tribes from the Gold Coast . . . before the Act takes effect."[77]

As abolition drew near, other steps were taken to assure the prescribed strength of the West India Regiments. The Mutiny Act of 1807, which was drafted under Windham's overall direction, stipulated that blacks be enlisted for unlimited service only.[78] Even the instrument used to deliver the *coup de grâce* to the trade, the Abolition Act itself, served the special manpower needs of the army: forfeited slaves and slaves taken as prizes of war could be enlisted into Britain's armed forces.[79]

What part did Lord Grenville play in this doubtful enterprise? Recent scholars have heaped praise on Grenville for his role in successfully and rapidly steering the abolition legislation through Parliament after Pitt's death.[80] But is this praise entirely deserved? Given his close personal and political relationship with Pitt, it is certain that he was aware of the policy of purchase. Indeed, as Colonial Office correspondence reveals, Grenville probably had the earliest and therefore longest association of any minister with the measure. In October 1790, as home secretary in Pitt's first administration, he authorized Governor Effingham of Jamaica to purchase on public account the slaves needed as pioneers to British troops on the island.[81] Nor is his abolition record in Parliament completely above suspicion. Given the changed circumstances of 1806—particularly the fact that abolition would actually facilitate African recruitment—the speed and success displayed by Grenville in the House of Lords at the end of the struggle to end the trade stand in bold contrast to his earlier efforts. His parliamentary record is still unexplainedly inconsistent. Nonetheless, of all the secretaries, Grenville's responsibilities as foreign secretary from 1794 to 1801 made him the least ministerially culpable for the execution of the recruitment policy. For this reason, his impact on the measure is more difficult to judge.

Let us return to Pitt. Enormous energies continue to be squandered in an effort to exonerate Pitt of the major responsibility for the delay in passing the Abolition Act.[82] But delay he did, for the trade was the mainstay of his policy of African recruitment. Within this context, then, the reason for Pitt's "ambivalent," "dilatory," and generally perplexing behavior becomes discernible. Two examples from this pattern of conduct illustrate my point. First, in 1796 Pitt failed to use privately his considerable talents and extensive political influence to persuade government supporters and others to vote for abolition and thereby forestall a free vote on the motion. He was certainly not restrained from lobbying on behalf of the motion by any political or constitutional conventions, and he had done so before. But if he had, *and* been successful, he would have worked against his own war effort. Secondly, in 1805 Pitt refused his official support of abolition at a time when the chances of its becoming a government measure appeared excellent. But appearances were deceiving. How could abolition become a general measure at a time—beginning in 1805 and continuing into 1806—when the number of Africans being purchased on public account was the largest it had been in the entire operational life of the policy of purchase? (See Table 1.) By these and related actions Pitt demonstrated clearly that his first priority was winning the war, not ending the slave trade. Until some other exploitable source of African manpower was discovered, abolition would have to be delayed.

Pitt is not exonerated; rather, he stands condemned as a man who led a double political life. In deciding between principle and interest, Pitt, like many identically confronted politicos before and since, chose the latter. In anyone else this conduct would have deserved a mild rebuke. But for Pitt—who was so ostensibly wedded to the cause of abolition—to be guilty of such unprincipled deportment is reprehensible. In the words of one observer of political behavior, "politics are, and have always been, a perilous sacrifice of morality to expediency in the pragmatist and a painful conflict between morality and expediency in men of conscience. Most politicians solve the matter by doing away with conscience and identity altogether."[83] This description would not be an untrue or unfair assessment of Pitt's actions.

Abolition of the trade became law in March 1807, with a suddenness that surprised even some abolitionists.[84] What factors produced this historic occasion? The coalition ministry that came to power in 1806 and shepherded the abolition bill through Parliament contained many who favored abolition. Other reasons included the improved tactics and lobbying efforts of the abolitionists, as well as the political leadership of Grenville. But to these factors must be added another: abolition was no longer a threat to national or imperial security on military grounds. The removal of the danger, therefore, ended the need for the quiet agreement among abolitionists and anti-abolitionists in the cabinet. Abolitionists were now free to pursue their cause unencumbered. The elimination of the military argument weakened the opposition program by removing a major plank and may substantially account for the rapid success of abolition in 1806 and 1807. How did this finally come about?

Actually, the revitalization of the abolition movement in 1804 prompted considerable activity in London; alternative sources of non-European manpower for West Indian defense were sought.[85] By June 1806, it was decided that the slave trade was still the best bet; only now the (still) hapless Africans taken as contraband would become the new recruits. To the executing clauses in the 1807 Mutiny Act and the Abolition Act was added an Order in Council of 16 March 1808; it directed that all fit Africans taken from slavers be turned over to military and naval authorities for enlistment into Britain's land and sea services.[86] Although it was no longer sanctioned in Britain, the trade would continue to serve British imperial interests.

4

SLAVES OR FREEDMEN?

We have seen that the decision to raise the West India Regiments was greeted by firm and immediate opposition—both in the colonies and in Britain. However, only after the critical first phase of the war (1793 to 1798), when the defeat of France in the West Indies was assured (for the time being) and British sugar islands were once again calm, was the collective strength of the West Indian interests marshalled to rid the plantations of the black regiments. By 1800, the island assemblies were proceeding with efforts to bring the black soldier under the jurisdiction of local slave laws and thus to destroy the regiments.

Under certain circumstances and for specific offenses the British soldier was already amenable to civil courts. His military status did not provide complete immunity from their jurisdiction, even though the military exercised the predominant judicial authority. The civil and military sharing of legal responsibility for the British soldier was based on the principle that he was not only a soldier but also a citizen, and therefore subject to civil as well as military law.[1] In the following description, Brigadier General Hislop dramatically described the tense and delicate dilemma of the West India soldier during the controversy over his legal status:

> When violent prejudices are imbibed by People of confined habits and notions, they are undoubtedly very difficult to remove. By persuasion there is little chance of succeeding. Nothing can more strongly prove the truth of this assertion, than the aversion, which many residents in the West India Islands still possess, against the

Black Regiments, and when it falls, in any degree, within their power, they will gladly seize the occasion to deprive them of that consideration and respect, which as constituting a part of His Majesty's Army, should be extended to them.

Under the aforesaid impression it has been asserted, and in some instances I have understood the principle has been acted upon, that Soldiers of West India Regiments are amenable to the Slave Laws, and therefore subject to every degradation, that the unfortunate and wretched Slave is doomed to endure. If such a principle were established, how could confidence be justly placed, or indeed with what Justice could it be expected from such Soldiers. The same Duties fall to their lot to perform, as are confided to the European Troops. The same vigilance and exactness in the discharge of them is alike expected, and the same degree of punishment awaits their disobedience or neglect. How then could it be possible, if such were admitted as a fact, that a West India Soldier, could with safety to himself perform his Duty? For instance, if a white Man insults him on his Post, or attempts to act there contrary to the orders he has received, he could not resist him, and if even struck, or any attempt is made to disarm him, he could not oppose with the firmness his duty as a Soldier would demand, and for the neglect of which, the Law by which he is governed, would award him a severe punishment.[2]

To simply declare West India soldiers slaves would leave them at the mercy of the civil authorities and the literal enforcement of the slave laws. As Hislop's example points out, such a status would seriously impede their effectiveness as soldiers. Moreover, the penalties inflicted on a slave for striking or even insulting a white person in the British West Indies at this time were whipping, mutilation, and sometimes death.[3] By the turn of the century, the situation was compounded by the fact that, as a result of the government's recruiting policy, the vast majority of West India soldiers were indeed purchased slaves.[4] To this volatile situation was added the possibility of a wholesale disbanding of the black corps into the plantocracy if the peace preliminaries of 1801 proved successful. It was clear that the continued existence of the West India Regiments depended upon establishing the black soldier a freedman.

There was apparently some confusion, even within the Army in the Caribbean, about the legal status of black soldiers. Hislop's description, written in 1801, states that on *some* islands they were considered amenable to slave laws. Yet the same year, a despatch from the Commander in Chief of British forces in the Caribbean indicates that there was almost universal agreement in the British islands that West India soldiers were subject to slave laws. The West India soldier, on the other hand, not only considered himself free (and therefore superior to those blacks in bondage), but he also believed himself the equal of white soldiers in every aspect of military service. As a result the black soldier was both proud and jealous of his unique station.[5]

The West India soldier had every reason to believe that he was a freedman or at least enjoyed a special status. Black soldiers were treated in the same hospitals in which European troops convalesced.[6] The fact that he wore the same uniform and enjoyed the same pay, allowances, and privileges as his white comrade-in-arms naturally tended to confirm this view. In addition, blacks were subjected at enlistment to a program of indoctrination; they were told by their officers that their position vis-à-vis slaves was superior because they served the King in a military capacity.[7] These proofs of equality, which were routinely accepted by the West India soldier and daily contrasted with the brutal realities of slavery,[8] did not come about by chance. From the raising of the first West India Regiments, the British government wisely committed itself to a policy of equality in the governance of its black and white soldiers. Occasionally, London chose to remind the army in the West Indies that white regiments should not be shown preferential treatment; the West India Regiments should receive equal "attention and favor."[9]

Within the walls, then, of British garrisons, the West India soldier lived under egalitarian conditions of military discipline, implying, at least, that he was a freedman. But no similar pronouncement covered him once he stepped beyond the gates of the post. The ambiguous status of the black soldier demanded clarification. Nonetheless, not until 1799 did London begin to break its official silence on this question.

In the subsequent struggle, the British army, endeavoring to protect the regiments from the grip of hostile colonial legislatures, achieved only the dubious success of shielding a specific and comparatively small segment of West India soldiery. Before the issue was finally resolved in 1807, soldiers belonging to the Fifth West India Regiment were incarcerated in a civil jail; some were held without trial for about a year.[10] The local legislatures held that, as soldiers were also citizens, military courts should not be allowed to try them for the most serious civil offenses—such as treason, murder, or rape—if they could be tried conveniently in a civil court. Yet it had been established that even these offenses, when committed by soldiers in active service, came under the jurisdiction of military courts. Early in the eighteenth century, the British government had acquired, in effect, complete statutory power over its troops, both at home and in the colonies, by means of the annual Mutiny Act.[11] Still, in spite of the jurisdictional primacy of military courts elsewhere, the legal status of black soldiers in West India was as undetermined, and there was considerable doubt in the British army as to how far they were amenable to military law.[12]

Colonial obstructionism could have been anticipated as one result of colonial participation in the enlistment process of the regiments. The Mutiny Act of 1694 prescribed that the enlistment of each soldier be attested before a civil magistrate so as to protect the enlistee from being duped into service.[13] The local magistrate or justice of the peace was to certify the enlistment and witness the attestations of the recruit, one of which was an oath of fidelity. The recruit also had to disclose his age, place of birth, and occupation, and swear that there were no restraints on his enlistment into military service.[14] West Indian justices of the peace, who were generally among those whites opposed to garrisoning British islands with black regiments, could be expected to use their participation in this process to block the recruiting of the regiments. Nonetheless, even at the height of the controversy, several thousand slaves were enlisted, and not a fragment of evidence remains of precisely how the legally required presence of West Indian civil magistrates was avoided or circumvented. Intent on bringing the regiments up to their prescribed strength, army recruiters probably simply paid the enlistment bounty but never brought the black recruits before the justice of the peace. Nor would this method have prevented the enlistment from being legal; according to a clause in the Mutiny Act of 1735, anyone who received enlistment money from an officer and knew it to be such was considered an enlisted soldier, even if he did not go before a local magistrate.[15]

It is also likely that a number of slaves enlisted during this period went through the prescribed process with the cooperation of justices of the peace from the parishes in which the garrisons were located. Colonial assistance in connection with the West India Regiments was perhaps rare, but it was not impossible. Moreover, it seems almost certain that cooperation between military and civil authorities occurred on islands that were the scenes of military operations. Where plantations were in ruin, slaves were in open rebellion, and whites had only recently been massacred, the inhabitants were not likely to refuse military assistance, even from armed blacks. St. Vincent, for example, appears to have cooperated steadily with enlistments for the Fourth West India Regiment after that corps was transferred there from St. Kitts.[16] On other islands, which had been spared the ravages of the war, the authorities might have been willing to assist the army in its recruiting efforts as long as they did not have to receive a West India Regiment as part of their own garrisons. Once this possibility was raised, however, the colonists would go to almost any length to prevent the arrangement. Jamaicans, on the other hand, were consistently uncooperative, and the number of blacks enlisted on their island was minimal.

Before the government finally asserted its power and influence to settle the legal status of the West India soldier, several other issues intervened to aggravate an already strained relationship. A chief complaint of the local populations was the army's policy of purchasing almost exclusively "New Negroes" as recruits for the regiments. Prevented from purchasing native West Indian blacks in significant numbers by the recalcitrance of local proprietors and colonial assemblies, the army's later recruiting efforts rapidly transformed most of the West India Regiments into African regiments—that is, corps composed predominantly of newly imported African slaves. Table 2 shows the preponderance of African-born recruits enlisted into the Fifth from 1798, when for all intents and purposes recruiting began, until 1807.

Table 2. Regional Origins of Recruits for the Fifth West India Regiment, 1798–1807

	1798	1799	1800	1801	1802	1803	1804	1805	1806	1807	Total
Africa	172	1	2	119	100	–	296	20	–	–	710
West Indies (blacks)	74	1	–	9	1	1	–	–	2	–	88
Europe	3	3	1	–	–	–	–	–	–	–	7
East India (lascars)	4	3	–	–	–	–	–	–	–	–	7
Total	253	8	3	128	101	1	296	20	2	–	812

Source: W.O. 25/656, folios 1–27.

A few regiments retained a largely Creole character, although the available, albeit incomplete, records show that even these corps had a good many African recruits.[17]

Colonial sensibilities, already excoriated by the establishment of the regiments, were irritated further by this additional "affront." The awkward and disoriented "raw" Africans, incommunicative even with the officers because of their ignorance of English,[18] were viewed by white West Indians with an explosive mixture of contempt and terror. The Fourth West India Regiment, in effect an African regiment, was suddenly removed from the Leeward Islands in 1797—the victim of chicanery and aroused colonial passions. Nor did the composition of the Eighth Regiment, which replaced the Fourth, escape the unceasing scrutiny of white inhabitants. Local criticism of this corps too was directed at the allegedly "barbarous" and "uncivilized" Africans who comprised it; even, the senior British officer in the West Indies in 1798 was wary of the "uncivilized" character of the "New Negroes" in this corps.[19] The rapid transformation of the formerly Creole regiments into African corps further alienated white West Indians and made them even more anxious to bring West India soldiers under the regulation of local slave laws.

Situations seemed to arise with a kind of conspiratorial regularity to focus attention on the West India soldier and to keep the issue of his legal position alive and in the public consciousness. Naturally, a few serious offenses were committed by black soldiers. A member of the Seventh Regiment was charged with murder of a civilian at Barbados in 1798;[20] and Private Charles Miller of the Second was indicted for assault and battery at Grenada in 1800. Initially Miller was summoned before a Court of General Sessions, but when he was presented to hear the charges it was decided that the slave court had juris-diction.[21]

The disposition of worn-out West India soldiers, whose numbers steadily increased as the war continued, also helped to rivet attention on the black soldier. Blacks who were unfit for further regimental duties but capable of light garrison tasks were retained and drafted into garrison or invalid companies. Those found totally unfit for mili-tary service, however, were the subject of much concern to the army and hostility from local proprietors. Occasionally, special arrange-ments were made to look after old and disabled soldiers. In one such situation, the veterans of a black corps were provided not only with the usual inadequate and temporary pension of "a bitt a day," but were also placed under the supervision of an English merchant.[22] Most, it appears, were simply left to their own devices. According to His-lop, a discharged black soldier often settled near or even on a planta-tion on which he had acquaintances among the slaves. The influence of the idleness, independence, and ideas of this intruder on the slaves naturally aroused the animosity of the proprietor, and the old soldier might be harried from estate to estate before being driven finally to seek refuge in town.[23] Reviled by the white populace, the West India soldier often found that only his discharge certificate stood between his free, if harried, existence and confinement in a workhouse for suspected runaways.[24]

The government's policy of distributing its white and black soldiers among the garrisons—in the ratio of two to one, respectively—made the legal status of the black soldier a universal issue in the British West Indies.[25] And yet the policy was clearly an effort to *conciliate* white colonists by preventing the islands from being almost completely garrisoned by blacks.[26] We have already seen that when Jamaicans were confronted with this policy in 1796, they combined crafty legal maneuvering with bluff to gain a brief period in which they were permitted to have an all-white garrison.[27] This merely postponed the issue until April 1801, when the last remaining significant British West Indies possession with an all-European garrison was ordered to abide by the imperial policy. In May, amid cries of consternation from local whites, 272 rank-and-file members of the much-abused Sixth West India Regiment went ashore in the Bahamas.[28]

In 1797 the British army in the West Indies took an extraordinary step to protect the most vulnerable of its black soldiers from falling under the jurisdiction of the local slave laws. In April of that year, Sir Ralph Abercromby, apparently on his own authority as Commander in Chief in the West Indies, declared that all West India soldiers found totally unfit for further military service were freedmen. They were to be provided with a pension of one shilling per diem, payable every two months, and, eventually, a conditional discharge that made the old veterans liable for service in invalid companies. The precedent was continued by Abercromby's successors,[29] but the effect of the effort was marginal at best. Not only did the colonial legislatures refuse to acknowledge the free status of discharged black soldiers, but the British government—though it did not repudiate it—never officially endorsed the action. The conspicuous absence of this important sanction, the reasons for which the law officers of the Crown were about to explain, no doubt encouraged the colonists to challenge the legality of the army's decision.

Continued failure to ensure the safety of invalid black soldiers goaded the army into a sustained effort to persuade the government to declare all West India soldiers, both fit and unfit, to be freedmen in all matters of civil concern. Towards the end of 1798, certain high officials in the government and the army in London were convinced of the need to exempt Britain's black troops from colonial slave laws. Among the former was the Duke of Portland who, since the beginning of the debate, had taken the position that as British soldiers raised by royal prerogative, blacks were subject to military law and regulations.[30] By the end of 1798 three methods of enfranchising West India soldiers had been repeatedly recommended by the army in the West Indies. These options ranged from the rather unlikely colonial acts and manumissions to the introduction of a clause in the annual Mutiny Act.[31]

An official decision as to whether West India soldiers were amenable to military law or to colonial slave laws was imminent as the last year of the eighteenth century passed into history. Until then it was necessary to prevent clashes between black soldiers and colonists, and officers with blacks under their command were instructed to keep these troops in the strictest discipline and good order.[32]

In early January 1799 the first of several legal opinions was presented to the British government. On January 10, in a decision which clearly influenced most of the subsequent ones, Attorney General Gloster of St. Vincent found that black soldiers purchased as slaves were indeed amenable to colonial police regulation. As a result, the opinion continued, cases involving West India soldiers should be adjudicated in slave courts or in Petty Sessions by one or more justices of the peace. General Henry Bowyer, Commander in the West Indies, cautioned Dundas against accepting Gloster's opinion because of the latter's position as public prosecutor and his long residence in the West Indies.[33] Two months later, on 11 March 1799, the law officers of the Crown rendered the first of three official opinions, all of them essentially the same. The first opinion was the result of a query put to the Crown's attorney and solicitors general by the Duke of Portland on 12 November 1798. At this time Portland had requested their advice on the two crucial points. (1) Does military service in the British army free blacks serving in West India Regiments from colonial slave laws? (2) If West India soldiers, despite their military service, are subject to colonial police regulations, can they be enfranchised by an act of the King or would it be more advisable to do so by an act of Parliament?[34]

Whatever hopes Portland and others may have had of using a favorable reply from the Crown's chief legal advisors to refute colonial arguments against the West India Regiments were dashed by the opinion of March 11. Regarding Portland's first question, the law officers were unequivocal: being in British military service did not release black soldiers from the operations of the slave laws insofar as those laws affected them personally. As to the second question, West India soldiers could be released from the jurisdiction of colonial slave laws only by manumission according to the laws of the various islands. Portland was also warned that manumission would not relieve West India soldiers of all legal disabilities, since they would still be subject to the restrictive colonial laws that regulated the activities of free blacks. Portland was further cautioned that his suggestion to enfranchise black soldiers by an act of Parliament was not in keeping with Parliament's policy of legislative noninterference in the internal government of the colonies.[35]

Twice during 1801 similar questions were put to the attorney and solicitors general. Exactly two years from the date of the first opinion the law officers were forwarding their second opinion to the Duke of Portland. It was a duplicate of the first. The jurists even acknowledged that Gloster's opinion had had a considerable influence on their own.[36] On December 14 the law officers responded for the third time to almost identical questions. This time they were asked by Lord Hobart, the new Secretary of War in the Addington administration, which was formed in February 1801. The reply was essentially the same as the other two and equally unequivocating:

> We are therefore of opinion that they [West India soldiers] do not in consequence of their being employed by His Majesty in military service become soldiers within the Mutiny Act; and we think they remain to all intents and purposes slaves, and that their condition as slaves is in no respect altered in consequence of their being engaged in military service, but they remain precisely subject to the same laws as they would have been subject to had they been the property of His Majesty and employed in agriculture or public works or in any other species of civil service. . . . It seems to us that they cannot cease to be subject to such colonial slave laws as immediately respect the police and internal government of the colony, and must be subject to every species of personal incapacity which attaches upon the slaves of any other proprietor.[37]

Implicit in the query asked repeatedly by Portland and Hobart was the basic question: were West India soldiers serving under the Mutiny Act? The reason for seeking legal counsel on this point was that Portland and others wished to know if the words contained in the Mutiny Act, "in pay as a soldier," applied to black soldiers. According to military law, the acceptance of pay for soldiering placed the recipient of this money under the jurisdiction of military law.[38] Thus a man who chooses to serve and to take pay as a soldier must be considered to have accepted the conditions under which he is paid and treated as a soldier, and therefore he is subject to military law. The chief justice's opinion in the case of Grant *v.* Gould in 1792 upheld this law when it was ruled that receiving pay as a soldier "fixed the military character" on Grant and was sufficient to give jurisdiction to a court martial.[39] The status of soldier was also fixed if, within four days of receiving enlistment money, the enlistee does not dissent before either a civil magistrate or a military judge advocate and return the enlistment money, minus the subsistence charge.[40] Blacks enlisted into the West India Regiments were paid the usual bounty or enlistment money. The change in status of a man who becomes a soldier was emphasized by a contemporary authority of British military law. According to Scott, a man who enlists into the British army relinquishes his present situation or status as a civilian—and with it the jurisdictional supremacy of civil courts—and assumes that of a soldier —who is subject to military courts.[41]

In arriving at their opinion of 14 December 1801, the law officers categorically disclaimed the argument that West India soldiers were serving in the British army under the conditions established in the Mutiny Act. Their argument was brief and employed as its rationale the British West Indian legal view of the slave. The slave was considered a *non persona*—a special category of property part chattel and part real property—who was incapable of making decisions and acting on his own initiative.[42]

It appears to us that the Mutiny Act relates to persons capable of being enlisted and becoming soldiers by their voluntary consent, which capacity certainly does not belong to the negro slaves of which these regiments are stated to be composed. We are aware indeed that words 'in pay as a soldier' which are used in the Mutiny Act were in the case of Grant *v.* Sir Charles Gould before the Court of Common Pleas held to fix the military character on the person who had received such pay—but then it was in the case of a person who was in a capacity to have elected originally whether he would have received it or not; and we do not think that the words can be understood to mean the receipt of pay by a slave who has no other source of maintenance, has no legal means of resisting the commands of his master, has no capacity of electing whether he will receive it or not, and has no free agency with respect to this or any other condition in which his master may think proper to place or employ him.[43]

The major basis of the law officers' position was the established political principle that Parliament should not interfere in the internal affairs of the colonies. In all three opinions, the law officers reminded the government that parliamentary enfranchisement of West India soldiers would constitute "interference" with the colonial legislatures. The advisability of passing such an act was not even considered as a question of law. It was, they concluded, a question involving political expediency, on which they felt themselves incompetent and therefore not obliged to offer an opinion.[44] Even though efforts were underway that would soon lead to an assertive role in colonial government, most ministers and members of Commons were also still reluctant to recommend such parliamentary action.

The legal opinions of 1799 and 1801 did not, however, result in the immediate colonial legal assault on the West India Regiments anticipated by the army. In fact, there was a noticeable waning of colonial efforts to rid the British Caribbean of black regiments. There were several reasons for this unexpected softening of the colonial attitude. First, hostility toward the regiments appears to have been moderated by the three favorable and unequivocally stated opinions of the Crown. Armed with the strength of these opinions, the colonists were apparently—and momentarily—disarmed by their own success and in no haste to confront the army with the ramifications of this legal victory. Second, the government was making a number of concessions on deployment of the West India Regiments, in hopes of placating the colonists into accepting, however grudgingly, the permanent presence of the black regiments. These concessions included the periodic relocation of black regiments and the isolation or confinement of these corps, whenever possible, in garrisons removed from populous areas. (The "incarceration" of the Second West India Regiment at Fort Augusta, Jamaica, was an example of this practice.)[45] The policy of limiting the number of blacks in each garrison to one-third the total force was another such conciliatory measure. The concessions, bolstered by the outstanding service record of most of the regiments, appear to have achieved their goal, at least for a time. Third, an important defection from the ranks of the colonists over the legal-status issue probably weakened colonial resolve. In September 1801, Attorney General Burke of Antigua claimed that the black soldier was legally a soldier within the Mutiny Act and as such was subject to military law. Although he recognized the distinction between a British soldier and a slave as it pertained to the voluntary act of enlistment, Burke nonetheless argued that when a slave purchased by the King is afterwards employed and paid as a soldier, this action ought to be considered an "implied or virtual manumission."[46] And finally, there was Trinidad's acceptance of black troops as part of its garrison.

In spite of the 1799 and 1801 opinions there was still much uncertainty about the legal status of the black soldier. The confusion probably stemmed from the fact that officers in West India Regiments continued to indoctrinate their troops in the belief that their position, vis-à-vis ordinary field slaves, was very superior. In a debate on the slave trade abolition bill in the House of Lords on 6 February 1807, Lord Hardwiche asked if West India soldiers were freedmen or slaves. Lord Grenville replied that he had always considered them to be freedmen.[47] No such uncertainty confused senior British officers in the West Indies. In October 1806, Lieutenant General Henry Bowyer wrote to William Windham, Secretary for War and Colonies, of his sorrow that even the King and his government considered West India soldiers to be slaves.[48]

The army remained undaunted by the legal setbacks; black soldiers were still treated equally with European troops.[49] Commanders in the West Indies repeatedly reminded the government of the need to provide legal protection for discharged black soldiers.[50] London was also informed that black soldiers testified under oath at courts-martial and that black sergeants were given commands of considerable importance. "Ought such people," Bowyer queried his superiors in London, "to be deemed and treated as slaves?"[51]

We have seen that the questions of the legal status of the black soldier provoked the ire of the colonies and resulted in an equivocating response from a divided imperial government. But how did the black soldier perceive his own situation? Just how vigilant of status was he? Moreover, precisely how was he likely to receive information about his, at best, dubious legal position, particularly news or rumors of impending disbandment.[52] And, finally, what voice did he raise in his own behalf?

During the evening of 9 April 1802, troops belonging to the elite flank companies of the Eighth West India Regiment mutinied among the fortifications at Prince Rupert's Bluff, Dominica. Before the mutiny was crushed on April 12, several whites and, it is alleged, over a hundred mutineers were killed.[53] A general court-martial was convened at Prince Rupert's from 15 to 20 April. Seven privates were found guilty of "exciting and joining in mutiny" and murder and were sentenced to death.[54] The Eighth was ordered to Martinique, where the executions were carried out the morning of April 27.

Several months later, in conformity with British practice, the regiment was broken. Those officers desiring to remain in British service in the Caribbean were placed on the establishment of other West India Regiments. The number of rank-and-file to be disposed of was 393. The manner of disposal depended on whether or not the particular soldier was implicated in the mutiny. As a result of interrogations, 209 noncommissioned officers and men were found not to have been involved and were drafted into other black corps. The remaining 184 were implicated. Of these, some were attached as laborers to the quartermaster general's department. The rest were distributed as pioneers among European regiments in the Windward and Leeward Islands.[55]

Why did the Eighth mutiny? The most important documentary evidence dealing with the incident is the Proceedings of the Court of Inquiry held at Port Royal, Martinique, April 28–30, 1802.[56] This record not only sheds considerable light on the causes of the mutiny, but also contains one of the very few recorded, albeit brief, accounts by West Indian slaves of their own personal condition. Although twenty-five black soldiers were interrogated, only seventeen declarations were transcribed. Judging from the incomplete identifications of the witnesses, the Eighth was an amalgam of mainly African-born soldiers and some English- and French-speaking Creoles. Unfortunately, testimonies were not recorded verbatim. The answers to questions put by the court were recorded either as rough general translations, if the witness was African or francophone, or paraphrases, if the witness spoke English. The result is rather lifeless prose; the African linguistic and Creole pidgin-patois expressions, the *lingua franca* of these troops, were lost in translation and transcription. Nonetheless, the evidence is unique.

According to Sergeant Gold, slaves from plantations in the vicinity of the forts at Prince Rupert's and slaves at the Portsmouth market had told the soldiers that they were to be reduced and then sold as slaves. The work in which detachments of the Eighth had been lately employed—toil considered by the soldiers to be slave work—lent support of the disquieting rumor. The Proceedings reveal that for several weeks prior to the mutiny soldiers had been regularly used in removing brush wood and draining the swamps contiguous to the fortifications. The army had in fact authorized this work in an effort to eliminate the marsh and thereby reduce mortality and sickness in the nearby posts. But, according to Private James Chottet, the soldiers believed that the job was merely a ploy to determine if they could cut cane. Private Stuart, described as a "creole from Dominique," thought the mutiny stemmed directly from the manner in which the troops were employed. Even the tool used to carry out the fatigue, the billhook, aroused consternation among the troops. The testimony of one officer disclosed that the soldiers were sure the billhook would soon be replaced by the hoe, the loathsome tool of the field slave. The same officer informed the Court that the soldiers had been in an uncompromising and defiant mood regarding their future as British soldiers. They, he further testified, had grown too accustomed to carrying a musket; they would not now replace it with the hoe.

The Court concluded that the cause of the mutiny was the fear of being sold into slavery. The alarm was confirmed by rumors circulated by the slaves and aggravated by the mode of work in which units of the Eighth had been employed.[57]

The mutiny had at least one immediate effect: any intention the Addington administration may have had of discharging black soldiers into the uncertainties of West Indian society as a result of the Amiens peace was scrapped. By the end of 1802, the number of West India Regiments had been reduced from twelve to eight, but none of the troops were discharged. The policy was to retain the soldiers of eliminated regiments—such as the broken Eighth Regiment—on the British Establishment.[58]

Notwithstanding the legal opinions of 1799 and 1801 and the British government's concessions to the colonies, the legal status of West India soldiers remained uncertain and again became a cause of conflict. In spite of the opinions, the army continued its unendorsed practice of declaring black soldiers to be free,[59] and there was renewed colonial hostility toward the black regiments. (The fact that the government chose not to disallow the declarations was an indication of some ministerial support.) As before, the army found the atmosphere of conflict incompatible with its responsibility of protecting British possessions in the West Indies. In December 1805, the commander of British forces, George Beckwith, complained to Viscount Castlereagh, Secretary for War and Colonies from 1805 to 1806, that the question of the legal status of black soldiers had been "some time in agitation, but never perfected." He recommended that the troops be protected by the introduction of a clause in the annual Mutiny Act. Three months later, in dispatches to Castlereagh and the Duke of York, he requested authority to enfranchise all West India soldiers and predicted trouble if his recommendation was not heeded.[60] The trouble Beckwith had in mind, no doubt, was another mutiny of black troops similar to that which occurred in the Eighth Regiment.

The years 1806 and 1807 were years of the underdogs. Moved by the principles of Charles James Fox, the British government made important efforts on behalf of blacks and Roman Catholics. The efforts proved far more successful for the former. Although already certain of victory by June 1806, the abolitionists finally achieved their goal the following year on March 25, when the act forbidding British subjects to trade in slaves received the King's assent. Borne on the enthusiasm for reform then affecting the supporters of Grenville's government, but nearly obscured by the success of the abolition movement, was yet another victory for the African. As had been promised by Grenville on February 6 and by the Secretary at War, the Right Honourable Richard Fitzpatrick, on March 9,[61] the Mutiny Act of 1807 contained a clause declaring all blacks in the King's service free to all intents and

purposes. In the *Tobago Gazette* of 11 December 1807, the following
notice appeared:

BY ORDER OF THE COMMANDER OF THE FORCES
EXTRACT from the Mutiny Act 47 Geo. 3d. cap 32–102 AND
be it further enacted that from and after passing of the ACT, all
Negros purchased by or on account of His Majesty, His Heirs, and
Successors, and Serving in any of His Majesty's Forces, shall be,
and be deemed and taken to be free, to all Intents and for all
purposes whatever, in like manner in every respect as if such Negro
had been born Free in any part of His Majesty's Dominions, and
that such Negros shall also to all Intents and Purposes whatever
be considered as Soldiers, having voluntary enlisted in His Majesty's
service.

THOMAS WHITE
Acting Assistant Commissary[62]

African slaves, who had been chosen by chance to take the King's
shilling instead of the yoke of the field slave, were now freedmen.
Thus, about 10,000 West India soldiers were enfranchised in what
must certainly have been one of the largest number of slaves freed by
a single act of manumission in preemancipation society in the Caribbean.[63]

Committed to a measure that saved the lives of countless Europeans
in the West Indies, the government had no choice other than to
enfranchise its black soldiers. Moreover, a subsequent study showed
that black regiments could be more economically maintained in the
tropics than white regiments.[64] But there was also a strategic reason
for the decision. The West India soldier had gradually assumed a larger
share of the burden of imperial defense in the West Indies; and after
the resumption of the war in 1803, Britain's major military effort
shifted from the Caribbean. Nelson's victory at Trafalgar in 1805
opened up other areas in which to engage France and her allies. Efforts
to establish a "disposable" or expeditionary force, which eventually
led to a sustained and major British effort in Portugal and Spain
beginning in 1808, led to a reduction in the number of "genuinely"
(that is, white) British troops in the West Indies. Between 1804 and
1807, this reduction was partially balanced by augmenting and

modifying the establishment of the West India Regiments.[65] Troops from the British Isles were also replaced by large numbers of prisoners of war and French deserters. According to Fortescue, by the end of the war, British garrisons in the West Indies were defended chiefly by African soldiers and foreigners in British pay.[66]

But what was the significance of enfranchising blacks in Britain's military services by an act of Parliament? Considered together with developments such as the anti-slavery movement, the establishment of the West India Regiments, and the founding of the Colonial Office in 1801, it was a clear indication that the initiative in colonial government was indeed shifting from the colonial governments to London. The principle of legislative noninterference, which had become fixed as a consequence of the American Revolution and which provided the political basis of the legal opinions of 1799 and 1801, was being abandoned. The impetus for change in Britain was the growing dissatisfaction with ineffective colonial governments.

In reversing this policy, the government actually reverted to legal principles that were established before the shock of the American Revolution. In the eighteenth century, members of Parliament were certain of their abstract right to legislate for the colonies; and the sovereign power vested in the King and Parliament was assumed in Britain to extend naturally to the colonies. This view of Parliament's legislative supremacy was made explicit by the Declaratory Act, which declared the colonies "subordinate unto, and dependent upon, the Imperial Crown and Parliament of Great Britain."[67] It also claimed that King and Parliament had "full Power and Authority to make Laws and Statutes of sufficient Force and Validity to bind the Colonies and People of America, Subjects of the Crown of Great Britain, in all Cases whatsoever." Furthermore, William Blackstone, the eminent jurist, had asserted that there must exist in every state "a supreme, irresistible, absolute, uncontrolled authority in which the *jura summa imperii*, or right of sovereignty, reside."[68] Even during the period beginning with the events of the American War—when the practice of noninterference in colonial affairs was in accord with opinion in Parliament—members of Parliament agreed that Parliament could legislate for the colonies in cases of emergency. In the case of the

Mutiny Act of 1807, it was assumed (based, no doubt, on Blackstone's assertion) that Parliament was exercising its transcendent powers.

The enfranchisement of thousands of black soldiers was part of a new epoch in interracial relations that had begun with the creation of the West India Regiments in 1795. But freedom for Britain's black troops was not the end of the controversy surrounding their presence in the Caribbean. The equally contentious question of disbandment had yet to be resolved.

5

CAMPAIGNS

In terms of the conduct of military operations the war between Britain and France in the West Indies, which lasted almost continuously from 1793 to 1815, went through an almost complete cycle. It began as a traditional West Indian war—that is, one of combined amphibious assaults on key coastal objectives. In 1793 and 1794, operations of this type were usually terminated by a brief siege or a formal clash between opposing corps of, mostly, European soldiers. The war resumed its traditional character from about 1798 to the conclusion in 1815, but during the interim years, a revolution in West Indian warfare occurred. With the abolition of slavery in the French possessions and the successful efforts of Jacobin agents to foment rebellion among the slave populations of certain British islands, the fighting took on the character of large-scale guerrilla warfare.[1] Large numbers of slaves, most of them with no previous military training or experience, were recruited by Britain and France. Protracted operations against insurgent slaves and Carib Indians were conducted for the first time in the mountainous, almost inaccessible, and largely uncharted interiors of the embattled sugar islands. Long columns of hundreds of troops moved through hot, airless woods, often along precipitous, narrow trails. Soldiers carrying full battle equipment scrambled back and forth across countless steep and boulder-strewn ravines and up and down rugged peaks in the enervating heat of the tropics. Under these conditions men and equipment deteriorated rapidly; deaths from heat and exhaustion were not uncommon.

It was not accidental that Britain and France were locked in a viciously waged guerrilla struggle from 1794 to 1798. Revolutionary

France had in fact called this type of war into existence. First, slaves at St. Domingo had rebelled in 1791; then, in February 1794, the Convention had abolished slavery in the French West Indies, and former slaves were called to arms to protect the new order against invading British forces. Seizing the initiative, France proclaimed and promoted a war of black liberation in the British West Indies. Little wonder, then, that a guerrilla struggle of concealment and ambush increasingly set the tone of the war.

The center of French military operations and revolutionary propaganda in the West Indies was Guadeloupe, from which British troops had been driven early in December 1794. Under the determined and capable leadership of Victor Hugues, a mulatto, Guadeloupe served as an *entrepôt* of arms, men, and Jacobin propaganda aimed at receptive slaves in the West Indies. For unexplained reasons, no immediate attempt was made to recapture the island, and it remained a thorn in Britain's side during much of the war. Not until 1810 was Guadeloupe again brought under British control. It was returned to France in 1814, then retaken by Britain for the third time in 1815.

The mode of military operations directly affected the tactical role played by the West India Regiments during the war. In the second or insurgent phase, the regiments served as rangers or counterinsurgent troops; and during the third and longest phase of the war, when operations were once again conducted in accordance with West Indian tradition, the West India Regiments were trained and deployed as regular British line regiments.

Because of dismal recruiting results from 1795 to 1797, the West India Regiments collectively saw rather limited service against the insurgents. Although a few of the corps were actively engaged during this period, other ranger corps bore the brunt of the fighting from 1794 to 1798. The latter units will be considered as West India Regiments as some of them were drafted into existing corps while others themselves became entire, new West India Regiments.[2]

Despite the climate of the West Indies, the lush green vegetation, and the rugged landscape of the islands, the rank-and-file of the West India Regiments were issued the standard British uniform. Perhaps the only remaining and reliable depiction of the uniform is the embroidered centerpiece of the regimental color of the Fourth West

India Regiment; it shows that in 1795 West India soldiers dressed much as other British troops did. The two figures wear short red coats with lapels to the waist and collars, cuffs, and lapels in the distinctive regimental facing. The uniform was completed by short black Hessian-styled gaiters, which came to a point in front and behind, and a large and most improbable looking hat with a large shaggy bearskin-type crest that ran the full height of the headpiece.[3]

The helmet supports the argument that these corps were among the first in the regular British army to be trained as light infantry. The hat shown in the embroidered centerpiece of the regimental color of the Fourth is the type of headdress worn by the infantry of light companies; the universal headdress of regular line infantrymen at this time was the enormous and unserviceable cocked hat. In addition, the short jacket worn by West India soldiers was issued only to light infantrymen; line regiments were not issued this item until 1796.[4] It seems unlikely that the two embroidered figures would represent only the single light infantry company that was then part of the establishment of a regular line regiment. This would mean that the West India Regiments were line regiments when they were first raised. Most of the men originally recruited into West India Regiments came from the ranks of various ranger corps and were, by virtue of their training and employment, light infantrymen. Moreover, we have already noted that the West India Regiments did not have the usual flank companies as part of their original establishment. Clearly, they were special battalions raised to fight a special kind of war. Even so, the West India Regiments were never officially designated as light infantry corps, and, when the style of conducting the war changed at the end of the eighteenth century, they relinquished the light infantry role in favor of that of a line regiment. Probably for these reasons, neither past or present military historians consider them light infantry regiments.[5] Judging from their training and deployment during the insurgent phase of the war, however, they were among the first regular light infantry regiments in the British army. I believe it is also significant that the officers who played such key roles in the creation of the famous Light Brigade at Shorncliffe, England in 1803—John Moore and Coote Manningham—served in the West Indies, where they personally conducted extensive operations utilizing light infantry principles. [6]

The West India Regiments saw very little service in the tumultuous struggle in St. Domingo for several reasons. The general failure to raise the regiments in the Windward and Leeward Islands in 1795 and 1796 was also experienced in St. Domingo. Moreover, most of the corps originally earmarked for St. Domingo were frequently relocated to other islands. The Third and Fifth regiments especially were shuttled back and forth between St. Domingo and Jamaica from 1795 to 1797. A comparison of the Jamaica monthly returns and commissary records for St. Domingo even shows that the Third and Fifth, or rather their recruiting cadres, were simultaneously divided between the islands. [7] The Fourth, which was formed later, apparently never served in St. Domingo.

Not only were West India Regiments seldom on the island, but very few St. Domingan blacks were recruited into any of them. This is clear from the *Description and Succession Books*, as well as the periodic returns. The books for the Fourth West India Regiment, which had been ordered to recruit in St. Domingo, show that in 1797 not one of the 252 blacks in the regiment were from St. Domingo. [8] Recruiting officers were unwilling to enlist blacks suspected of having been impregnated with the pernicious ideas of the French Revolution, for fear they would infect British slaves when called upon to guard British islands. Any connection with St. Domingo, therefore, was viewed with utmost caution. Jamaica made it very clear that any of its slaves taken to St. Domingo for service would not be permitted to return. [9]

The chief reason for the limited service of West India Regiments in St. Domingo was, however, the policy of retrenchment that, ironically, coincided with the corps' first significant recruiting success in 1797. In spite of the raising of numerous black and white colonial corps, the pouring into the island of thousands of British troops and much British wealth, and the efforts to seduce rebellious mulattoes and blacks with promises of amnesty and money, [10] by 1796 it was clear that Britain was no longer waging a war of conquest. It had become a costly war of self-preservation, a struggle to simply maintain a rapidly diminishing presence on the island.

A steadily deteriorating military situation from 1795 to 1798, when the colony was evacuated, led to the policy of retrenchment. Toward the end of 1795, Britain irrevocably lost the initiative; after that its forces were mostly confined to the coast.[11] By 1797, the insurgents, chiefly under the command of Toussaint L'Ouverture, greatly outnumbered the British. There was also some evidence of an impending invasion of Jamaica by blacks from St. Domingo, who would be assisted by insurgent Jamaican slaves and Maroons.[12] By 1797 the British army had in effect acknowledged the loss of St. Domingo; all outlying posts were abandoned and its troops were concentrated in a few coastal places to afford protection to British navigation and commerce.[13] Finally, in 1798, under the realistic and cost-conscious direction of Brigadier General Thomas Maitland, British forces were evacuated—first from Port-au-Prince, St. Marc, and the parish of Arcahaye, then from the island as a whole. The evacuation was complete by October 1798.[14]

The situation in St. Domingo was futile and leading to an overwhelming defeat for Britain; but even then there was some reluctance in London to withdraw from the island. Four years later, the Duke of Portland confessed to Governor Nugent that black rule in St. Domingo, or anywhere else in the Caribbean, was even more dangerous to Jamaica than the re-establishment of French power; he therefore instructed Nugent not to hinder French efforts to retake the colony.[15]

Retrenchment particularly affected colonial corps, black as well as white, including the West India soldiers serving on the island. Prior to Britain's withdrawal, Maitland had instructed the commissary general to prepare an estimate of the total future expenses to be incurred by the force the government deemed requisite for the defense of St. Domingo. A force of almost 6,500 troops would cost the Treasury £700,387 sterling annually. The colonial contingent alone was projected at 4,664 and would cost the British taxpayer £405,631 each year. The annual cost of a colonial corps with a strength of 379 officers and men was put at £23,998.19.1. It was Maitland's opinion that the "advantage to be derived [by keeping the colony] is not equal to the Expence to be incurred."[16] Bleak military prospects finally made these expenses unacceptable in London too. In 1797, royalist French officers were already being forced to resign their commissions in British service, and a return dated 1 July 1798, shows no West India troops among the colonial corps then on St. Domingo.[17] Probably the only West India Regiment that saw any significant service there was the Seventh. According to commissary records, it served in the district of Mole St. Nicolas.[18] The Seventh's service record, however, remains a mystery, for it was apparently never mentioned in dispatches.

Other West India Regiments narrowly missed serving in St. Domingo. In August 1798, Dundas ordered the Ninth and Twelfth West India Regiments to St. Domingo; the slowness in communications made it impossible for him to know that on July 31 Maitland had decided on total evacuation.[19] The Ninth and Twelfth would have to serve elsewhere.

The removal of West India soldiers from St. Domingo did not, however, solve the very sensitive issue of the several thousand blacks and mulattoes who were serving in other colonial corps. Their precise numbers are unknown, but of the 6,019 colonial troops listed by Maitland in July 1798, at least 3,000 were non-whites.[20] When news of a likely British withdrawal reached Jamaica, Balcarres warned Portland that the island was opposed "in the extreme" to accepting any troops who would fall "within the legal line of [the] Negroe Race." (It will be remembered that Jamaica had just dissuaded the government from attaching the Sixth West India Regiment to its own garrison.) Yet, as Balcarres quickly added, Jamaicans were very uncomfortable with their decision to refuse entry to St. Domingan blacks; for it seemed certain that if the corps were disbanded in St. Domingo, Toussaint would take them into his own service and might even use them against Jamaica.[21] Furthermore, as Bryan Edwards noted after his visit to the colony, the colonial troops were disciplined and intrepid soldiers.[22] Jamaicans could not have it both ways, however, and fear won out over reason; the majority of blacks and coloreds in the British colonial corps in St. Domingo were simply set adrift. Many did indeed join Toussaint's victorious army.

Unlike St. Domingo, the Windward and Leeward Islands were the scene of sharp and sustained fighting by West India Regiments and their predecessors, the ranger corps. Offensive operations utilizing these troops coincided with the arrival of Sir Ralph Abercromby's relief expedition in 1796. Delayed four months by violent Atlantic storms, this force finally straggled into Carlisle Bay, Barbados, in April. Subsequently, it would permit Britain to regain the initiative in the war; when it arrived, however, preparations were already under way at Barbados. Among the forces assembling there was a brigade of black troops that included the Dominica, the Guadeloupe, and the Royal Island Rangers—later the Eighth, Ninth, and Tenth West India Regiments, respectively.[23] Quartered at Constitution Hill near Bridgetown, these units mustered a total strength of 1,210. Before sailing with the British expedition against the Dutch Guianas, Dr. George Pinckard, who arrived in the West Indies on one of Abercromby's transports, observed the training of these predominantly French blacks. His letter of 29 February 1796 provides us with one of the few substantial eyewitness descriptions of West India soldiers.

> They are a fine body of men, who have been enlisted from the revolted French islands, or brought away on the evacuation of them by our troops. They are active and expert, and are training into a formidable corps to assist in our intended expeditions. About sixteen hundred of them bear arms; besides whom there are twelve hundred to be employed as pioneers. They have all the vivacity and levity of the French character about them; and it occasionally, affords us amusement to observe the Barbadoes negroes regard them with evident amazement, gaping with wonder at their volatility and alertness.[24]

None of these corps participated in the attack on Abercromby's first objective, St. Lucia, on 27 April 1796. However, two companies of Malcolm's Royal Rangers, about 250 men who were then in the process of being drafted into the First West India Regiment, joined the expedition. They were constantly employed, either on military operations or on the customary but grueling fatigue details.[25] With the siege and capture of Morne Fortune, the principal defensive work, the island capitulated on May 26; 2,000 men, the vast majority of them well-disciplined blacks, surrendered.[26] But the rugged country prevented British troops from establishing a cordon around Morne

Fortune and the other fortified bluffs quickly enough to block the enemy's escape into the craggy interior of the island. Abercromby sailed victorious from St. Lucia on June 4 to the relief of Grenada and St. Vincent, but the bitter task of pacifying the island, especially the interior, was left to Brigadier General John Moore. Moore—who was later appointed colonel of the Ninth—was fortunate that the Ninth and Twelfth West India Regiments were among the troops eventually attached to his command. They helped fight what proved to be a punishing guerrilla war.

Moore, who very nearly succumbed to yellow fever, quickly assessed the situation on St. Lucia and made his dispositions. His observations and arrangements are worthy of review because they were characteristic of British experience on other islands. Moore's first and perhaps most important decision was to assign his black and white regiments to quite different operational functions. Less than three months after taking up his command, he had already found, "from experience," that his European troops were incapable of acting against the insurgents in the interior; he succinctly described the rugged and broken terrain as "prodigious." Only his black rangers could operate successfully there. His assessment of the reasons for the ineffectiveness of the European regiments was also discerning: poor diet, rum, a general lack of discipline and economy among the troops, and a dispirited and incompetent officer corps were explicitly cited by Moore. Implicit in his remarks was the crucial need of light infantry training for British troops—the type of training necessitated by guerrilla warfare. On the other hand, West India soldiers, who in 1796 were principally Creoles, knew the habits of the insurgents, and they combined personal knowledge of tracking through the bush with their recent experiences as rangers. Moore assigned his white battalions to the equally important task of occupying coastal positions in the hope of intercepting French efforts to aid the insurgents with men and supplies.[27]

On 18 January 1797, Moore wrote to his father that he had employed his two black corps "for the more active service" against the "Brigands." According to the November 1796 return, the total strength of the Ninth and Twelfth West India Regiments was 874 men.[28] The presence of insurgents, who still held on to certain areas in the deep woods, combined with the death of about half of Moore's

white troops, placed the British in an extremely weak position. "The
Blacks," Moore confessed dejectedly, "to a man our enemies."[29]
Nonetheless, his high opinion of the West India Regiments remained
unchanged. Several months earlier he had written to Abercromby:

> In this Country much may be made of Black Corps. I have had
> occasion to observe them of late. They possess, I think, many
> excellent qualities as Soldiers, and may with proper attention
> become equal to any thing. Even at present as they are, for the W.
> Indies they are invaluable.[30]

Actually, by October Moore had experienced the worst of the fighting. The rest of the year was spent in desultory mopping-up operations
against the insurgent blacks.

Among the units in Abercromby's relief expedition to Grenada on
9 June 1796 were units of the First West India Regiment. In addition
to the white regiments, Webster's and Angus's locally raised Black
Rangers were already on the island. Efforts to end the rebellion at
Grenada before Abercromby's arrival had met with the same difficulties experienced at St. Lucia. Not until July 1795 could British
cruisers succeed in preventing the French from landing supplies; even
then the blockade could not be maintained during the hurricane
season, when the French brought in supplies from Guadeloupe and
Cayenne.[31] But even without regular French support and living partly
off the land, the insurgents were still in control of practically all of
Grenada as 1795 came to an end.[32]

Not only were there insufficient numbers of troops on Grenada to
mount a serious offensive against the insurgents, but local British commanders had yet to learn, as Moore had at St. Lucia, the best disposition of their black and white troops. Instead of being sent to scour
the woods for freedom-minded slaves and Frenchmen, black soldiers
constituted the major part of the garrison of St. George's, the capital
of Grenada.[33] Meanwhile, ill-prepared white troops floundered on
expeditions into the interior. Writing his battle report "in a negro hut,
on the top of the highest mountain in this rugged island," Brigadier
General Campbell provides us with a vivid picture of the desparate
situation of untrained troops after an encounter with insurgents in the
woods and among the precipices:

We seem entirely left to poke out our own way in the dark wilds, and fastnesses, not yet having found a guide who knows a yard beyond the beaten tracks, which are here improperly called roads; neither can you get for love of money a person who will venture a hundred yards to gain intelligence, consequently we either fall into ambuscade, or are led to error, through false information.[34]

By December 1796, however, the principal bands of insurgents had been systematically tracked down by detachments of the First West India Regiment and the local ranger corps in a struggle white inhabitants had come to refer to as an "unnatural war." Small groups held out for some time, and the Second West India Regiment was employed from June 1797 to August 1800 in stamping out the last traces of the rebellion. According to the commander of the Second at this time, the fighting occurred in such broken country that the officers of his corps had to be assisted personally by black soldiers in order to traverse the rugged landscape.[35]

Given the character and locale of the war against the insurgents, and the general inability of most European troops to undertake counter-insurgency operations, it is not surprising that West India soldiers bore the brunt of much of the fighting.[36] The following account, taken from the regimental history of the Forty-second Royal Highland Regiment, illustrates the predicament in which untrained troops frequently found themselves. It is a good example of the type of operation gone awry that West India soldiers were often called on to rescue.

The outposts being frequently alarmed by parties of the enemy firing at the sentries at night, a sergeant and twelve Highlanders . . . penetrated into the woods at 9 o'clock in the evening with short swords, to cut their way through the underwood to discover the position or camp from whence these nightly alarms came. After traversing the woods all night an open spot with a sentry was discovered. This man fired his musket at a dog which accompanied the soldiers, and then plunged into the wood, as the sergeant ran forward to cut him down. The soldiers were at the edge of a perpendicular precipice of great depth, at the bottom of which was seen a small valley crowded with huts from whence issued swarms of people, on hearing the report of their sentry's musket.

Having made this discovery the soldiers commenced their journey back, but when they were about halfway, they were assailed by a fire of musketry on both flanks and in the rear. The Caribs were expert climbers, every tree appeared to be manned in an instant: the wood was in a blaze but not a man was to be seen, the enemy being concealed by the thick and luxuriant foliage. As the Highlanders retreated, firing from time to time at the spot from whence the enemy's fire preceeded, the Caribs followed with as much rapidity as if they sprung from tree to tree like monkeys; in this manner the retreat was continued until the men got clear of the woods.[37]

A small party of the Second West India Regiment was sent in support of this harassed band of Scots. The total loss for the Second and the Highlanders during the engagement was six killed and eight wounded.

By mid-January 1798, Dundas began to note a pronounced tranquillity in the once-turbulent sugar islands. In April General Cornelius Cuyler, who had replaced Abercromby in 1797, could confirm that the rebellions had been crushed. Even Dominica, which was only about twenty-one nautical miles from the still unsubdued and bustling Guadeloupe, was peaceful. By January 1799, St. Vincent and Grenada had reportedly already recovered from the devastations caused by the insurrections.[38]

What were the consequences of the war against the brigands? According to Abercromby, prior to the insurrections, the military knew little of the interior of the Windward and Leeward Islands. The operations conducted during earlier wars had been confined to the vicinity of the principal towns. Abercromby, somewhat exaggeratedly, considered that these islands were all "now well known." "It remains," he correctly concluded, "to fix and perpetuate that Knowledge by good Plans."[39]

The experiences of the war against the insurgents and the critical need for light infantry troops is thought to have had an impact on the subsequent and permanent establishment in the British army of the the Rifle Corps, in 1800, and the Light Brigade, in 1803. Of course, there is no doubt that the lessons learned from French *Voltigeurs* during the Holland or Helder Expedition of 1799 were foremost in the minds of the Duke of York and others when these corps were raised. Nonetheless, the two men who organized and trained these corps were themselves veterans of the insurgent phase of the war in the West Indies. Moore, who served in Holland in 1799 and was also commander at St. Lucia, later commanded the Light Brigade at Shorncliffe. Colonel Coote Manningham, who commanded the Rifle Corps —which eventually became part of the Light Brigade—trained and commanded several light companies in Grey's army in the West Indies.[40]

Yet British military historians have been reluctant to acknowledge the impact of West Indian service, more specifically the long, hard-fought insurgent campaign, on the permanent establishment of light infantry regiments. Fortescue mentions the need for light infantry-men only in reference to the Holland Expedition. However, in Moore's letters (and we can presume that Fortescue read them too) one is constantly reminded of the conspicuous deficiency of this type of training among British soldiers. This lack was partially offset by bringing the several black ranger corps on to the British Establishment as West India Regiments and by the periodic drafting of the German Jaegers into the Sixtieth Regiment. The reason for this lack of recognition of the impact of West Indian service on the development of the army can be found only in the professed disinterest of professional British military historians in the British army's campaigns in the West Indies.

The experiences and lessons of the insurgent war did not have the expected long-term effect on the establishment of the West India Regiments. In spite of the recommendations of some officers, the West India soldiers were not provided with formal light infantry training, with rifles instead of the traditional smooth-bore, and with green uniforms instead of red tunics.[41] Efforts were undertaken, instead, to transform the regiments into regular British line regiments. There were two reasons for this decision. First, although the war against France was to drag on until 1815, the slave populations were never again a military factor. As a result the conflict took on, once more, the traditional character of West Indian warfare, and the need was for line regiments, not light infantry corps. Second, as the focus of the war gradually shifted from the West Indies to Europe, the number of British line soldiers in the Caribbean was reduced, while the permanent presence in the West Indies of several battalions of the Sixtieth Regiment made additional corps of light infantry troops unnecessary.[42]

The outstanding service of the West India Regiments during the insurgent war was acknowledged in January 1797, when Abercromby informed West Indian governors that the regiments were to become a permanent branch of the British Establishment for the defense of the islands.[43] They were no longer fencibles. By December 1799, every major British garrison in the West Indies had its complement of black soldiers, usually constituting about one-third of the force. In several posts in the Windward and Leeward Islands Command, black soldiers outnumbered white troops.[44] Dundas himself wrote that "the formation of such Corps is so essential (if not absolutely necessary) to their [the colonies] Preservation."[45]

Thus, more than sixty years before a similar event in the United States Army, black regiments became a permanent part of the British Establishment.

The brigands' war, the most intense period of military activity during the long struggle, was followed in 1798 by a period of relative calm, although hostilities between Britain and the Northern League and the Batavian Republic led to a brief skirmish in 1801. West India Regiments served with distinction in several small expeditions against the Swedish, Dutch, and Danish West Indies.[46] In March 1802, a peace treaty was concluded between France and Britain; Britain returned all conquests in the Caribbean, with the single exception of Trinidad. By May 1803, the fragile Peace of Amiens was shattered, and war was renewed. The diminishing numbers of European regulars stationed in the Caribbean after 1805 meant that the West India soldiers saw increasing service and participated in nearly all of the expeditions mounted from 1803 until the war's end in 1815. During these campaigns, the West India Regiments won no fewer than three coveted battle honors.[47]

Among the numerous expeditions launched between 1803 and 1815 in which black troops took part, was the ill-fated campaign against New Orleans. The employment of West India Regiments at New Orleans is particularly significant, since it marks the first time these troops, which were raised originally to serve only in the West Indies, were used outside the region.[48] Plans to give the West India Regiments a broader imperial military role were under consideration only a few years after their creation. In November 1799, Abercromby recommended that "Black Troops" be employed in the proposed "liberation" of Spanish South America. Several memoranda written between 1806 and 1808 by Arthur Wellesley, the future Duke of Wellington, also suggested using "Negro infantry" in the conquest of Spanish Central and South America.[49] However, the only British expedition sent against Spain's American possessions during the war ended in the British fiasco at Buenos Aires in 1807, and it did not employ West India soldiers.

In addition to Latin America there were other, and frequent, requests to send West India Regiments to other parts of the expanding British Empire. In October 1802, the Sierra Leone Company petitioned the government to send a black regiment to that territory.[50] At the same time, plans were being shaped to send a West India Regiment to Gibraltar.[51] The following year the governor of Ceylon requested a black regiment for service against the king of Kandy.[52] And in 1804, Castlereagh toyed with the incredible idea of exchanging West India Regiments with the sepoy battalions of the East India Company. He cautiously put forward this most unlikely idea because, in his opinion, West India soldiers were the only substitutes for the reduced number of European troops in India.[53]

There were several reasons behind the requests for West India Regiments. Malarial-type diseases, the bane of European soldiers, were present in all of the stations seeking black troops. There was also the perennial shortage of European troops, coupled with the growing demands of an expanding imperial design.[54] The Sierra Leone Company wanted West India troops to hold in check the turbulent Maroons and hostile Africans that lived in and around the territory.[55] Whatever the reasons, most of the requests were refused by the government. The governor of Ceylon, for example, was authorized to recruit the Ceylon Regiments by purchasing African slaves from Portuguese East Africa. The proposal to swap West India troops for sepoy soldiers was dropped hastily when an indignant Arthur Wellesley flatly rejected it in 1805.[56]

Near the end of the war, the West India Regiments finally were given a broader operational mandate. In 1812, a recruiting depot for the regiments was established at Bance Island, Sierra Leone. This recruiting establishment eventually led to a permanent presence of West India troops on the West African coast. In 1818, it was decided to garrison Britain's West African possessions with West India soldiers; and in May 1819, headquarters and five companies of the Second Regiment arrived at Sierra Leone from Jamaica. This contingent included twelve officers and 341 other ranks, the majority of which were quartered at Sierra Leone, with small detachments on Banana Island and Isles de Los. Another 106 men were sent also to Gambia, further up the coast.[57] The Second was soon involved in military operations: the Rio Pongo Expedition of 1820 and the disastrous Ashanti War of 1823. Throughout the nineteenth century, West India soldiers were employed in numerous campaigns in West Africa, several of them against the Ashanti.

The principle of enlarging the operational sector of troops originally raised to serve in specified areas or garrisons had earlier been applied to the East India Company's sepoy armies. The new principle was necessitated by the increasing commitment of Britain's European regiments to other theatres of war. Moreover, strategic thinking in regard to India now held that the war in the East should be carried to enemy-held islands in the Indian Ocean from self-supporting bases of operation on the subcontinent. Increasing numbers of sepoy troops were thus used on overseas campaigns. By the turn of the century, a dual function had evolved for the company's armies: they were considered an internal defense force and an imperial instrument for overseas expeditions. Early in the war the sepoys were permitted to volunteer for these expeditions, since, according to their enlistment, they were not bound to serve abroad. Sepoys participated in the capture of Ceylon, Amboyna, and the Spice Islands in 1795, the Egyptian Campaign of 1801, the occupation of Macao in 1808, and the captures of Mauritius and Java in 1810 and 1811, respectively.[58] The West India Regiments were given a similar dual function, with the defense of the West Indian area the regional commitment and West Africa the overseas responsibility. By the end of the nineteenth century, however, this operational duality was no longer applicable; by then West India Regiments were considered as regular troops capable of serving in any part of the world.[59]

The end of the war with France found the West India soldier in a uniform that had evolved only slightly and was still essentially a copy of the one worn by British line regiments.[60] In 1811 the "Waterloo" or "Wellington" shako replaced the "stovepipe." The short red or scarlet jacket was still worn, but without some of the horizontal white piping and lace that adorned the tunics of Britain's European troops. Instead of the heavy gray overalls, short gray spats, and boots or shoes officially sanctioned for British soldiers on active service, the rank-and-file of West India Regiments wore jodhpur-styled white or blue cotton trousers—which were also worn by European regiments in the West Indies—and black slippers. The latter, a regimental peculiarity, were a necessity, since West India soldiers were unaccustomed to wearing boots and probably could not have campaigned in them. A contemporary drawing of a private of a battalion company in the Fifth West India Regiment appears in Colonel Hamilton Smith's *Costume of the Army of the British Empire*, a very limited number of which were published in 1815.[61]

Nowhere was the value of West India Regiments more evident then in the elemental ability of the black soldier to outlive his white counterpart. Numerous medical reports and returns, several fastidiously prepared, document this simple fact. (See table 3.) In one three-year study of the Windward and Leeward Islands Command, the proportion of mortality among the European rank-and-file in general, garrison, and regimental hospitals was nearly one in ten. The mortality rate among West India soldiers was only about one in twenty-two. During this period, 4,055 white soldiers died of disease, compared with only 578 blacks. In a seven-year study of the health of the troops of the same command, disease-related deaths reduced the number of white troops annually by an average of almost 25 percent. The average annual decrease reported for West India soldiers was but 6 percent.[62]

What conditions produced such grim statistics within the European

A Private of the Fifth West India Regiment, 1814

garrisons in the West Indies? Contrary to popular knowledge, the destruction of the British army during the French Revolution and the Napoleonic Wars—and, no doubt, previous conflicts as well—began before these men ever reached the Caribbean. Although efforts were made to screen out the unfit, recruits at this time were usually the refuse of British society, and they were frequently physically incapable of enduring the hardships of West Indian military service. Abercromby's army, for example, which was being collected at Cork, Ireland in the autumn of 1795, suffered 3,500 casualties—including

Table 3. British Military Casualties in the West Indies, 1793–1815

	Europeans (British and foreign)	Blacks (West India Regiments)	Total
Total casualties	352,000	72,000	424,000
Deaths (included above)	70,000	5,000	75,000

Source: John W. Fortescue, *A History of the British Army*, vol. 4 (part I); pp. 496, 565; William A. Young, *The West India Common-Place Book*, p. 218; and numerous periodic returns enclosed in P.R.O. Colonial and War Office despatches.

Note: I have estimated that about 97,000 European troops served in the West Indies during the war. Slightly more than 70 percent of them died there. This figure is based on the number of troops required to maintain a European garrison strength of about 11,500.

500 deaths—before its departure for St. Domingo.[63] According to Pinckard, who accompanied the expedition, their initial poor health, combined with inadequate diet and long confinement on crowded and unsanitary transports, resulted in more than 1,000 sick soldiers on arrival at Barbados. Their illness had no relation to the climate of the West Indies; Pinckard diagnosed it as "Common . . . shipfever" or typhoid.[64]

Large-scale troop movements in disease-ridden ships had long been attended by appalling waste of life. Of the 5,000 troops shipped from the West Indies to Newfoundland in 1702, slightly more than 1,000 survived the grisly voyage.[65] By the time of the American Revolution, losses among troops in sea transit had been significantly reduced. Nonetheless, despite improvements and the issuance in October 1795 of War Office regulations governing overseas troop transportation, British soldiers continued to be conveyed in infectious vessels. In 1797, an officer steadfastly refused to put his men on board one of these ships. Some five years later the commander of garrisons in the Windward and Leeward Islands reported somewhat quizzically that several contaminated transports and men-of-war could be used to ferry healthy troops but not invalids. One reason given for the continued use of these vessels of death was the shortage of transports in the West Indies.[66]

Those fortunate enough to survive the severities of eighteenth-century ocean transit were exposed upon arrival in the West Indies to even more gruesome rigors, which frequently resulted in death. Many thousands, already weakened by the long, arduous voyage from Britain, were rapidly carried off by acute infectious diseases. The spread of these diseases was immeasurably facilitated by the location of many barracks in low, swampy areas. The need to protect strategic military points and plantations, both of which were usually laid out in low-lying areas, resulted in the building of barracks and posts at these unhealthy sites. Military posts were frequently situated near estates to make it possible to police the slave population.[67] But even when troop accommodations were built on more suitable terrain, the interior construction often encouraged the spread of disease. According to an inspection report of the barracks at Up Park Camp, Jamaica, in March 1806, the mode of sleeping was on damp fixed platforms or, more commonly, on damp floors.[68] Many years after the war, Dr. John Davy described the famous fortification at Brimstone Hill, St. Kitts, in these words:

> The barracks of this fortress are a striking example of defective construction in a sanitary point of view: the worst of them have undrained and unventilated ground floors, the flooring of boards, pervious to exhalations from beneath and to all liquid impurities from above: this is, or was the case even in the elevated citadel.[69]

In spite of these miserable conditions, and, again, contrary to public knowledge, it appears that more British soldiers succumbed to diseases caused by chronic alcohol and lead poisoning than to malignant fevers. This mass poisoning resulted from the inordinate consumption of "New Rum," a liquid that plagued the Army in the West Indies even before 1793. According to Dr. Theodore Gordon, Deputy Inspector General of Hospitals in the Windward and Leeward Islands in 1803, this "poison" was devoured with "a degree of desperation that is scarcely credible."[70] Its availability and alleged antiscorbutic properties, plus the boredom of garrison duties and the immoderate drinking habits of eighteenth-century Britons, fostered the unrestrained consumption of this toxic beverage. Because it was also believed by the troops to be a prophylactic medicine against yellow fever and other illnesses, rum was even smuggled into hospitals. Several veterans of West Indian service cited rum as the most deleterious factor affecting the health of British troops. Dr. Gordon, for instance, concluded after careful study that alcohol-related diseases destroyed more soldiers than disorders associated with the climate. And Major General Hugh Carmichael, one-time Commander in Chief of the Jamaica Command, and veteran of more than fifteen years of service in the West Indies, considered the "corrosive and insidious Effects of Rum" to be nothing less than the principal cause of disease and mortality.[71]

Acute intoxication did not result simply from excessive consumption of alcohol. Several eyewitness descriptions of the long-term and, particularly, the immediate effects of the beverage, make it apparent that the rum issued to the troops was usually of the "moonshine" variety. It was improperly distilled and contained deadly fusel-oil alcohols that, in large doses, are convulsive poisons. The high concentrations of lead found in rum samples toward the end of the eighteenth century came from the widespread use of lead and pewter components in distilling and sugar-producing machinery. Worms, gutters, and the housing of sugar boilers were frequently made of lead.[72] Heat, acidity, and alcohol combined to quickly dissolve dangerous amounts of lead into the final product. Moreover, diseases such as encephalitis, liver cirrhosis and necrosis, nephritis, anemia, peripheral neuritis, and even gout—although imperfectly diagnosed during the war—all have links to alcoholism and plumbism (chronic lead poisoning). Thousands of European soldiers were discharged from British military and naval service with symptoms of the advanced stages of these disorders.

The dangers attending the consumption of rum contaminated with high concentrations of lead were known in military circles, even during the American Revolution. John Hunter, an army doctor who served in Jamaica, discovered that stills made of pewter were heavily adulterated with lead. From chemical tests, Hunter discovered that the rum available to British troops on the island contained large amounts of the metal. His findings were incorporated into a paper printed in 1788 in his *Observations on the Diseases of the Army in Jamaica.* A second edition was published during the war in 1796.

Unfortunately, either there was no system of disease identification in the British army at the time, or, if such a procedure did exist, it was seldom adhered to. Very seldom do regimental returns include this type of information; as a consequence, we have no way of knowing precisely how many casualties were caused by which diseases. Given our present knowledge of the health of the army in the West Indies, however, it seems highly probable that many of the deaths ascribed to yellow fever were in fact caused by a disorder resulting from rum intoxication; the symptoms are very similar. A deeply jaundiced complexion, thirst, and dark-colored vomit (the result of internal hemorrhaging) are signs of both yellow fever and alcohol-induced necrosis of the liver. Yet the cause of death of a jaundiced soldier in a British army barracks in the West Indies would be readily imputed to "yellow jack."

In addition to the effects of various fevers and contaminated rum, other diseases in their chronic state assisted in the appalling destruction of the British army. Dysentery, enteritis, leg ulcers, venereal disease, smallpox, lung ailments, rheumatism, and anemia were but a few. The latter, which was promoted by long-lasting alcoholism and nutritional deficiency stemming from a heavily salt-provision diet, is thought to have earned thousands of soldiers a speedy dismissal from military service.[73] The salting method of preserving beef and pork not only considerably reduced the nutritional value, it also heightened thirst, which was quickly quenched with the ubiquitous rum.

A considerable effort was made to save lives. It was recommended that convalescents be removed to Nova Scotia from the West Indies because, during the early years of the war, two-thirds of those hospitalized in the islands eventually died. A series of long-overdue reforms were instituted in the army's medical services with immediate results. When barracks and hospitals were constructed at higher altitudes, the frequency of fevers was noticeably reduced. Barracks too were to undergo structural modifications; at Jamaica, for example, it was ordered that ground-level sleeping platforms give way to hammocks. And, because hammocks occupied more space, each room in the newly constructed barracks had to be larger and could accommodate fewer soldiers. There was also a requirement that barracks be built with greater ground clearance. [74]

Other efforts were directed at improving the diet of the soldier. Several regulations were issued to reduce the prodigious amount of rum consumed and improve its quality. These included: the sale of good proof rum only at regimental canteens, to insure the quality of the beverage and to prevent the troops from drinking to excess; the prohibition of rum less than a year old; the partial substitution of rum with Fayal wine; and at Jamaica, at least, a reduction in pay as a way to limit the purchase of poisonous rum. In the latter case, the troops were compensated with additional food. [75]

Supplies of fresh provisions, fruits and vegetables, were to be furnished to the troops upon their arrival in the West Indies. Fresh meat, acknowledged as essential to the preservation of health, was to be provided as a regular part of the soldier's diet. At Jamaica, fresh beef would be issued three days a week instead of the customary two. Other proposed remedies included modifications of the uniform to make it more suitable to the climate; frequent fumigation of troop ships; and, again at Jamaica, the abandonment of posts deemed unhealthy to European troops. [76]

But many of the regulations proved useless, and some were based on incorrect, sometimes disastrous, information. Directives framed, for example, on the belief that dysentery was caused by abdominal chill and that yellow fever could be treated successfully with repeated doses of mercury and an almost limitless array of emetics, purgatives, and stimulants probably hastened the death of numerous soldiers. [77] It appears that other regulations and recommendations were, at best, only partially implemented. New rum continued to find its way into the barracks of the army, with the same grisly results. [78] Yet, the commissary general, one Samuel Chollet, opposed the substitution of Fayal wine for rum; he claimed that the troops complained of its poor taste and, besides, its cost was high because of a local tax of 4s. 1d. per "Pipe." Although it never completely replaced the rum ration,

Fayal wine was furnished to the troops. In 1806, some 221,400 gallons were sold to Windward and Leeward Island garrisons.[79] Nevertheless, despite the evidence regularly forwarded to London linking the deplorable health of the army to, among other causes, rum intoxication, rum remained the staple drink of European troops in the West Indies.

In addition to the army's inability or, perhaps, refusal to eliminate rum from its garrisons, the diet of British troops remained heavily salted. The high cost of fresh beef undoubtedly worked against its regular addition to the soldier's diet: in 1808, the cost per pound was reported as 1s. 6d. as compared to 7½d. for salted beef.[80] The putrid, disease-laden transports continued in service, usually unfumigated; and the most notable example of a barracks complex built at a high altitude, the Newcastle Barracks, St. Andrew, Jamaica, was not erected until decades after the war. The delay in construction resulted from the traditional dispute between the government and the local legislature over how colonial grants for local defense were to be spent. The colonies gave priority to the erection of a series of small, tactical posts to preserve internal security against slave disturbances. The imperial government wanted to construct or renovate existing strategic fortifications, provide better provisions, and improve troop accommodations. At Jamaica, where barracks and hospitals came under the supervision of the local board of works, they were useful pawns to secure Jamaicans their priorities.

Blacks of the West India Regiments were superbly suited for service in the Caribbean. The minimal casualties sustained by these troops throughout the war stemmed in large measure from their relatively high resistance to malarial diseases. But the durability and suitability of West India soldiers was equally the result of their avoidance of other silent killers, namely rum poisoning and poor diet. Although rum was served at the mess and canteens of the West India Regiments, the black soldier, unlike the white, was not addicted to it. Medical reports confirm this as fact. A senior and experienced commander admitted that black soldiers were more reliable than Europeans, largely because the latter were addicted to rum, which adversely affected not only their discipline but also their health and, subsequently, their usefulness as soldiers.[81] The black soldier also consumed little of his salted provisions, preferring to barter them for fresh vegetables. And, probably because of his familiarity with tropical foodstuffs, the West India soldier, both Creole and African-born, appeared to rely more heavily on locally grown roots and fruits to supplement the army diet.[82]

The longevity and fighting qualities of the black soldier demonstrated the utter folly of garrisoning the West Indies with Europeans. Appreciation of this fundamental feature of West Indian service led some to recommend the establishment of an all-black garrison.[83] But London was not prepared to implement what was probably considered a Draconian measure. Nor were metropolitan officials prepared to duplicate in the Caribbean the East Indian model in which sepoys greatly outnumbered Europeans. London's decision was largely influenced by the still-powerful voice of the West India interests, which were never reconciled to the creation of a standing force of armed blacks. Thus, the appalling human waste continued throughout the nineteenth century. From 1826 to 1836, the average annual replacement for European regiments in the Windward and Leeward Islands was about 19 percent; during the same period, it was approximately 26 percent for the Jamaican Command. The reported rate for the West India Regiments was 4½ percent.[84] The incredible suffering of the European soldier in the West Indies wrote, without qualification, the grimmest chapter in the long history of British tropical garrisons.

6

AN INTERIOR VIEW

Until recently little was known about the crucial early history of the West India Regiments. The only substantive accounts of these corps, those of Ellis and Caulfield, were traditional regimental histories that emphasized the campaigns. There is, of course, much more to a regiment than a simple register of its victories and defeats; in peace and even in war, a regiment is absorbed in daily problems of discipline and internal administration. A view of this wider aspect of regimental life is best achieved by an examination of the records of the interior economy and management of a regiment. The two chief sources for this information—which were apparently not consulted by Ellis and Caulfield—are the *Description and Succession Books*, and particularly the invaluable semi-annual Inspection and Confidential Reports.

The reports were usually compiled in early May and October to acquaint the commander in chief of the British army with the actual state of every regiment: its field exercises, interior economy, discipline, and the merit and capacity of officers for command. Inspections were undertaken by general officers commanding brigades, and the resulting reports were forwarded to the adjutant general, London, together with any observations it was judged important enough to include. The reports were not considered simply assessments of a regiment at a particular time, but rather, the result of a continuous process of inspection. Some of the specific categories of inspection were officers, staff, noncommissioned officers, musicians, enlisted men, men to be discharged, recruits, field exercises and movements, arms and ammunition, colors, clothing, mess, books and accounts, complaints and courts-martial, medical department, and religious service. Part of the inspection required the regiment to be formed-up, drilled, and instructed to carry out various maneuvers and firing exercises under the scrutinizing gaze of the inspecting officer. Regimental books were minutely examined for completeness and accuracy; and officers were questioned on points pertaining to field duty and to the economy of their respective units.

The Inspection and Confidential Reports show that for the most part West India Regiments were reliable and efficient corps composed of blacks noted for their bravery and very soldierly appearance.[1] This was the consequence of a policy to recruit, whenever possible, only men of a certain height who were members of the most warlike African nations. The reports also indicate the key problems associated with the internal economy of the regiments. These problems, and other important aspects of this establishment—notably the unique impact of these corps on the surrounding slave society—are discussed below.

DISPERSION

A policy with serious consequences for the efficiency of the West India Regiments was that of dividing these corps into several detachments and dispersing the units among the garrisons of different islands, often for extended periods. The men of these detachments could expect to be separated for several years; and, after the insurgent phase, their war experience was likely to be comprised of an unbroken string of tedious and monotonous garrison duties. Only occasionally, as a result of sporadic French offensive operations or British expeditionary activity, was a regiment reunited. Dispersal was a logical consequence of the regiments' assignment to protect proprietors against raids by garrisoning a multiplicity of installations, forts, and posts. Moreover, as internal security forces with major responsibility for policing the local slave populations, British regiments, particularly West India Regiments, were required to man widely scattered police posts.

This arrangement frequently led to difficulties. All the detached units of a regiment, except one, had to operate without the assistance of the regimental staff, which remained with headquarters.[2] Detachments experienced frequent changes of their commanding officers, and there was an inevitable relaxation of military deportment among troops locked up in remote posts. Arms and accouterments were indifferently kept, and discipline rapidly diminished. Barracks at some posts were nonexistent; at others they were temporary constructions and often in a ruinous state. A regiment reunited after several years of dispersion required complete reorganization to restore efficiency and unity as a corps.[3]

An examination of the periodic returns show that West India Regiments were almost always scattered among garrisons on two or more islands. The same, it appears, was seldom true of the European regiments. The "General Half Yearly Inspection Report of the Army in the Windward and Leeward Islands" for December 1805 provides a case in point. Of the fourteen European regiments serving under this command, only two were garrisoned on more than one island.[4] Of the six West India Regiments—the First, Third, Fourth, Sixth, Seventh and Eighth—four were dispersed, as follows:[5]

First West India Regiment	6 companies/Dominica
	3 companies/Trinidad
	1 company/Tobago
Third West India Regiment	5 companies/Dominica
	5 companies/Antigua
Fourth West India Regiment	6 companies/Surinam
	4 companies/Demerara
Sixth West India Regiment	5 companies/St. Lucia
	2 companies/St. Vincent
	3 companies/Grenada

The Seventh, one of the two West India Regiments not dispersed, had only recently been reunited. According to the Inspection Report, it had been dispersed since its formation in 1802.

Two policies established at the creation of the West India Regiments caused these corps to be splintered among the garrisons and posts of different islands. First, the numbers and locations of posts assigned for occupation by West India soldiers were to be determined, to a great degree, by the casualty records of the European soldiers. Strategically important posts that were notoriously unhealthy for white soldiers—and these were numerous throughout the Caribbean—would

be garrisoned, at least in part, by black troops. The policy of limiting the number of West India soldiers attached to any one garrison further guaranteed that the corps would be dispersed.

As might be expected, dispersion had its most serious impact on discipline. A detachment of the Sixth Regiment at Dominica, which had been separated from its headquarters for several years, was reported in 1809 to be poorly disciplined as a result.[6] Among the less serious crimes reported in the court-martial returns were selling regimental necessaries, "disobedience to Orders," and theft. Offenders found guilty of minor infractions were usually sentenced to be flogged with hundreds of lashes, but in most instances their sentences were remitted. Private Joseph Derby of the First West India Regiment, for example, was tried and found guilty on 12 April 1809 of "tempting to conceal 3 Women out of a number he had in charge." Private Derby's original sentence of 300 lashes was commuted to 75.[7] (Sentences for more serious violations, such as desertion, were carried out with no remission.) After the flogging, the offender was examined by the regimental surgeon or his assistant. Soldiers guilty of minor infractions were subject to other forms of punishment. During his eleven years as lieutenant colonel of the Second West India Regiment, Major General Hugh Carmichael found that an effective way to punish incorrigibles was to reduce them to a position resembling that of a field slave. The soldier was deprived of his arms and appointments and employed only on fatigue duties.[8] At Jamaica, instead of corporal punishment, offenders were incarcerated in "black holes." One inspecting officer considered these structures so effective a deterrent he regretted they were not built at other garrisons.[9]

Desertion from isolated detachments was a relatively easy matter, but the records indicate that escape was rarely attempted, from either detachments or large garrisons.[10] The reason is simple: there was no place to go. The ceaseless, strength-sapping labor and brutality of the plantation-slave system did not provide the would-be deserter with a viable alternative to his disciplined regimental existence. The body of that worn-out, dying slave dumped along the roadside near a post at Barbados, was probably not an infrequent sight. No doubt it served as a grisly deterrent to desertion. The few who did desert, such as Private Hypolite of the Fourth West India Regiment, usually joined

Maroon bands. Hypolite was among a group of runaways who surrendered at Dominica in March 1814.[11] Occasionally even white
deserters were found among bands of captured or surrendered runaways.

The problem of maintaining discipline among detachments of West
India soldiers was magnified by officer absenteeism. The Inspection
Reports make repeated references to the impossibility of instituting
courts-martial when not enough officers are present.[12]

The lack of permanent barrack structures was yet another serious
problem associated with the policy of dispersion. The smaller and
more isolated the post, the greater the likelihood that it was totally
lacking in housing good enough to preserve the health as well as the
discipline of the troops. For example, in July 1804, a detachment of
the Seventh West India Regiment stationed on the Chagauramas
Peninsula, Trinidad was reported to be "hutted" because the post was
without barracks. A unit of the First West India Regiment in July
1805 was also reported to be "Hutted [in] Slight cane Huts, and
much out of repair."[13]

Inadequate accommodations for detachments had its roots in the
historic dispute between the government and the local assemblies
over the expenditure of colonial defense grants. Permanent troop
accommodations at the Honduras Settlement, whose protection and
other forms of military assistance were provided largely by Jamaica,
were nonexistent for most of the war, even though the superintendent
of the Settlement had announced in February 1798 that barracks
would be constructed.[14] By 1808, no construction had taken place
anywhere in the Settlement, and the entire Fifth West India Regiment,
which had provided the garrison for several years, was reported to be
in a distressed state. According to the superintendent, the men were
living in "miserable detached Huts." Naturally, such conditions made
it impossible to maintain discipline and the good appearance of arms
and accouterments.[15]

Jamaica's refusal to accommodate these troops properly resulted
not only from the annual debate with London over defense, but also
from the island's intent to rid the British Caribbean of black regiments. Withholding the annual grant could achieve local objectives
and, simultaneously, cripple the regiments attached to the Jamaica

Command. It apparently mattered very little to Jamaicans that their actions threatened the security of the whole British Caribbean.

The government's commitment to the dispersal of the West India Regiments was irrevocable, but there were officers who hoped it could be modified. In October 1809, the officer inspecting a detachment of the Sixth Regiment at Dominica pointed out the evils of dispersion to the commander of British forces in the Windward and Leeward Islands. In the same report he recommended that the detachment be returned periodically to headquarters and that other detachments of the Sixth be rotated among the posts garrisoned by the regiment.[16] These were sound proposals that, if accepted as a policy for all detachments of West India Regiments, would have gone a long way towards improving discipline and efficiency. However, probably because of the expense involved in the frequent rotation of large numbers of troops and equipment and the perennial shortage of military transport in the West Indies, the recommendations were shelved. Dispersion of West India Regiments continued. Three years later, an officer inspecting a detachment of the Sixth Regiment—about 229 men at St. Lucia—noted that the unit had been separated from its regimental staff for some time.[17]

ILLITERACY AND LANGUAGE

During the French Revolution and the Napoleonic Wars there were probably few soldiers in Britain's regular European regiments, excluding officers and noncommissioned officers, who could both read and write. All notices and orders needing the direct attention of the troops were read aloud by officers or sergeants. Communication between officers and men was, however, naturally facilitated by the fact that both groups spoke English. In short, then, although illiteracy was almost universal throughout the rank-and-file of the British army, the problems it posed were not overwhelming.[18] At the worst, the situation was only irksome and time consuming.

The problem of illiteracy in the West India Regiments, however, was enormous and was not mitigated by a common language. Before 1800, the vast majority of West India soldiers were not only unable to read and write English, but they could not converse in it. English was a

completely foreign language. Nor were these troops tied together by
the bond of any one common language; a large number of African
languages and dialects were spoken. The inability of officers and men
to communicate created immense problems. All orders had to be
translated into innumerable languages and dialects. Numerous commands had to be memorized by disoriented African recruits, who then
had to respond to these harsh sounds with strange, abrupt movements.

The first reference to this dual problem, which, like officer absenteeism was to remain characteristic of the West India Regiments until
well after 1815, was provided by the alleged conspiracy to mutiny of
the Fourth West India Regiment in 1797. At that time, the services of
an interpreter were required to crossexamine the soldiers who were
implicated. The *Description and Succession Books* of the Fourth for
1797 show that of the 253 blacks enlisted, 155 were "New Negroes."
Less than a year later, Bowyer noted that most of the blacks recruited
into West India Regiments had no knowledge of any European
language.[19]

The consequences of the West India soldier's unfamiliarity with
English abound in the Inspection Reports and other official dispatches. An inspection of the Fifth West India Regiment at Spanish
Town, Jamaica, in June 1812 disclosed that because of illiteracy
among black noncommissioned officers, they were not supplied with
the customary written abstracts of rules and regulations. Earlier, an
officer who had never before inspected a West India Regiment confessed that the Fourth, which he reviewed at Surinam in January
1806, was unlike any regiment he had ever seen.[20] Illiteracy among
the noncommissioned officers, he discovered, resulted in the accounts
being in a highly confused state. Unless this situation were corrected,
he warned somewhat exaggeratedly, the Fourth would not be "like
other Regiments." Seven months later another officer inspecting a
detachment of the Fourth at Post Brandwaght, Surinam, noted:

> The few Officers Effective, and the entire want of *white* Non-
> Commissioned Officers, with a corps composed of raw Africans,
> totally ignorant of the English language, are disadvantages which
> the Regiment labours under, and which the utmost assiduity in
> other respects appear scarcely sufficient to counterbalance.

The same officer was

> Very doubtful . . . how far it is possible according to the Existing
> System and present Establishment of Black Corps, for a length of
> time, to make the Black soldier so completely serviceable and of
> real use, which habits, Constitution, and nature seem evidently to
> point out and admit.[21]

Settling the pay accounts of the soldiers and attempting to explain
related and complex items such as stoppage were particularly difficult
if not impossible under these conditions. Black noncommissioned
officers, who were appointed to that rank in large measure because
they could speak and understand English, had to be present as inter-
preters, since officers were unable to communicate directly with their
own men.[22] The African's different system of measuring time only
complicated matters, as is evident in the following report of a unit of
the Sixth West India Regiment in 1806:

> Half these Men cannot speak an intelligble Language, and as their
> Ideas of time are different from ours, it is extremely difficult at
> present to make them comprehend what they have a right to in
> money matters.[23]

Occasionally a positive result could be derived from the communications gulf between officers and men. According to Brigadier General
Wale's inspection of nine companies of the Fourth West India Regiment at Pointe à Pitre, Guadeloupe, in November 1810,

> the Non commissioned Officers and Privates are in general
> extremely sober, quiet and docile and as tractable as it is possible
> for men to be, who have so slight a knowledge of the language of
> their Officers, being most of them Africans by birth, and pur-
> chased by Government out of Guinea Ships.[24]

This awkward situation, which steadily worsened as Creole recruits
were killed or discharged and replaced by blacks born in Africa, was,
of course, a direct result of the policy of purchasing "New Negroes."
By September 1798, nearly all of the eight West India Regiments had
already become African regiments. We have seen how this alteration
in the regional origins of the West India soldier was assisted by the

unwillingness of planters to sell Creole slaves to the army. Creole ranger corps were added, as we have seen, to the British Establishment at the end of 1798 as the Ninth, Tenth, Eleventh, and Twelfth West India Regiments. But they were all disbanded by 1804, and the troops from these regiments provided drafts for the renumbered Seventh and Eighth Regiments. By the end of the war attrition among these troops had transformed all but one of the remaining eight corps into African regiments.

What, indeed, were the national or ethnic origins of the African recruits? Because the British army evinced a distinct preference for Africans from certain areas, particularly the Gold Coast, the supposed origin of each recruit was recorded in the several *Description and Succession Books* of the West India Regiments.[25] (See table 4.) But just how exact are these recordings? According to Alfred Burdon Ellis, who was a nineteenth-century soldier, officer in, historian of the First West India Regiment, as well as an ethnographer of West Africa, it was virtually impossible to distinguish the ethnicity of the mass of African recruits. Slave dealers who collected them for sale in the New World identified their human cargoes only by the name of the port from which they were shipped, for example, "Senegal." In the eighteenth century, the name "Senegal"—now a river and a republic—meant first the town of Saint-Louis and secondly the river. Thus, a slave identified as Senegalese might be: (a) an individual transported from Saint-Louis, whatever his nationality; (b) a Wolof of Cayor from the immediate vicinity of the town; or, (c) a Pular-speaker from Futa Toro in the middle valley of the Senegal. Individuals who originally recorded the alleged nationality of the slave obviously recognized cultural variants; but they seldom knew much about Africa, and the typology they employed was neither that of their African contemporaries nor that of present-day ethnographers.[26]

Professor Philip Curtin's synthesis of various West African ethnographical studies also points to a second and equally confusing European habit of identifying African nationalities. This was to choose one ethnic or linguistic designation to distinguish a much larger group, as in the case of, for example, "Bambara," "Mandingo," "Coromantee," "Nago," "Congo," "Moco," "Popo," and "Chamba." "Bambara" was a catchall term for slaves brought from the interior and sold near the mouth of the Senegal River.[27] Far removed from the slave-hunting

Table 4. Ethnic-Regional Origins of African-Born Recruits
of the Fifth West India Regiment, 1798–1808

Tribe/Region	1798	1799	1800	1801	1802	1803	1804	1805	1806	1807	1808	Totals
Eboe (Ibo)	12	—	—	45	66	—	110	1	—	—	—	234
Congo	44	—	—	23	—	—	35	1	—	—	—	103
Hausa	9	—	—	3	2	—	24	11	—	—	30	79
Moco (or Ibibio)	6	—	—	15	21	—	28	—	—	—	—	70
Mungola	35	1	1	16	—	—	1	—	—	—	—	54
Mundingo	10	—	1	4	1	—	24	—	—	—	—	40
Popo	7	—	—	2	—	—	11	4	—	—	2	26
Nago (Yoruba)	8	—	—	—	—	—	13	2	—	—	3	26
Mandingo	6	—	—	2	—	—	14	—	—	—	—	22
Coromantee	9	—	—	1	—	—	7	1	—	—	—	18
Mocha	—	—	—	3	3	—	6	—	—	—	—	12
Chamba	5	—	—	—	—	—	4	—	—	—	—	9
Fulla	1	—	—	—	—	—	6	—	—	—	—	7
Waree	6	—	—	—	—	—	—	—	—	—	—	6
Mozambi	2	—	—	1	1	—	1	—	—	—	—	5
Isa	—	—	—	1	2	—	1	—	—	—	—	4
Baraba	—	—	—	—	1	—	2	—	—	—	—	3
Olle	—	—	—	2	—	—	1	—	—	—	—	3
Occum	—	—	—	—	—	—	2	—	—	—	—	2
Brehar	2	—	—	—	—	—	—	—	—	—	—	2
Bona	—	—	—	—	2	—	—	—	—	—	—	2
Bambara	1	—	—	—	—	—	1	—	—	—	—	2
Wambre	1	—	—	—	—	—	—	—	—	—	—	1
Beeros	1	—	—	—	—	—	—	—	—	—	—	1
Banjah	1	—	—	—	—	—	—	—	—	—	—	1
Quajsee	1	—	—	—	—	—	—	—	—	—	—	1
Nogaba	1	—	—	—	—	—	—	—	—	—	—	1
Jarman	1	—	—	—	—	—	—	—	—	—	—	1
Matambee	1	—	—	—	—	—	—	—	—	—	—	1
Matamba	1	—	—	—	—	—	—	—	—	—	—	1
Senegal	1	—	—	—	—	—	—	—	—	—	—	1
Obano	—	—	—	—	—	—	1	—	—	—	—	1
Osohaba	—	—	—	—	—	—	1	—	—	—	—	1
Omoza	—	—	—	—	—	—	1	—	—	—	—	1
Sardrah	—	—	—	—	—	—	1	—	—	—	—	1
Otam	—	—	—	—	—	—	1	—	—	—	—	1
Yala	—	—	—	—	1	—	—	—	—	—	—	1
Beeby	—	—	—	1	—	—	—	—	—	—	—	1
Totals	172	1	2	119	100	—	296	20	—	—	35	745

Source: W.O. 25/656

Note: The spelling of the names, except for those in parentheses, are as they appear in the returns.

grounds in Africa, the army recruiter was dependent on this ethnic data and re-recorded it in the *Description and Succession Books* (see table 4).

Despite the ambiguity and overlapping terminology that resulted from these novice typological efforts, recognizable ethnic information was noted, and it too found its way to the pages of the *Description and Succession Books*. This was the case for the "Eboe" (Ibo) and Hausa, and this data is significant, for Ibos and Hausas comprised a sizable proportion of the Africans recruited into the West India Regiments during the war. (The pattern which results from this data, as well as the information on the origins of African recruits contained in the *Description and Succession Books,* corresponds with the general pattern of Britain's and France's slave shipments to the Caribbean during this period.[28]) Equally significant is the listings in these books of the birthplace of recruits, expressed in terms of towns or districts and regions. The place of birth of Private James Adams of the Fifth West India Regiment, for example, is listed as "Congoki, Mongola"; and Private Charles Baillie, also of the Fifth, is listed as being from the district of "Moano" in "Eboe" country. This specific data could have been easily and accurately obtained by interrogating a slave-informant, either through a member of his own language group or another knowledgable African. The interrogators could be either West India soldiers or members of the slave or free black population.[29]

The *Description and Succession Books* of the West India Regiments abound in descriptions, often fastidiously recorded, of the body decorations of the African recruits, especially teeth cuttings and cicatrices. Private Robert Barrett of the Second West India Regiment, a "Congo," was described as having "Two upper Foreteeth Filed," while Private Samuel Alderly, also of the Second, and identified as an "Ebo," was decorated with "37 Small Cuts on [his] Right Shoulder."[30] How useful is this information in helping to retrieve the apparently lost identity of recruits whose ethnicity was so inexpertly determined? Authorities differ on this question. According to an older study, body decorations at one time were recognized tribal badges and set one group off from another; the original significance of the practice of cicatrizing the face and torso in West Africa was, however, lost during the pre-European era. By the late eighteenth century the scars had become mere adornments. More recent scholarship, on the other hand, suggests that scarification does have ethnological importance.[31] Although further study of these curious national distinctions might prove useful, an examination of the numerous descriptions of cicatrices in the *Description and Succession Books* shows that in most cases soldiers with the same ethnic or regional designation usually had different facial and body marks.[32]

If body decorations served no useful ethnological purpose, their recording did afford at least one benefit to the army. In the event of desertion, an offender could be more readily identified. Private Edward Gload, a deserter from the Second West India Regiment, was described in an advertisement in a Kingston, Jamaica, newspaper as five feet six inches tall, a member of the "Maraba nation," and the bearer of "a scar on the left side of his mouth, marked also on both sides of the forehead."[33] The army's assiduity in such matters also disclosed that many of the African-born recruits had suffered from highly infectious diseases characterized by skin eruptions, since there are numerous references to recruits being scarred and "Pitted with . . . Small Pox."[34]

Although the West India Regiments were composed chiefly of recruits from various African nations, as well as a diminishing number of Creoles, no apparent attempt was made to form companies of Africans belonging to a single national or language group, or even of Creole soldiers. On the contrary, the *Description and Succession Books* show that companies were heterogeneously formed of, for instance, Ibos, Hausas, and Creoles.[35] The reason for this organization was, no doubt, the time-honored principle of divide and rule. At a time when mutinies were frequent events in nearly all British garrisons and even in the Royal Navy, the ethnic and regional heterogeneity of each company in the West India Regiments worked against a mutiny. The policy of dispersion also tended to reduce the chances of collective action with mutinous intent.

The records give no evidence whatever of friction among Africans of different groups or between Africans and Creole soldiers. This is extraordinary since, as Orlando Patterson has shown in his sociological study of slavery in Jamaica, there was serious dissension between Creoles and African slaves, particularly Ibos. His study also shows that antipathy existed among Africans of different nations.[36] Yet there is not a single reference to this sort of disharmony in the numerous and candid Inspection and Confidential Reports, nor in other official correspondence. Perhaps the incomparably better position of both Africans and Creoles as British soldiers vis-à-vis the slaves eliminated serious discord within the ranks.

In spite of the language problem and concomitant difficulties (one of which was the slowness of African recruits to learn their musket drill),[37] there were certain advantages in recruiting Africans. These were summed up by Hislop in 1801 in his invaluable "Remarks on the Establishment of West India Regiments."

> Among other circumstances favorable to the measure of forming the Regiments from new imported Africans, one deserving notice is, that they are received, wholly unacquainted with and uncontaminated by the Vices which prevail among the Slaves in the Towns and Plantations, having no acquaintance or connection of any sort, but such as they form in the Regiment. I have invariably found them to make the most orderly, clean and attentive Soldiers. Out of two hundred and upwards, which have been received into the [Eleventh West India] Regiment in the course of Five years and a half, there are not above three or four instances of any of them being punished, and not one for any serious offence, whereas many of those who are furnished by the Planters, when the Regiment was formed, have very frequently deserved (as some have met) Capital punishment.
>
> The new African recruit becomes gradually initiated into the habits of a Military life, and ere' long discovers the superiority of his situation above the Slave, whose debased state he has never been subject to. He likewise feels himself proportionably elevated, from the rank which his officers hold in Society, and the respect which he sees is paid to them.[38]

Efforts to overcome the dual problem of language and illiteracy were undertaken somewhat late and achieved limited success. In August 1811, the Duke of York sought official sanction from the secretary for war and colonies to attach a literate and disciplined European sergeant to each company of every West India Regiment.

These noncommissioned officers were to be attracted to this service by additional pay of a shilling a day.[39] In the past white sergeants had occasionally transferred into West India Regiments from European line regiments stationed in the Caribbean; but, because of poor discipline and irregular habits, these men were frequently court-martialed and reduced to the ranks.[40] The establishment of a regimental school for each British regiment, white and black, and headed by a "Serjeant Schoolmaster" was also considered. In order to run the schools, it was hoped that the attraction of extra pay would encourage noncommissioned officers to join the West India Regiments.[41]

Once the recommendations had been made, efforts to provide them with official approval moved swiftly. In December 1811, the cost of augmenting the establishment of the eight West India Regiments by one European sergeant major per company was computed at the modest annual sum of £1,460.[42] On 23 January 1812, a circular letter from the secretary of war notified the colonels of the West India Regiments that the establishment of their respective corps would be augmented in accordance with the Duke of York's proposal.[43] Swift official sanction was not, however, followed by equally rapid implementation. The major obstacle was that the circular letter of 23 January 1812 stipulated that a European sergeant major not be attached to a company until a vacancy had occurred. Furthermore, according to another War Office circular to the colonels, the extra allowance of one shilling per diem for the sergeant majors, would not begin until 25 May 1814, more than two years later;[44] no official explanation for the lag was offered. Under these circumstances, it is unlikely that more than a few of these men had joined the West India Regiments before the war ended in 1815.

Attempts to reduce illiteracy in the West India Regiments by means of regimental schools were slightly more productive; nonetheless, there was much room for improvement by 1815. In January 1812, a circular letter from the Duke of York had established these schools for the West India Regiments.[45] It appears that none of the eight regiments had been able to open their schools during the first year. The reason usually given was the inability to find a "fit Person" to take charge.[46] The lamentable fact was that, even by the end of the war, most of these corps had failed to establish their regimental schools. A "Confidential Report on the Inspection of the 7th West India Regiment" at Curacao on 30 September 1815, for example, disclosed that the Seventh was unable to find anyone in the regiment capable of conducting the school; nor could anyone on the island be procured.[47]

Only the Fourth and Fifth Regiments seemed to have been at all successful. By May 1815, the Fourth, then based at Antigua, had enrolled fifty-seven men and boy "scholars." Many were reportedly progressing extremely well at learning to read and write. Even though the "School Master Serjeant" had been reduced to the ranks by a court-martial on charges of drunkenness and neglect of duty, the school was convened twice a day by a company sergeant major and a corporal. It was also visited regularly by the officer of the day, who was responsible for reporting on its progress. The commander of the Fourth was also preparing to set up a trade school for younger soldiers. His fledgling curriculum would include instruction in shoe-making, tailoring, and military armoring.[48] The Fifth Regiment's success in establishing its regimental school was cut short by the death of its schoolmaster, then interrupted again when the corps was ordered to join the expedition against New Orleans. During the time the school was in operation, privates, drummers, and noncommissioned officers had made progress. The plan was to re-establish the school as soon as a capable instructor could be obtained.[49]

The long-term success of the army's plans to combat illiteracy in the black regiments can perhaps be judged from the frank comments of Dr. John Davy. Davy was attached to the Windward and Leeward Island Command and observed these troops during his tour of duty from 1845 to 1848. Around 1853, Davy wrote that the West India Regiments were composed of blacks recruited in Africa. The majority of these men, he noted, were ignorant of the English language or at most were acquainted with it in the "most imperfect manner." As for the regimental schools, Davy had this to say:

> There is a school at the head quarters of each regiment, or a school room, but not always provided with a teacher: I can speak from my own knowledge of negligence of this kind, which is likely to be concealed from the higher authorities.[50]

CLOTHING

The problem of clothing, which Fortescue has so ably described, had serious consequences for the entire British army. The long war against France was an additional strain on an obsolete and cumbersome system. According to Fortescue, thousands of British soldiers died of exposure during Britain's three misadventures in Flanders and Holland (in 1793, 1794, and 1799) because of the wastefulness, inefficiency, and helplessness of the army's clothing system. And in the West Indies, because of inadequate supplies of shoes, additional thousands had to endure the attacks of insects, which often resulted in malignant ulcers and amputated toes. Hundreds of men were subsequently discharged from the Army because of infirmities caused by inadequate clothing.[51]

To be sure, the inability to properly clothe the troops stemmed in large measure from an ancient system, which permitted colonels of regiments to profit from clothing their men. This practice led to inefficiency, delay, and abuse. But the difficulties also resulted from the unexpected scale of the war and the inability of Britain's still-fledgling textile industries, in spite of the Industrial Revolution, to keep pace with the army's needs.[52] Between 1793 and 1795, army estimates called for more than a threefold increase in troop strength, to a total of about 318,000 regulars, fencibles, militia, and foreign troops in British pay.[53]

Little wonder then that the Inspection and Confidential Reports of the West India Regiments are filled with references to clothing shortages, particularly in 1806. During the early part of that year, the entire First Regiment was found to be suffering severely: three companies at Trinidad were reported in the "greatest want of clothing"; five companies at Prince Ruperts', Dominica, were lacking many articles, but especially trousers and shoes; and a clothing return for a single company at Tobago showed that all the men of this detachment were "wanting" in trousers and shoes.[54] Other West India Regiments suffered similarly. An inspection of a detachment of the Fourth at Surinam in August 1806 disclosed that "the Regiment have received no Caps for their Augmentation, and the men are furnished partly with old Caps of different Corps."[55] A detachment of about fifty recruits belonging to the Sixth were reported to be without uniforms.[56] As late as July 1812, the British commander in the Windward and Leeward Islands angrily informed the Duke of York that not only had the clothing for the Third West India Regiment not arrived on time but uniforms for the entire force under his command were late.[57]

A common cause for delays in providing clothing to British soldiers —who were supposed to be issued new clothing once a year—was the confused management of regimental accounts by their agency. One such case involved the Seventh West India Regiment and its agent, Patrick Campbell. The secretary at war had repeatedly ordered that all accounts prior to 24 December 1797 for regiments managed by Campbell be delivered to the War Office for examination and settlement.[58] In March 1800, Campbell was commanded by an irate Windham to turn in these records before 25 June, "in a proper state." Failure to comply, Windham threatened, would necessitate "taking further measures to enforce the delivery of the same."[59] Throughout 1800, Campbell continued to receive angry letters from the War Office.[60] Campbell's standing seemed threatened when it was revealed that Lieutenant Campbell of the Seventy-fourth Regiment, who as a cadet at the Royal Military College, High Wycombe, had incurred debts he had never paid, was the nephew of Agent Campbell.[61] In December 1800, Campbell was directed once again to comply immediately with an order from the Duke of York. He was told to "Communicate to the Colonel of the 7th West India Reg^t. His Royal Highness's most positive Injunctions, that the Regiment shall be completed with Accoutrements & every Article of Appointment, with all possible Dispatch."[62]

In 1798 several proposals for reforming the existing clothing system were recommended by the Finance Committee of the House of Commons. These were found unacceptable, however, and in 1801 the old system was continued with only a few minor changes.[63] For the West India Regiments, the problem of clothing persisted throughout the war.

The uniform of the West India Regiments, although frequently in short supply, had undergone some changes between 1795 and 1812. In February 1800, British regiments were issued the cylindrical black felt "stovepipe" shako. White cap covers were probably worn over them by West India soldiers and European troops stationed in the Caribbean. This shako, which remained the headdress of the British army until 1812, was adorned with regimental plates and colored hackles: white for grenadiers, green for the light company, and white with red base for the battalion companies. The huge bearskin hats worn by grenadiers in European regiments apparently were not issued to Britain's black grenadiers.

Two jackets, distinguished by the color of the regimental facing, were issued:[64] the customary short red jacket, which had "wing" epaulettes for the flank companies; and an equally short white jacket, worn for drill and fatigue with loose-fitting white trousers. Snug-fitting white breeches, which flared at the bottom to cover the shoes, gaiter style, were worn on more formal occasions. Great coats were also issued. All leather equipment was black; but in 1803, buff-colored accouterments were finally adopted.[65] Officers wore a long-skirted scarlet coat and a high black hat with a broad brim.[66] And, contrary to the belief of some who maintain that no information about the uniform of bandsmen of the West India Regiments exists, the color of the jacket of drummers, for instance, matched the regimental facing.[67]

Clothing, of course, was not the only, nor perhaps the major, cause of anxiety among officers of West India Regiments. When the war began, Britain lacked a modern small-arms industry, and there was a serious shortage of muskets until well after 1800.[68] The problem that affected the black regiments, however, was not the insufficient quantity of arms but rather the condition of the muskets issued to them. Nearly all of the complaints recorded in the Inspection Reports tell of old and unserviceable arms, many of which had formerly belonged to other regiments.[69] In some cases, West India soldiers were armed with captured Dutch weapons.[70]

CONTACT BETWEEN WEST INDIA SOLDIERS AND SLAVES

Because it was customary for British troops to police the slave population, in addition to fighting the soldiers of other colonial powers in the West Indies, numerous posts were sited close to plantations.[71] As

late as the governorship of Sir Eyre Coote at Jamaica (1806 to 1808),
a small post was erected at "Woodstock" in Portland, some "twelve
Miles from Port Antonio;" according to the Jamaica commander, there
was a conspiracy among the local slaves there.[72] Even large coastal
fortifications, like Fort Shirley at Prince Ruperts', Dominica, nestled
alongside plantations.[73] The distribution of West India soldiers among
these posts and forts assured frequent contacts between the black
troops and the plantation slaves. Even white troops readily established
relations with the slaves, particularly at the local markets, which have
been described as places of interracial concourse.[74]

Black soldiers also had the opportunity, on market days, to mix
freely with slaves who lived many miles away.[75] The investigation of
the alleged conspiracy of the Fourth West India Regiment at St. Kitts
disclosed that black soldiers often traveled around the island speak-
ing to the slaves and even dining with them.[76] After being discharged
from service, many soldiers settled on plantations near their posts,
where, during the course of several years, they had developed
acquaintances among the estate slaves.[77] Under these circumstances,
it was impossible to keep the two groups separate. Yet British commanders invariably tried. In the Windward and Leeward Islands, Sir
Thomas Trigge's "constant" policy was to instill a sense of pride in
the West India soldier only in order to give him a feeling of superiority
over the "generality of Negroes." Trigge confessed that he sought to
prevent the slaves and soldiers from making "common cause," which
would endanger Britain's position in the Caribbean.[78] (Dr. Pinckard,
it will be remembered, voiced a similar fear.) The government was
reminded by Jamaicans that planters and the army could agree on
one point: intercourse between black soldiers and slaves would under-
mine the planters' control over their bondsmen. Major General Hugh
Carmichael's first order of business on assuming command of the
Second West India Regiment in 1796 was to prevent, as much as
possible, all communication between the regiment and the slaves.
Like Trigge, he hoped to accomplish this impossible task by means of
indoctrination.[79]

Private Derby's crime of hiding three women slaves was perhaps not
an extraordinary incident. Numerous records indicate that the West
India soldier sought to establish ties with the slaves, especially black

women with whom he might form normal relationships. The army's effort to isolate the black soldier from the slave population meant that he was expected to live a celibate life, whereas among the European troops on overseas duty, six "lawfull Wives of Soldiers" for every hundred men were permitted to accompany the regiment.[80]

It was not surprising, therefore, that proprietors of nearby estates began to complain of female slaves being lured away by West India soldiers. Sir William Young claimed that black soldiers frequently intruded upon his estate in search of female companions. He also noted a resultant animosity between the soldiers and the male slaves. Although this divisiveness could be used to good advantage to prevent slaves and soldiers from joining forces, Young saw a potentially greater danger in the liaisons. This type of association, he warned,

> may be carried to an extremity, and have consequences, which make me doubt if it is wisely so considered; yet in the alternative of favorable reception, and domestication with the negro families, a connexion and common cause with armed men, at some critical period, might not be safe; and in the ordinary course of Nature and events, a rising generation of children, born and remaining slaves, with relation to a soldier-father, might at some time awaken feelings, and create consequences, endangering the whole colonial system.[81]

One of the first means proposed to remedy the situation was the establishment of something approaching a military brothel. In May 1799, President Ottley of St. Vincent recommended that black women be employed "about" the West India Regiment stationed on the island. It is not known what became of his suggestion, although slave prostitution had been condoned earlier in and around Fort Augusta, Jamaica.[82] In 1801, however, Hislop proposed a more respectable plan to purchase female slaves and attach a number of them to each black company. The women would be encouraged to marry the most well-behaved men in the companies. Severe punishment would be meted out to anyone interfering with the marriages as well as to married soldiers found guilty of adultery. Hislop's plan, which was subsequently implemented—decades before marriage among the slave populations[83] was seriously encouraged—was motivated by strictly practical considerations. His plan, he wrote, would be of "considerable advantage and profit to the Publick."

> The children would of course, be the property of Government, and whether Male or Female, should remain constantly with the Regiment, and be considered as belonging to it. Boys would be trained to arms, and become in time excellent Soldiers.
>
> The Girls, when at a proper age, would be allowed to marry in the Regiment, and during their younger years might be taught such employment as would make them useful to it. It would also be but just to allow the same ration of provisions to them, as to the Wives and Children of Soldiers in European Regiments.[84]

So the West India Regiments were to recruit themselves!

Records of black women associated with the West India Regiments are fragmentary at best; they suggest that by the end of the war only a few women were attached to the black regiments. A return for 1804 includes 515 women and 535 children scattered among British garrisons in the West Indies, but it is not known whether they were blacks, whites, or both.[85] The same return shows a separate listing of 535 "Negroes"; since their sex is not indicated, it is safe to assume they were "fort Negroes"—military slave laborers that were attached to every garrison in the Caribbean.

Periodic regimental returns offer somewhat more information, but since data on black women were not systematically recorded—or were not adequately preserved—the records do not provide precise figures for any given year. What we have confirms the suspicion that very few West India soldiers had wives. A return for the Fifth West India Regiment for December 1807 shows only forty-one women accompanying their "reputed" husbands at Honduras. Twenty-seven children were also present. A return for the First Regiment for October 1815 lists fifty women and twenty-three children as drawing rations. In December 1819, when postwar military reduction was in effect, Governor Woodford of Trinidad noted that few black women had married West India soldiers.[86]

Unfortunately, little else is known of the relationship between West India soldiers and the slaves nor of the consequences of their association. Notwithstanding the disdain with which the West India soldier was taught to view the slave, and the animosity that existed between male slaves and soldiers, the slaves must have greatly admired the soldier for his freedom and his comparatively pampered life-style. At least one slave was discovered attempting to enlist illegally into a West India Regiment.[87] There were many conditions that would tend to unite soldier and slave in friendship, not the least of which was a common nationality and memories of a lost African homeland.

RELIGIOUS SERVICE

Very little is known about religious service or instruction offered to West India soldiers. Apparently, chaplains were usually present in black regiments, for there is not a single reference to a clerical absenteeism. Yet the Inspection and Confidential Reports are conspicuously silent on this aspect of regimental life; only two references have been found regarding this topic.[88] Inspection of the Seventh West India Regiment in October 1812 disclosed that the corps was composed mainly of Roman Catholics. A more informative report on the Fifth Regiment, stationed at Fort Augusta, Jamaica in June 1812, revealed that the entire regiment attended divine service every Sunday. This service was conducted by the rector of Spanish Town on the parade ground at Fort Augusta. This is a most interesting disclosure since the Established Church had theretofore completely neglected the slave. In 1816 a local act was passed appointing curates to assist the rectors in propagating the gospel among the slaves in Jamaica. They were paid a salary of £300 per annum, which was increased to £500 in 1818. Their efforts, it is said, bore few results.[89] It would seem that the same rector who refused, or was not permitted to provide religious instruction to slaves journeyed from Spanish Town to Fort Augusta every Sunday to instruct the West India soldiers.

WEST INDIA REGIMENTS AS LABOR BATTALIONS

It was customary for the British army to employ troops on unusual work details or fatigues, a practice that probably sprang from periodic efforts to avoid the high costs of the army's early dependence on contracted civilian labor. Work of this type was eagerly sought after, for in 1800 the extra pay for the rank-and-file was ninepence per day. By the end of the war, fatigue pay had been somewhat modified—to tenpence per day in the summer and eightpence each day during the winter months.[90] The fact that British soldiers received only a small fraction of their regular pay directly in hand—because of various stoppages for food, uniforms, etc.—greatly encouraged them to undertake fatigue work.

Since it had long since been recognized that it was more economical to employ blacks on military fatigues than whites, West India soldiers were frequently employed as artificers during the many lulls in the war. Reluctance to undertake this type of work apparently was limited to the corps serving under Andrew Cochrane Johnstone at Dominica, and for good reason. The willingness of blacks to perform fatigue work was probably also affected by the continuous and extensive use made of them on active military operations. The numerous battle reports and the several battle honors won by the regiments attest to their proud status. Quite a different situation prevailed in World War I, when black West Indian soldiers were largely viewed by the War Office as service troops and so employed—with serious social and political repercussions at the end of the war in Europe and the Caribbean.[91] West India Regiments were regarded by the army as important fighting formations, and their military standing was not lowered by fatigue work. At Trinidad, black soldiers were continually employed on all sorts of projects; the Eleventh built roads and public buildings in addition to constructing fortifications. At one time, 300 men of the Eleventh worked every day for four hours clearing the heights above Port of Spain to strengthen the fortifications protecting the city.[92] Later the Ninth and Twelfth Regiments removed brush at Chaguaramos preparatory to building a defensive work.[93] At the Honduras Settlement, the Fifth West India Regiment dug a canal, for which they were paid 1s. 8d. in local currency each day.[94]

The rising cost to the army of hiring slaves increased the use of West India Regiments as service corps. By 1800, the regular pay of the British soldier was one shilling per diem; in 1802 the reported daily cost of a hired slave was three shillings.[95] Deducting the regular daily soldier's pay of one shilling and the ninepence extra paid for fatigue duty from this sum, the additional cost of a hired slave was 1s. 3d. a day. Moreover, based on the slightly higher 1805 cost for hired slaves, the difference, for example, between employing 1,000 soldiers for 182 days and hiring an equal number of slaves for the same duration was £23,508.6.8! Although the availability of black soldiers was dependent on the state of relations between Britain and her neighbors in the Caribbean, and although the amount claimed to feed one hired slave per day was probably excessive, the savings realized by employing West India soldiers were substantial. No cost-conscious government could ignore these simple computations. It has already been noted that many of the men implicated in the mutiny of the Eighth Regiment at Dominica in 1802 were punished by being reduced to pioneers. There is no question that the decision was motivated entirely by the army's need to limit spending on labor; the inclusion of these unfortunate men in the army's permanent but small pioneer corps would lessen proportionately the dependence on hired slaves.[96]

Finally, although official records are silent on this point, it can be safely assumed that such extensive dependence on the West India Regiments as labor battalions resulted in at least some abusive practices.

Some of the problems discussed in this chapter affected all British regiments serving in the West Indies. Most of the issues, however, were unique to the black units because of the type of soldier recruited, the kind of service he was expected to perform, and the restrictive character of the society in which these regiments were raised.

7

RECRUITING AND DISBANDMENT, 1808-1815

Passage of the act outlawing the slave trade on British vessels aroused immediate concern in the army. After 1807 the army could no longer rely on the slave ships to furnish a steady stream of African recruits for its West India Regiments.[1] Foreseeing the difficulties of maintaining the prescribed strength of the corps after the trade ceased, the government provided that Africans would continue to be enlisted for lifetime service; by this time, as a result of the Mutiny Act of 1806, Europeans were being enlisted for limited service of seven years only.[2]

The British government also provided for the West India Regiments to receive new African recruits even after the act was put into effect on 1 January 1808. Anticipating that enemy shipping interests, as well as a few brazen British speculators, would continue the trade in slaves, an Order in Council of 16 March 1808 established a vice-admiralty court at Sierra Leone to which all illegally transported or condemned slaves captured by Royal Navy ships or privateers along the African coast were to be taken for adjudication. All fit liberated (recaptured) Africans would there be turned over to British military and naval authorities for enlistment.[3] The decision to enlist Africans taken from captured slavers required one further step to guarantee recruits for the regiments: since it was illegal to enlist aliens into the army—and since captured slaves were classified as aliens—a special relaxation in the law was arranged.[4]

Despite these measures, abolition resulted in a permanent reduction in the overall strength of the West India Regiments from 1807 until the end of the war. In August of 1807, the total effective strength of these corps was about 7,950. In January 1809, this force returned 7,488 total effectives. Eleven months later the number had dropped to 7,149; and by November 1810, the total effective strength of the eight regiments had further shrunk to 6,745.[5] This decline reflected casualties sustained by the West India Regiments in a series of campaigns fought between 1808 and 1810. A steady attrition is also apparent in specific regimental returns. In May 1808, the First West India Regiment returned 1,057 other ranks; by October 1815 there were only 722 sergeants, corporals, drummers, and privates in the First.[6]

How many recruits were actually provided for the regiments between March 1808 and the end of the war by the policy of enlisting so-called liberated Africans? According to a return prepared by the Liberated African Department at Sierra Leone, 2,009 men and boys were enlisted into the West India Regiments, the Royal African Corps, and the Royal African Colonial Corps during this period. Unfortunately, there is no indication of the distribution of recruits among the three corps (see table 5). Nor are Kuczynski's and Johnson Asiegbu's tabulations of any assistance, for their figures are also composite enlistments for the three corps and even include the Royal Navy.[7] What is more important, neither Kuczynski nor Asiegbu made use of the incomplete but, nonetheless, significant recruiting records of the African Recruiting Establishment at Bance Island, Sierra Leone.

Although the recruiting depot was not established until 1812 and several of the monthly returns are missing, the records do provide some assistance in determining how many recaptured Africans were enlisted into the West India Regiments from 1808 to 1815. The actual number will probably never be known, but it appears that of the estimated 2,009 men and boys enlisted at Sierra Leone, about 1,600 went into the West India Regiments. In addition, a number of free Africans, who probably lived in Sierra Leone or the nearby regions, voluntarily enlisted into the West India Regiments; it is thought that the volunteers numbered about 200. A total, then, of some 1,800 men and boys were recruited on the West African coast for service in the West India Regiments.[8]

During the same period recruits for the corps were obtained from a variety of other sources. Vice-admiralty courts in the British West

Table 5. Slaves Captured and Condemned, and Their
Disposal at Freetown, Sierra Leone, 1808–1815

	Total					Recruited				
Year	Men	Boys	Women	Girls	Total	Men	Boys	Women	Girls	Total
1808	39	16	12	11	78	—	—	—	—	—
1809	86	80	57	57	280	—	—	—	—	—
1810	471	281	195	140	1,087	70	—	—	—	70
1811	246	114	121	64	545	45	—	—	—	45
1812	1,265	408	337	180	2,190	959	122	48	7	1,136
1813	227	117	57	45	446	144	17	6	2	169
1814	1,017	426	270	157	1,870	445	13	15	—	473
1815	583	253	277	183	1,296	191	3	4	—	198
Totals	3,934	1,695	1,326	837	7,792	1,854	155	73	9	2,091

Source: C.O. 267/127, "Return showing the Number of Liberated Africans received into the Colony of Sierra Leone specifying the Name of the Vessel from which they were landed, the state of Adjudication and the manner in which the said Persons were then and subsequently disposed of as appears by the Register kept in the Office of the Liberated African Department." These figures are not thought to be complete. Nor were they tabluated correctly in the original.

Note: Those recruited "Entered His Majesty's Land Service as Soldiers for the West India Regiment, Royal African Corps, and Royal African Colonial Corps with their wives and Children."

Indies turned over about 300 captured blacks;[9] a few slaves owned by army officers in the West Indies were purchased by the commissary general in 1812.[10] Even a few slaves incarcerated in a Kingston, Jamaica, jail on charges of conspiring to rebel were subsequently enlisted into the West India Regiments.[11] And finally, a few hundred West Indian slaves, chiefly from the Dutch islands, were brought into the corps.[12]

A grand total, then, of about 2,500 men from all recruiting sources were enlisted into the West India Regiments during the entire eight-year period.

If it is understandable why there was an initial diminution in the strength of the force, we may still wonder why recruiting failed to produce sufficient numbers of Africans to maintain the prescribed establishment of the regiments? The chief reason is that the recruiting depot at Sierra Leone was not established until four years after the Order in Council of 16 March 1808; in the interim the need for a recruiting center on the African coast had been repeatedly advanced.[13] There was also some confusion as to where this depot should be located; from 1800 to as late as 1811, Goree, an island off the coast of modern Senegal at Cape Verde, was considered.[14] Bance Island, however, was finally selected and the depot opened there in April 1812. Poor recruiting in Africa, especially during 1808 and 1809, was the result of the policy of Thomas Perronet Thompson, the first governor of Sierra Leone appointed by the Crown. Disturbed by the existence of slavery in the colony, Thompson forbade the recruiting of liberated Africans into British military service on the grounds that lifetime service was a form of apprenticeship.[15] In August 1808, the month after Thompson assumed office, an ordinance was passed declaring the system of apprenticing liberated Africans within the colony illegal.

The need to recruit the West India Regiments and other colonial corps was of primary importance to the British government, and Governor Thompson was eventually recalled. In February 1810, Captain Columbine of the Royal Navy took over the administration of the colony. Columbine was instructed to reinstate immediately the recruitment of liberated Africans into the services, as set forth in the Order in Council of 16 March 1808. He was cautioned to implement fair methods of inducing Africans to enlist but not to overlook any proper means in re-establishing a strong recruiting organization.[16] There had been virtually no replacements for two years, and the need for African recruits was desperate.

In 1811, the Duke of York proposed a bounty of eight guineas to be paid to each recruit as an inducement.[17] Enlistments finally began in 1810, although the numbers were insignificant for at least another year (see table 5). Apparently none of the men recruited during this time were enlisted into the West India Regiments.

Involuntary enlistment of liberated Africans continued. According to Dr. Robert Thorpe, the chief justice of the colony and judge of the vice-admiralty court at Freetown from 1811 to 1813, the consent of a captured slave was never sought. Even Ellis, the historian of the First West India Regiment, admits this.[18] Asiegbu claims that Britain's essential interest in the colony was as a recruiting area and that as a result coercion was employed to obtain recruits. He also points out that the 1808 change to Crown Colony status for Sierra Leone marked the beginning of the end of the humanitarian and philanthropic spirit that had guided its early development.[19] Crown Colony status in effect meant that imperial needs would shape the substance and tone of metropolitan policy regarding Sierra Leone. The evidence on recruitment clearly supports Asiegbu's assessment.[20]

There were additional factors explaining the poor recruitment results from 1808 to 1815. Apparently not all of the slaves taken from slavers seized on the African coast were brought to Sierra Leone. According to one dispatch, fifty Africans taken from French slave ships were detained by the customs collector at the Cape of Good Hope and subsequently attached to British regiments there as laborers. They were given uniforms and the same pay as British soldiers.[21] Moreover, the seized slavers frequently contained only a few men and boys judged fit enough for military service; the inmates of these ships existed under appalling conditions. Hundreds were found dead, and many of the survivors suffered from dysentery, scurvy, smallpox, and ulcerations. Some of the adults asked to be returned to their homes, and many others were indentured as apprentices at Sierra Leone.[22]

According to one authority, the total number of liberated Africans recruited into Britain's military services up to 1833 was only 3,147.[23] Although this figure appears to be a bit low, it is certainly true that recruiting in Africa proceeded very slowly indeed. It may have even prompted the eventual establishment of a second recruiting depot at Havana, Cuba, where other Africans may have been purchased by the government.[24]

Despite the difficulties associated with recruiting on the African coast, the British experiment encouraged the Dutch to begin intensive military recruitment at St. George d'Elmina, on the Guinea coast around 1836; the new troops were to see service in the Dutch West Indies. Following the pattern established by Britain at Sierra Leone, the Dutch, and later the French, liberated or manumitted prospective recruits after purchasing them. Yet many of these so-called liberated slaves are said to have been transported to Surinam and the Dutch and French West Indies in chains or under guard.[25]

The end of the long war produced the inevitable retrenchment in British military spending. For the West India Regiments this meant first some disbandments, then a reduced peacetime establishment, and finally wholesale disbandment. In May 1817, the Seventh and Eighth Regiments were ordered disbanded. The ranks of the Eighth, except for those no longer fit for active service, were drafted into various West India Regiments in the Windward and Leeward Islands Command. The officers were paid until 24 December 1816 and issued passage money to Britain, as were those of the Seventh Regiment. Most of the other ranks of the Seventh were drafted into the Fifth. An immediate consequence of the disbandments of these two corps was the disestablishment of the recruiting depot at Sierra Leone on 7 March 1816.[26]

In January 1817, the remaining six West India Regiments were granted a peace establishment of 800 rank-and-file each, and a circular to this effect was forwarded to the colonels of the regiments on 5 February.[27] The supernumeraries from the reduced corps and the disbanded regiments were drafted into six garrison-pioneer companies. These troops, numbering 1,212 in both commands, were paid threepence per day and were issued clothing and rations. Pecuniary considerations dictated the formation of these companies, which helped the army realize a considerable saving over the old, expensive system of hiring slave pioneers.[28]

Troops discharged because of old age or wounds were permitted to settle on the islands of their choice. Their disability would determine the size of their pension: eightpence per diem for those rendered totally incapable of self-support and fivepence to those capable of maintaining themselves. It is not known how many disabled West India soldiers were in fact discharged into West Indian society at this time. The number certainly was not large. Establishment of a facility at Barbados to maintain soldiers judged insane was also proposed.[29]

The reduced establishment was followed almost immediately by general disbandment. Between March 1817 and October 1818 the Third, Fourth, Fifth, and Sixth West India Regiments were ordered disbanded. Five companies of the Third were retained until 1825.[30] The remaining two regiments, the First and the Second, were further reduced to 650 rank-and-file members. Thereafter, each command would have but one West India Regiment among its troops. Britain's special European regiments—the Royal York Rangers, the Royal West India Rangers, and the York Chasseurs—were also disbanded, although not in the West Indies. Probably because they contained numerous "culprits" and Frenchmen, they were disbanded in Canada.[31]

General disbandment of the West India Regiments created the major problem of disposing of these troops. Where and how would they live? According to the original plan, the disbanded troops, several thousand of them, would each be allowed to choose an island home.[32] Hostility towards the black regiments persisted, however, and there was nearly unanimous colonial opposition to this scheme. Only Trinidad, which saw the troops as sources of much-needed labor and as militiamen, favored the plan.[33] Rather naively, the Duke of York requested Earl Bathurst, Secretary of War and Colonies, to remind the colonial governors of the great service performed by these troops; he insisted that because of their faithfulness, they should be permitted to settle peaceably in the West Indies. In the same letter, the Duke noted the dissatisfaction among the ranks with any plan to send the African-born soldiers back to their homeland. Although Bathurst concurred, a compromise solution was worked out.[34] Some of the soldiers were permitted to remain in the Caribbean, but only on Trinidad or in the remote Honduras territory. The third area selected for settlement was Sierra Leone. Creole soldiers and those brought from Africa at an early age were to remain in the West Indies; the remainder would be removed to Sierra Leone.[35]

Some 350 soldiers of the Third and an undisclosed number of troops from the disbanded Sixth, along with their families, were eventually settled on Crown lands in Trinidad.[36] Settlements were located on several sites about two miles distant from each other and located eight to twelve miles east of Arima. In addition to the pension, one pound of salt meat, eight plantains "or the equivalent," and an undisclosed amount of rice was temporarily provided for each man and woman daily. Children received half of this ration. Rum was also issued at the discretion of the governor. Each settler was to receive a grant of land in the area of the settlement and was expected to quickly become self-sufficient.[37]

Although the old soldiers were encouraged to settle on the island, there were still some lingering doubts about their loyalty. Accordingly, some of these soldiers were not immediately given arms, and a superintendency was established to administer the settlements. The superintendent, a former officer of the disbanded regiments, was to receive his half-pay as well as an additional salary of £500 sterling. He too was provided with a land grant in the vicinity of the settlement and a small staff, including a surgeon.[38]

These settlers were not unique newcomers to Trinidad. Several hundred freed American blacks who had served with British forces during the War of 1812 had already been added to the population. The latter founded the famous "company towns." Nor were the military settlers of 1819 to be the last; disbanded West India soldiers were almost continuously settled on the island. One authority claims that in 1862 one-eighth of the population was composed of discharged soldiers.[39]

British Honduras was selected to settle soldiers from the Fifth West India Regiment. Although information surrounding the disposal of this corps is incomplete, its *Description and Succession Book* lists approximately 169 soldiers who were settled in the territory during the early months of 1817.[40]

The other area in which large numbers of discharged West India soldiers were settled was, of course, the colony of Sierra Leone. Records show that the majority of disbanded West India soldiers were settled here. In 1818, for instance, 1,222 black men and their families —soldiers from the Third and Fourth Regiments and the Bahama Garrison Company, as well as, probably, pioneers and musicians from other British regiments—were settled in Sierra Leone. Unfortunately we do not know exactly how many of these were West India soldiers. In April the following year 1,030 more soldiers, chiefly from the disbanded Fourth and the reduced Second Regiments, arrived in the colony. As in Trinidad, several military communities were established. During the early days of settlement, the majority of the former soldiers were located at Freetown, probably with a view to the defense of the capital. Later, some of them settled on new lands ceded to Great Britain. The villages of Waterloo, Gibraltar Town, Wellington, York, and Hastings are among those founded by discharged West India soldiers.[41]

Provisions for these settlers were similar to those made for their comrades in Trinidad and British Honduras. Every soldier in good health was to receive an allowance of fivepence a day for the rest of his life. Those suffering from wounds or other disabilities were to receive eightpence. Food was also issued, exclusive of rum, but money allowances did not begin until the provision allowance had ceased. And, since it was intended that these soldiers should become self-sufficient farmers, they were granted consignments of land and agricultural implements. In 1822, they were reported to be content and industrious in their new vocation.[42]

The value of the West India Regiments, after twenty years of arduous service, was undisputed. Even that early critic of the metropolitan measure to establish permanent black garrisons in the British Caribbean, Lieutenant General Henry Bowyer, acknowledged the African soldier as an undoubted asset in the West Indies.[43] Sir John Fortescue was at times critical of the West India Regiments, an attitude that was, surprisingly, largely a consequence of ignorance and prejudice. Nonetheless, he also recognized their significance.

> The formation of those native levies for the garrison of our tropical possessions is one of the most important facts in the military history of this period. The principle has since been indefinitely extended, though [he added] it is still subject to temporary limitations owing to the reluctance of white settlers to put arms in the hands of the coloured races.[44]

Even the Jamaica *Royal Gazette* came out with a surprising tribute to a West India Regiment, which underscored the *modus vivendi* eventually reached between the colony and the imperial government. Although the *Gazette* was still not prepared to support what it termed the "un-Jamaican" argument of accepting West India Regiments in principle, it did admit that black troops were highly useful in the Caribbean. Referring to the Second Regiment, which was leaving the island in 1819, the *Gazette* noted:

> The departure of the Second West-India Regiment from this island affords a proper occasion for speaking with approbation of the discipline and deportment of that Corps. It is perhaps peculiarly just that this tribute to the good conduct of the Regiment should emanate from the press of this city. No other part of the island

has had an equal opportunity with this vicinity of observing the demeanour and regularity of the officers and men. If prejudices have existed towards troops of this description, the conduct of the Second West-India Regiment has deservedly made a most favourable impression in their favour, at least upon those who have had opportunities of observing their habits and manners.[45]

8

CONCLUSION

The fear of arming indigenous peoples or peoples recruited from oppressed populations is as old as colonial or imperial armies—or, for that matter, as old as national armies. Giving guns to Africans, slave or free, in the New World or in Africa itself, was opposed by European settler groups and metropolitan factions alike. Both rebels and royalists in the rebellion against the rule of Spain in Latin America were uneasy with their decision to rely on slave troops. As late as the nineteenth century, and even well into the twentieth, the British in southern Africa were intensely uncomfortable with armed blacks in their midst. Similar anxieties were registered in the German Cameroons at the end of the nineteenth century; and efforts to minimize the alleged danger of arming Africans—while maximizing their indispensable utility—paralleled British efforts in the West Indies during the 1793-1815 war. Fearful lest retiring black soldiers should lead a rebellion to end German presence in the Cameroons, efforts were taken to keep them under immediate imperial control—offering inducements to re-enlist and special compensation for long-term military service.[1]

Nonetheless, this historic fear of arming blacks, particularly slaves, which was fueled by the cataclysmic events of the St. Domingo Revolution, was unfounded. On the contrary, by establishing the West India Regiments in 1795—in the midst of the struggle in St. Domingo —the British government effected a solution for the very problem most feared by the colonists: slaves, henceforth, would police the huge slave empire in the Caribbean. By 1800, the solution was in effective operation. However unpalatable to some at the present time, it is true that, with rare and inconsequential exceptions, the blacks of the West India Regiments upheld the plantocracy and thereby initiated a tradition passed on to Britain's colonial armies in tropical Africa. (Like the *askaris* in the West Indies, the *askaris* in Africa preserved law and order at home and fought with distinction abroad. No armies in British southern Africa played a revolutionary or liberating role, and none had any discernible effect on the pace or character of decolonization.[2]) The West India Regiments were a new army, and they were reflective of a new and expanding black society. Yet a black army did not spell the end of the plantation-slave system, as opponents of the regiments had wildly predicted.

Too much has been made of the St. Domingo experience as an argument against arming slaves. White colonists in the British West Indies opposed the establishment of slave-recruited regiments for essentially economic and commerical reasons, but they used the St. Domingo nightmare, conveniently and temporarily, to mask their real motives. Perhaps historians, who are generally ignorant of military matters in the Caribbean, were mesmerized by colonial rhetoric and the events occurring in St. Domingo between 1789 and 1804. Ragatz himself concluded, incorrectly, that colonial objections to the West India Regiments were "well-founded."[3] Such fears, if they ever existed, could only have been based on rebellions of the retainer contingents that were privately raised and maintained by proprietors during periods of emergency. Yet, Professor Ragatz would have been hard pressed indeed to find a significant number of incidents, if he found any at all, in which trustworthy slaves had turned on their masters *en mass*. So it was with the West India Regiments. The mutinies that did occur among these troops were not savage acts against the civilian population of the type that frequently occurred during the Sepoy Mutiny in 1857.[4] Instead, there were a handful of contained affairs, limited to military personnel within military environs; moreover, they occurred during a highly unstable period in the history of Britain's armed forces, an era notable for mutinies and desertions of mammoth proportions. Not only did the West India Regiments not jeopardize the slave system, they in fact buttressed (and simultaneously modified) it with tough and dependable African soldiers.

Not even the most obdurate colonial critic of the garrisoning of the British Caribbean with black regiments could deny their usefulness. The *modus vivendi* eventually worked out between the colonial party and London—whereby the proprietors grudgingly accepted the presence of West India Regiments in exchange for periodic relocation, limited numbers, and isolation or confinement of these troops—was largely a result of this readily demonstrable situation. To be sure, the compromise between London and the plantations did not prevent the colonists from bitterly denouncing black troops, particularly if they were guilty of mutinous behavior, such as when thirty-three newly acquired African recruits of the Second West India Regiment mutinied in Jamaica in May 1808. To placate Jamaicans and thereby maintain the shaky agreement, London ordered the garrison commander, Hugh Carmichael, to testify before the Assembly and to furnish it with all documents requested. In addition, Carmichael, a veteran of many years service in the West Indies, was quickly relieved of his command and given a staff post in the Windward and Leeward Islands. It mattered little to local whites that the disturbance (a more appropriate word than mutiny) resulted in the death of only two Europeans, was confined to isolated Fort Augusta, and was quelled immediately by troops of the same regiment.[5]

The creation of the West India Regiments was one of the most important (and certainly the most dramatic) forces shaping the new society in the British Caribbean as the Napoleonic Wars came to an end. The determined efforts of the government to strengthen its *askari* or African corps—by manumission of all black soldiers through an act of Parliament in 1807, by providing the troops with rudimentary education and religious instruction, and by putting them on an equal footing with white soldiers in all matters—were fundamental challenges to the basic underlying principle of racial inequality intrinsic to West Indian slavery. Except for occasional manumissions, none of these efforts were officially extended to the civilian slave until 1833, when a significant beginning was made to emancipate them. However unwittingly, the army was an agent of reform: it created in the very midst of a society of enslaved blacks a small but highly visible community, a military caste of free blacks enjoying equal rights and privileges with its white members.

No other socializing experience so jolted the sensibilities and long-held racial attitudes of local whites as did the daily humiliating sight of European soldiers under the command of proud, perhaps even boastful and splendidly dressed and accoutered black noncommissioned officers. It is not surprising that white spectators were revolted by the sight of the dejected group of pinioned white deserters escorted by a detail of black troops. Yet, with black troops now forming a major and permanent part of the garrison in the West Indies, such sights must have been common. Of course, more research is needed before a clear understanding of the impact of the British garrison on the development of West Indian racial attitudes is available; nonetheless, the constant sight, repeated over many years, of blacks expertly leading and commanding whites must have taken some toll of the then-current view that blacks were lazy, cowardly, and inferior to whites.[6]

The establishment of the West India Regiments also created a large black elite of disbanded soldiers; their impact on the surrounding society in the West Indies and Sierra Leone is thought to have been significant and has yet to be fully investigated. Merely their exposure to other cultural areas of the Caribbean and to West Africa and their immense status in the eyes of other blacks would have placed them socially above their fellows. In addition, their organizational competence, technical-administrative experience (however limited), and educational training (however rudimentary) provided these troops, particularly the noncommissioned officers, with an immense potential for effective communal leadership.[7] Like his future counterpart in British armies in tropical Africa, the West India soldier is thought to have been detribalized; that is, he lost his tribal identification and, in the process, his narrower, ethnocentric habits, thought patterns, and attitudes, at the same time gaining a broader worldview and a new set of loyalties.[8] He continued to live in a disciplined and cohesive state, within a complex of closely linked military settlements.[9] The constantly replenished community of disbanded West India soldiers, which rivaled the other and older native elite groups in size and organizational-leadership skills, might be said to resemble an organized trade union, a potent pressure group competing, like any other special-interest group, for its slice of the pie.[10]

The academic's neglect of the military factor in West Indian history obliges one to speculate somewhat more broadly than usual about the impact of the long war against France on this new native elite. But one need only remember the galvanizing effect of World War I on the political development of Captain Arthur A. Cipriani, the Trinidadian hero, and numerous others who served in the British West Indies Regiment during the war. One writer, commenting on how profoundly the war had affected those who had gone overseas, concluded that it would be difficult to exaggerate the effect of the experience in generating revolutionary ideas.[11] Yet, could any conflict have had a more revolutionary influence than the French Revolution? As a British soldier, the *askari's* duty was to uphold the plantocracy, the very antithesis of the new society proclaimed by the revolution. The *askari* performed his task well and unflinchingly, as the records indicate. This obligation, however, did not and could not prevent the West India soldier, in the seclusion of his barracks and away from his British officers, from speculating wildly on the questions raised by the revolution and the long war. And once he was out of uniform, the former West India soldier had an even greater opportunity to develop and test his political ideas.

We have seen that the establishment of the West India Regiments was central to London's new and more forceful policy of greater initiative in colonial government. Risking censure abroad and at home, and violating an important political convention, the British government under Pitt demonstrated uncommon toughness in the face of determined colonial opposition, while successfully consolidating the black regiments in the Caribbean. From a metropolitan viewpoint, the results were well worth the effort: the defense of the plantations was stiffened with dependable and durable troops who provided a proven model for future British conquest and control in tropical Africa.

APPENDIX A.

WILLIAMSON'S L'ORDONNANCE DE CREATION DES CORPS NÈGRES DU 26 JUIN 1795

EXTRAIT

De Registre du Greffe du Conseil Supérieur
De Saint-Domingue.

DE PAR LE ROI

Son Excellence SIR ADAM WILLIAMSON, Chevalier du très-Honorable Ordre du Bain, Capitaine-Général, Gouverneur & Commandant en Chef de l'Isle de Saint-Domingue, Ec. Ec. Ec.

Pénétré de la nécessité d'opposer promptement aux brigands qui infestent la Colonie de Saint-Domingue une force armée suffisante pour les réduire, Nous avions déjà donné des Ordres à divers Officiers, de lever des Corps de Nègres dans les paroisses soumises aux armes de Sa Majesté.

Cette mesure ne pouvant être considérée que sous le rapport qui lie le sort politique des Colonies à sucre au maintien de l'esclavage, Nous avons pensé qu'elle ne rempliroit entièrement le but que nous nous proposons, qu'autant que l'esclave recevroit son affranchissement de la libéralité de son maître, qu'autant qu'il seroit sans celle entretenu dans l'espérance qu'il ne pourroit acquérir une liberté légitime, qu'en se consacrant à la défense de la personne & des propriétés de son maître.

Source: W.O. 1/61, pp. 367–70.

C'est dans ces sentimens que nous avons agi jusqu'à présent.

Aujourd'hui que l'expérience & le desir même des Propriétaires de Saint-Domingue se réunissent pour justifiér l'utilité de cet armement, il devient convenable de lui donner une base uniforme & stable, & de fixer les règles qui doivent être suivies à cet égard: Mais avant tout, Nous annoncons aux Habitans qu'autorisé par Sa Majesté à ne rien épargner pour les rendre à la paix & au bonheur, le Gouvernement se portera à faire les avances nécessaires pour remboursement des Nègres que les Propriétaires euxmêmes donneront pour servir dans ces Corps armés.

En conséquence, Nous, en vertu des pouvoirs à nous donnés par Sa Majesté, & de l'avis du Conseil Colonial, avons ordonné & ordonnons ce qui suit:

ARTICLE PREMIER.

Tous les Nègres enrôlés jusqu'à ce jour dans les différens Corps de Chasseurs y resteront. Confirmons en conséquence lesdits enrôlement, & les déclarons bons & valables.

ART. II.

Les divers Corps de Nègres dont nous avons autorisé l'armement, seront, le plutôt possible, portés au complet.

ART. III.

Ces Corps de Nègres seront attachés à la Colonie, & ne pourront jamais en être distraits pour être employés ailleurs: Ils pourront seulement, d'après nos ordres, se porter dans toutes les parties de l'Isle où le bien du service l'exigera.

ART. IV.

Les Nègres devant composer les Corps dont nous avons autorisé l'armement, seront levés par forme de contribution sur chaque Propriétaire de Nègres, & la proportion sera d'un Nègre par quinze esclaves, sans distinction de sexe; & si ladite proportion ne suffisoit pas, il y a sera pourvu ultérieurement.

ART. V.

Tout propriétaire dans les Paroisses ou les enrôlemens seront ordonnés, sera tenu, dans le plus bref délai, de fournir au Colonel chargé du recrutement du Corps armé, un état exact de ses Nègres.

ART. VI.

Les Propriétaires resteront maîtres du choix des sujets, & aucun de ceux qu'ils présenteront ne pourra être refusé, à moins qu'il ne soit défectueux, ou hors d'âge & de force à porter les armes.

ART. VII.

La valeur des Nègres levés de cette manière, sera remboursée à leurs Propriétaires, à raison de deux mille livres, Savoir; un tiers comptant, un tiers dans six mois, un tiers dans un an.

ART. VIII.

Le Colonel chargé du recrutement délivrera au Propriétaire du Nègre recruté une reconnoissance, en vertu de laquelle il pourra se présenter devant Nous, ou devant le Commandant pour le Roi de chaque Paroisse, à l'effet d'obtenir son remboursement.

ART. IX.

L'enrôlement durera l'espace de cinq années, à compter du jour où le sujet aura été agréé.

ART. X.

Dès l'instant de l'enrôlement du Nègre, il lui sera, soit par son maître, soit par nos préposés, remis une promesse de liberté, & à l'expiration du tems fixé pour la durée de l'enrôlement, le sujet recevra du Gouvernement un congé, qui vaudra l'acte de son affranchissement absolu.

ART. XI.

Si pendant la durée de l'enrôlement, le Nègre déserte ou commet toute autre faute indigne du soldat, il sera déchu & privé de son droit à la liberté.

ART. XII.

Les dispositions des articles 7, 8, 9 & 10, seront observées à l'égard de tous les esclaves ci-devant enrôlés dans les divers Corps de Nègres.

ART. XIII.

Faisons expresses défenses à toutes personnes, de quelque qualité & condition qu'elles soient, d'armer ni de lever aucun Nègre, sans nos ordres, & si ce n'est en la manière prescrite par la présente.

ART. XIV.

Il n'y aura par Paroisse qu'un seul Corps de Nègres, lequel ne pourra être attaché à aucune autre troupe de quelque nature qu'elle soit, voulant & entendant que les Corps de Nègres fassent une troupe distincte & séparée de tout autre. Révoquons en conséquence tous les Ordres que nous avons donnés de contraires à la présente disposition.

ART. XV.

Pour être de l'Etat-Major de ces Corps, il faudra être Propriétaire, ou avoir résidé pendant cinq ans dans la Colonie. Exceptons du présent article les Officiers employés & qui servent déjà dans les corps formés.

ART. XVI.

Les Corps de Nègres ne pourront séjourner ou tenir garnison dans aucune Ville ou Bourg, sans un Ordre exprès émané de Nous, ou des Commandans pour le Roi dans lesdites Ville ou Bourg.

ART. XVII.

Les Nègres estropiés en combattant conserveront leur paye.

ART. XVIII. & dernier.

Autorisons au surplus les Colonels chargés du recrutement, à enrôler dans tous les Quartiers où ils jugeront convenable, pourvu qu'ils n'agissent que du consentement & de la volonté des Habitans dans lesdits Quartiers.

Prions MM. les Officiers du Conseil Supérieur de St-Domingue de faire enrégistrer la présente Ordonnance, & Mandons à MM. les Commandans pour le Roi de tenir la main à son exécution.

Donné en la maison du Roi, sous le sceau de Nos Armes & le contreseing de notre Secrétaire, le vingt-six Juin mil sept cent quatre-vingt-quinze.

Signé, ADAM WILLIAMSON.

Par ordre de son Excellence

WM. SHAW. secretaire.

Registrée a été la présente Ordonnance au greffe du Conseil Supérieur de Saint-Domingue, ce requérant le Procureur-Général du Roi, pour être executée suivant sa forme & teneur.

Collationné. D'AUBREMON, Greffier.

AU PORT-AU-PRINCE,

Chez THOUNENS & Compagnie, Imprimeurs du Gouvernement & du Conseil Supérieur de Saint-Domingue.

APPENDIX B.

THE CHARLES RANCE CONTRACT

Martinico.

Know all men by these presents that I, Charles Rance of the Town of St Pierre and Island of Martinique aforesaid, Merchant, Do hereby agree and Contract with Lieu^t General Thom^s Trigge, Commander in Chief of His Majesty's Forces in the West Indies, on the part and behalf of Governm^t to furnish and supply on or before the first day of April next ensueing, *Four hundred and Fifty new Negroe Slaves*, to be delivered in such proportions as may be required to the *First, seventh and Eight West India Regiments*, and in the Islands or places where they may be respectively stationed, in Consideration of receiving for each individual Negro so delivered, the sum of *Seventy seven pounds Sterling* in Government Bills, drawn by the Commissary General on the Treasury of Great Britain at Sixty days sight, which Negroe Slaves shall be of the description hereafter mentioned, and shall be subject to the examination, inspection, and approval of a Board of Military and Medical Officers to be appointed for that purpose;

1st   That the said Negro Slaves shall not be under the age of sixteen years, or exceeding Twenty two years old, so far as the same can be known or ascertained,

2nd   That they shall be of a late importation from Africa such as are commonly called "New Negroes" never having been employed in any of these Islands or plantations,

Source: C.O. 318/30, enclosed in Bowyer to Windham, no. 21, 21 November 1806.

3rd That they shall not be deformed, maimed or injured in any respect; but stout, able bodied healthy men, capable of bearing Arms;

4th That they shall immediately on their arrival (at such Island or Islands as the aforesaid Regiments may be stationed at) be brought before a board consisting of Two Army Medical Men, and the Officer commanding the Regim^t for which they are intended, which Board shall examine them, touching their fitness, to serve as Soldiers in any of His Majestys West India Regiments or Corps, as well as to the several particulars of the Articles of this Contract,

5th That the Negroes of about sixteen years old, shall be five feet three inches in height, and likely to grow, but full grown men must be Five feet five inches high, And furthermore that no Slaves shall be delivered but those of the Gold Coast, Coromantie, or Congo Nations,

That in case the said number of Four hundred and fifty Negroes shall [not] be delivered by the time herein specified, and agreeably to the other particulars required by this Contract, then this obligation to be void, In default of which, we the said Charles Rance, John Gay & Kenneth Mc Leay, do bind ourselves jointly & severally our Heirs, Executors, Administrators and Assign's, in the Sum of £1000 Sterling, Money of Great Britain.

In Witness whereof We have hereunto Set our hands and affixed our Seals, the 21st day of October 1799 and the 39th year of His Majesty's Reign,

Charles Rance
(Signed)   John Gay
K: Mc Leay

Signed Sealed & delivered in the presence of (Signed) R: Darling

A^s to Mr Rance

Signed by John Gay & Kenneth Mc Leay, in the presence of, (signed) Ja^s Lanne,

St Pierre, Martinico,
26th October 1799,

Registered in the books of this Office (Signed) P: R: Bearcroft, Comm^y of Accounts

APPENDIX C.

THE GORDON MEMORANDUM OF 8 APRIL 1807
AND THE
DAWSON-GORDON LETTER OF 9 NOVEMBER 1806

MEMORANDUM

April 8. 1807

It is so universally admitted that the Black Force in the W. Indies should be augmented as much as possible with a view to lesson the consumption of the European Troops, that it remains only to consider of the best means of effecting it.

Previous to the late Act for the abolition of the Slave Trade, The Officer Commanding in the West Indies was empowered to purchase Slaves to complete the Black Regiments to their Establishment, & that this had been nearly effected will appear from the marginal State of our Colonial Force, from which it seems that only 1,105 negroes were wanting by the last returns to complete the 8 West India Regiments to 1,000 men each.

1st	Dominica	780
2	Jamaica	780
3	Dominica	796
4	Surinam	1,003
5	Honduras	855
6	St. Lucia	911

Source: W.O. 1/634, pp. 317–25.

152

7	Barbados	984
8	Trinidad	786
	Effectives	6,895
	Establish!	8,000
	Wanting	1,105

It would be very desirable from the great extent of our Colonial Possessions, and indeed the impossibility of supplying them continually with European Troops, that the Black Force should be carried as high as 10 Regiments immediately, and if possible to 12.

The Bahamas being now garrisoned by a complete Black Regiment* has lessened the Establish^t of the Leeward Islands, which even before that diminution was short of the numbers required for its security.

The best mode of effecting this augmentation would be to take every advantage of the time allowed before the Act takes effect, and enter into a contract with the Merchants at Liverpool to furnish from 2 to 4,000 slaves of the tribes from the Gold Coast at Barbados from whence they could be distributed as The Officer Commanding should direct.

Half, or certainly one third of this number, might be taken at the age of 16, well made & healthy lads.

The average price of the men would be about £70 Sterling, the boys proportionally less.

WG

The enclosed copy of a letter from a Merchant of Liverpool will explain the means of that Town for the execution of this measure.

My Dear Sir,

Tho' I am not directly concerned in the African Trade, I will endeavor to reply to the Letter I had the Honor to receive from you

---

*In his marginal note on the strength and distribution of the West India Regiments, Gordon lists eight corps; the regiment he places in the Bahamas would raise that total to nine. The *Army List* for 1807 shows only eight West India Regiments on the British Establishment. The identity of this corps is a mystery. Conceivably, it could have been a corps privately raised and earmarked for regular British service. This was a common practice during the war. Some sources do indicate that black corps other than the West India Regiments were being raised continually in the Caribbean. One such corps was the "Bombor Regiment." It is possible that Gordon was referring to such a regiment.

this morning, in such manner as to enable you, I hope, to determine whether more minute information should be sought by my having any Conversation on the subject with any one to whom the communication may be confidentially made in order to obtain it.

About 130 sail of Vessels have been fitted out from this port this year for the Coast. The greatest part of them gone to the Bite & Angola, not above 12 or 14 of them, I should suppose to the Gold Coast.

The Gold Coast Negroes only, I presume, are wanted by Government. Calculating 12 Vessels to Carry on an Average 300 Negroes each, the number of able bodied Men would not exceed one third, or 1,200 in those Ships if so many, allowing for Women & Children & Youths from 12 to 16 years of Age, which from the circumstances of the increased attention to the Cultivation of Coffee have latterly been found to be the most saleable, as better calculated for that purpose & suiting better than full grown Men. These Vessels have probably already got their particular destinations, for it is no longer the practice, or very seldom as in peaceable times, for them to call at Barbadoes for Orders. Therefore very little dependence is to be had on any of these Vessels, certainly not as to any number of any consequence of such Negroes as are wanted, but enquiry may be quietly made, without the object being hinted at, as to what Vessels may have been ordered to proceed to Jamaica or to call at Barbadoes, or to which of them orders may yet possibly be conveyed, having Gold Coast Negroes or of the Corymante Tribe on Board, if you desire it.

There is at this moment only one Vessel fitting out for the Gold Coast to carry about 300 Negroes, & by a person of great respectability & of undoubted property.

There are also others of equal responsibility who I am sure would gladly accept the Contract for the number wanted or for a greater Number, Gentlemen with whom Government might Contract with the utmost Confidence, if Circumstances should permit its being deferred so as to be carried compleatly into effect only during the next Year. Under the late regulation on Vessels only which have been in the Trade and belonging to the original owners, can only now be employed in it, of such there are but a few only laying by in our Docks unemployed perhaps not exceeding 10 or 12 Vessels, these might be fitted out & sent to sea in about 3/m^s, perform the Voyage and deliver their Cargoes in Barbadoes in 1807. But were it possible, in consideration of its being a Contract on Government account, to obtain Licences for Vessels, which are at present restricted under the late regulation, to be employed in the Trade, a sufficient number might be procured, & the most respectable Men be found, with whom the contract might be immediately made, and the number of 2,000 be delivered much sooner than could possibly be done by any Contract to be made with those Gentlemen who could only engage in it on the return of those Vessels now out, whose arrival here cannot be looked for before the next April, when the greater part may be expected. If the Object will admit of delay, I have no hesitation to say you may depend upon being able to make a contract here for the number required, and of the Corymantee Tribe, to be delivered at Barbadoes or at any other of the Windward Islands as may be agreed upon. As to the terms I should suppose somewhere about £65 to £70 Sterl. per Head. I shall be happy to procure for you any information which may be required, or to assist in making the Contract. I beg you will present my Compliments to Mrs. Gordon & believe me. My Dear Sir

Liverpool
Saturday 9th Novr 1806.

[signed]

Pudsey Dawson

APPENDIX D.

BRIEF RECORD OF THE
WEST INDIA REGIMENTS DURING THE WAR

First West India Regiment Raised in 1795 as Whyte's Foot; Malcolm's Rangers (raised in Martinique in 1794) and Black Carolina Corps drafted into the First from 1796–1797; battle honors: "Dominica" 1805, "Martinique" 1809, "Guadeloupe" 1810.

Second West India Regiment Raised in 1795 as Myer's Foot; St. Vincent Rangers drafted into the Second in 1796; small detachment of the Second mutinied at Jamaica in 1808.

Third West India Regiment Raised in 1795 as Keppel's Foot; disbanded, 1817–1818.

Fourth West India Regiment Raised in 1795 as Nicolls' Foot; battle honors: "Martinique" 1809, "Guadeloupe" 1810; disbanded, 1817–1818.

Fifth West India Regiment Raised in 1795 as Howe's Foot; disbanded, 1817–1818.

Sixth West India Regiment Raised in 1795 as Whitelocke's Foot; disbanded, 1817–1818.

Seventh West India Regiment Raised in 1795 as Lewes' Foot; disbanded in 1802 with the rank-and-file drafted into several West India Regiments; re-raised the same year with drafts provided by the disbanded Ninth, Tenth, and Twelfth West India Regiments, the so-called "French" West India Regiments; disbanded in 1817.

Eighth West India Regiment Raised in 1795 as Skerrett's Foot; disbanded in 1796; re-raised in 1798 with drafts provided by the Loyal Dominica Rangers, a colonial corps; mutinied at Dominica in 1802 and subsequently broken the same year; re-raised in 1802 with drafts provided by the disbanded Eleventh West India Regiment; disbanded in 1817.

Ninth West India Regiment   Originally raised in Guadeloupe in 1794 as the Guadeloupe or Drualt's Rangers; taken on the British Establishment in 1798; disbanded in 1802 with rankers drafted into the Seventh.

Tenth West India Regiment   Originally raised in Martinique in 1794 as Soter's Royal Island Rangers; taken on the British Establishment in 1798; disbanded in 1802 with rankers drafted into the Seventh.

Eleventh West India Regiment   Formerly the South American Rangers, which was raised in 1796 at Demarara; taken on the British Establishment in 1798; disbanded in 1804 with rankers drafted into the Eighth.

Twelfth West India Regiment   Formerly O'Meara's Rangers; taken on the British Establishment in 1798; disbanded in 1802 with rankers drafted into the Seventh.

NOTES

CHAPTER 1

1. Benjamin Keen, ed., *Readings in Latin-American Civilization: 1492 to the Present*, p. 60.

2. George Sanderlin, *Bartolmé de Las Casas: A Selection of His Writings*, p. 101. For Spain's use of blacks and Indians on the mainland during the sixteenth century, see also Richard Price, *Maroon Societies: Rebel Slave Communities in the Americas*, pp. 36-37, 51.

3. Alan C. Burns, *History of the British West Indies*, p. 220.

4. C. R. Boxer, *The Dutch in Brazil, 1624-1654*, p. 140. War and emancipation practices in the New World are discussed briefly in connection with the revolutionary period in the Americas, in David B. Davis, *The Problem of Slavery in the Age of Revolution, 1770-1823*, pp. 72-83. Spain continued to free slave soldiers as late as the 1868-1878 Civil War in Cuba; see Franklin W. Knight, *Slave Society in Cuba During the Nineteenth Century*, pp. 175-76.

5. For example, see John W. Fortescue, *A History of the British Army*, vol. 1, p. 261; Eric Williams, *Capitalism and Slavery*, p. 215; and Minutes of the Council of Jamaica, 31 May 1694, in Fortescue, ed., *Calendar of State Papers, Colonial Series, America and West Indies*, vol. 14, no. 1074, p. 291.

6. Frank Cundall, *The Governors of Jamaica in the Seventeenth Century*, pp. 162-63; and Richard Pares, *War and Trade in the West Indies, 1739-1763*, p. 256. The word *colored* refers chiefly to the offspring of a union between a white and a black.

7. C.O. 137/61, Egremont to Lyttleton, January 1762; see also W.O. 1/51, Calder to Jenkinson, 29 October 1779; and ibid., Vaughan to Jenkinson, 21 September 1780. For a similar development in Cuba, see Herbert S. Klein, *Slavery in the Americas: A Comparative Study of Virginia and Cuba*, pp. 215-19.

8. W. Cobbett, *The Parliamentary History of England*, vol. 33, Debate in Commons on Mr. Ellis's Motion for the Amelioration of the Condition of the Negroes in the West Indies, 6 April 1797, Bryan Edward's speech, p. 280.

9. J. R. Western, *The English Militia in the Eighteenth Century*, pp. 189, 200, 203, 222, 236-37, 239, 245; cf. pp. 258-71, 442-43.

10. Arthur N. Gilbert, "An Analysis of Some Eighteenth Century Army Recruiting Records," p. 42.

11. Fortescue, *A History of the British Army*, vol. 4 (part II), p. 940. In the same year, the year France declared war on Britain, the French army numbered 500,000.

12. W.O. 1/51, Christie to Jenkinson, 18 May 1780.

159

13. Jackson, *A Treatise on the Fevers of Jamaica*, pp. 393–94, 410–24.

14. Piers Mackesy, *The War for America, 1775–1783*, p. 526. Chief among those reasons for high sea transit casualties were unsanitary troop transports and the poor health of the British regular at enlistment. See also Roger N. Buckley, "The Destruction of the British Army in the West Indies, 1793–1815: A Medical History".

15. W.O. 1/52, Campbell to Townshend, 20 July 1782.

16. By 1793, however, only eighty-seven black pioneers were serving with the British army in Jamaica. C.O. 137/107, Abstract of Jamaica's Defence Arrangements, 1790–1802, in Hobart to Nugent, no. 4, 4 February 1802.

17. W.O. 1/51, Calder to Jenkinson, 29 October 1779.

18. C.O. 152/60, Mathew to Germaine, no. 85, 4 July 1780.

19. C.O. 137/61, Lyttleton to Egremont, 12 May 1762, and Lyttleton's address to the Assembly; W.O. 1/51, The Memorial of John Brodbelt, 2 November 1778, pp. 586–94; and Pares, *War and Trade in the West Indies*, p. 256. See Elsa Goveia, *Slave Society in the British Leeward Islands at the End of the Eighteenth Century*, p. 219, for the humiliating experiences suffered by free coloreds (and presumably free blacks) as militiamen. According to Goveia, the free colored population was concerned primarily with increasing their property and removing the political and economic disabilities under which they labored because of their color (pp. 96–97).

20. W.O. 1/55, Shirley to Yonge, 11 February 1787; and ibid., Rowe to Yonge, 12 September 1787, p. 37, and 6 October 1787.

21. Goveia, *Slave Society in the British Leeward Islands*, pp. 145–51; and Lowell Ragatz, *The Fall of the Planter Class in the British Caribbean, 1763–1833: A Study in Social and Economic History*, p. 25.

22. For the Jamaica garrison during the late 1770s and early 1780s, see Edward Brathwaite, *The Development of Creole Society in Jamaica, 1770–1820*, pp. 278–79. One of the few important medical reforms around this time was the establishment of Up-Park Camp, in Jamaica, a "Remarkably Healthy Situation"; see C.O. 137/88, Effingham to Grenville, No. 8, 12 September 1790.

23. For example, "A Proposal to raise a Corps of Foot . . . in the West Indies, to consist of Free Mulattoes and Blacks," British Museum Add. MSS. 28062, fol. 378; and Reginald W. Jeffery, ed., *Dyott's Diary, 1781–1846*, vol. 1, p. 94.

24. "A Proposal to raise a Corps of Foot."

25. Alfred B. Ellis, *The History of the First West India Regiment*, p. 52; W.O. 1/55, Shirley to Yonge, 11 February 1787.

26. For the case of Antigua, see Goveia, *Slave Society in the British Leeward Islands*, pp. 78–79.

27. Pares, *War and Trade in the West Indies*, pp. 227–40; Ragatz, *The Fall of the Planter Class*, p. 31.

28. Jackson, *A Treatise on the Fevers of Jamaica*, pp. 249–50. For Jackson's publications and service record, see Leslie Stephens, ed., *Dictionary of National Biography*.

29. Henry R. Carter, *Yellow Fever: An Epidemiological and Historical Study of Its Place of Origin*, pp. 263–64.

30. Fortescue, *A History of the British Army*, vol. 4 (part I), p. 77.

31. C.O. 137/108, Hobart to Nugent, September 1802.

32. The best study on British military operations is still Fortescue's. For those conducted in 1793 and 1794, see Fortescue, *A History of the British Army*, vol. 4 (part I), pp. 134–35, 330–33, 350–65.

33. C. L. R. James, *The Black Jacobins: Toussaint L'Ouverture and the San Domingo Revolution*, pp. 128–29, 139–42; Thomas O. Ott, *The Haitian Revolution, 1789–1804*, pp. 65–72, 82–83.

34. P.M.G. 14/74, Extraordinaries Abroad 1792, 1793, 1794, pp. 85, 161, 165, indexed under "West Indies"; C.O. 318/12, circular letter from Dundas to General Cuyler, the Governors of St. Vincent, the Leeward Islands, and Barbados, and the Lieutenant Governors of Dominica and Grenada, "Private and Secret," 21 January 1793; ibid., Dundas to Prescot, "Secret," 12 October 1793; C.O. 318/13, Dundas to Vaughan, 7 October 1794.

35. Henry Dundas, *Facts Relative to the Conduct of the War in the West Indies*, pp. 185, 191, 193.

36. Fortescue, *A History of the British Army*, vol. 4 (part I), p. 356; C.O. 318/13, Grey to Williamson, 10 May 1794, enclosed in Grey to Dundas, "Secret," no. 28, 13 June 1794.

37. C.O. 318/13, Grey to Dundas, "Secret," no. 33, 17 July 1794, enclosure no. 2, "State of His Majesty's Forces in the West Indies Under the Command of His Excellency General Sir Charles Grey, 17 July 1794."

38. Ibid., "Secret," no. 28, 13 June 1794; ibid., "Secret," no. 33, 17 July 1794, and enclosure no. 1.

39. Ibid., Grey to Dundas, "Secret," No. 32; ibid., no. 38, 9 September 1794.

40. See C.O. 318/15, "Abstract of the Returns of His Majesty's Forces in the Island of St. Domingo—dated 31 May 1794," p. 301; Bryan Edwards, *An Historical Survey of the Island of Saint Domingo*, p. 195; and Gardner, *A History of Jamaica*, p. 224. According to one account, the average annual death rate from non-military causes among British troops serving in the West Indies at this time was 25 percent. See Arthur Bryant, *The Years of Endurance, 1793–1802*, p. 86.

41. C.O. 318/13, Grey to Dundas, "Secret," no. 37, 9 September 1794.

42. W.O. 1/83, Vaughan to Dundas, 24 November 1794.

43. Ibid., Vaughan to Dundas, "Secret", no. 6, 25 December 1794. In 1780, during the American Revolution, Vaughan had supported a plan to raise a regiment of free blacks to serve in the West Indies. C.O. 152/60, Mathew to Germaine, no. 67, 16 March 1780.

44. W.O. 1/31, Vaughan to Portland, 22 December 1794.

45. W.O. 1/83, Vaughan to Dundas, no. 6, "Secret," 25 December 1794. The quotas were as follows: Barbados 200, Grenada 200, Antigua 150, St. Kitts 150, and Dominica, St. Vincent, and Tobago 100 each. The same formula was to apply to any additional corps raised in the area.

46. Ibid. For the crucial importance of blacks in British service in St. Domingo, see W.O. 1/62, Williamson to Dundas, 14 January 1795. Vaughan was in error when he likened the corps he planned to raise to Indian sepoy regiments. Unlike the latter, Vaughan's West India soldiers were to be slaves, which would seriously impede their recruitment and complicate their maintenance and deployment in the Caribbean.

47. Coke, *An Account of the Rise, Progress and Present State of the Methodist Missions*, pp. 11–12.

48. W.O. 1/83, Vaughan to Dundas, No. 22, "Secret," 16 April 1795. For instance, the Leeward Islands: the First King's Regiment and the Second Queen's Regiment of Black Rangers; Dominica: De Vermount's and the Loyal Dominica Rangers; St. Vincent: Haffey's and Jackson's Rangers and the St. Vincent Rangers; Grenada: Webster's and Angus' Black Rangers; and the Tobago Jaegers.

49. C.O. 153/28, Leigh to Portland, No. 61, 15 July 1795; W.O. 1/769, Thomson to

Portland, no. 8, 10 October 1797, enclosed in King to Huskisson, 11 December 1797; C.O. 153/28, Thomson to Portland, no. 11, 19 February 1798.

50. C.O. 153/28, Stanley to Portland, 31 March 1795.

51. C.O. 285/4, Committee of Correspondence to Petrie, 15 March 1797 (enclosure). Colonial troops taken into imperial service apparently received the same pay as British regulars. In addition, the proprietors of these slaves received a fixed daily amount for each enlisted slave and the full price of all who died or were captured. See W.O. 1/83, Vaughan to Dundas, no. 9, "Secret," 11 January 1795; W.O. 1/86, Jones to Cuyler, 20 September 1797.

52. W.O. 1/86, Jones to Cuyler, 20 September 1797; P.M.G. 14/74, Extraordinaries Abroad 1792, 1793, 1794, indexed under "West Indies," p. 278; P.M.G. 14/75, Army Extraordinaries Abroad 1795 and 1796, indexed under "West Indies," pp. 52, 54, 58, 73, 244.

53. W.O. 1/60, Williamson to Dundas, no. 1, 13 September 1794.

54. Total is comprised of 980 blacks and 2,620 mulattoes; see ibid., p. 329.

55. "Return of the Black Corps formed and forming, St. Domingo," enclosed in W.O. 1/767, Williamson to Portland, no. 2, 12 July 1795. For additional information on Britain's effort to raise levies of slaves in St. Domingo for imperial service from 1794 to 1798, see W.O. 1/60, Williamson to Dundas, no. 1, 13 September 1794; ibid., Williamson to Portland no. 7, 10 October 1794, "M. de Charmilli's Proposals," pp. 581-86; A.O. 3/265, unnumbered expenditure abstracts, 1797-1798; T. 81/21, slave enlistment certificates. See also Fortescue, *A History of the British Army*, vol. 4 (part I), pp. 333-42, 457-59; and Edwards, *Historical Survey of St. Domingo,* p. 386; W.O. 1/62, Williamson to Dundas, 14 January 1795; W.O. 1/60, Williamson to Dundas, no. 1, 13 September 1794; W.O. 6/5, Dundas to Williamson, 6 November 1794.

56. W.O. 1/62, Forbes to Dundas, no. 1, 9 December 1795.

57. W.O. 1/83, Vaughan to Dundas, no. 6, "Secret," 25 December 1794.

58. Ibid., Dundas to Vaughan, no. 9, 19 February 1795.

59. Ibid., Vaughan to Dundas, no. 22, "Secret," 16 April 1795.

60. W.O. 1/767, Mackensie to Portland, 24 April 1795; C.O. 101/34, Mackensie to Portland, 11 August 1795, enclosure no. 4.

61. C.O. 140/85, Votes of the Assembly, p. 324.

62. W.O. 1/31, Vaughan to Portland, 16 June 1795; W.O. 1/83, Vaughan to Dundas, no. 22, "Secret," 16 April 1795; ibid., Vaughan to Dundas, 25 April 1795.

63. C.O. 153/30, Grey to Dundas, no. 38, 9 September 1794.

64. W. Cobbett, *The Parliamentary History of England*, vol. 32, Debate in Commons on Wilberforce's Motion for the Abolition of the Slave Trade, 18 February 1796; Wilberforce's speech, p. 739.

65. See W.O. 1/82, "Notes from Sir Ralph Abercromby about the West Indies. London, 10 November 1797," pp. 626-27. On the British army's topographical inadequacies in 1795, see Richard Glover, *Peninsular Preparation: The Reform of the British Army, 1795-1809*, pp. 75-80.

66. See George Pinckard, *Notes on the West Indies*, vol. 2, p. 243.

67. C.O. 137/126, Carmichael to Castlereagh, 26 January 1809, and 11 April 1809.

68. W.O. 1/31, Vaughan to Portland, 26 January 1795; C.O. 152/77, Vaughan to Byam, 14 March 1795 (enclosure); W.O. 1/83, Vaughan to Dundas, no. 13, "Secret," 25 February 1795; no. 22, "Secret," 16 April 1795; "Most Private," 18 April 1795; 19 and 25 April 1795; "Most Secret," 12 May 1795.

69. W. O. 1/83, Dundas to Vaughan, no. 14, 17 April 1795.
70. W.O. 6/5, Dundas to Williamson, no. 5, 17 April 1795.

CHAPTER 2

1. W.O. 6/131, Dundas to Duke of York, 16 April 1795; Dundas's letter, no date, enclosed in W.O. 1/617, Brownrigg to Huskisson, 14 August 1795.
2. W.O. 4/158, Windham to Whyte and Myers, 24 April 1795. Although coloreds were also to be recruited, these regiments will be increasingly referred to as black corps, as the vast majority of those enlisted were blacks.
3. W.O. 4/337, circular letter from Lewis to colonels of West India Regiments, 3 October 1795; *The London Gazette*, 2 May 1795.
4. W.O. 1/83, Dundas to Vaughan, no. 14, 17 April 1795.
5. W.O. 4/337, Windham to Colonels Stephen Howe, Oliver Nicolls, and William Keppel, and Lt.-Col. John Whitelocke, 29 May 1795; ibid., Lewis to Skerrett, 15 September 1795; ibid., Lewis to Lewes, 15 September 1795; Great Britain, War Office, *Army List*, 1796.
6. *Army List*, 1799; W.O. 4/337, Lewis to Lewes, 15 September 1795.
7. See, for example, W.O. 1/770, King to Brownrigg, 12 July 1799, and enclosures. A careful examination of PRO materials discloses that commissioning blacks as officers in the West India Regiments was never considered by the government.
8. W.O. 25/653, f. 25. Durant was discharged from the Fourth on 1 June 1801, after twenty-one years of military service.
9. There is no evidence to indicate that commissions held by blacks and mulattoes in the colonial corps in St. Domingo were obtained by purchase.
10. Edward Curtis, *The Organization of the British Army in the American Revolution*, p. 160. The price of an ensign's commission increased only slightly during the period between 1776 and the end of the Napoleonic wars. According to the *General Regulations and Orders for the Army* (the "King's Regulations"), published by the War Office in 1822, the price of an ensign's commission in a line regiment was £450 (p. 46).
11. J. Stewart, *A View of the Past and Present State of the Island of Jamaica*, p. 157.
12. Skerrett's Regiment had an abbreviated establishment of only five companies. W.O. 4/337, Windham to Portland, 16 September 1795; W.O. 4/158, Windham to Whyte and Myers, 24 April 1795; W.O. 4/337, Windham to Howe, Nicolls, Keppel, and Whitelocke, 29 May 1795; ibid., Lewis to Lewes, 15 September 1795. See also W.O. 24/594, pp. 51–54. The pay of a private in the British army in 1795, over and above all allowances, was six pence per day. This was raised to one shilling per diem in 1797. Fortescue, *A History of the British Army*, vol. 4 (part II), p. 935.
13. For Jamaica, see Philip D. Curtin, *Two Jamaicas: The Role of Ideas in a Tropical Colony 1830-1865*, pp. 31–32; and Burns, *History of the British West Indies*, pp. 560, 594–95.
14. The Bishop of London appears not to have held an official appointment as military vicar; nevertheless, overseas chaplains were in the habit of bringing grievances to his attention. There is, apparently, no single study which explores the special relationship between the established Church and the British army. Robin Higham, ed., *A Guide to the Sources of British Military History*, p. 129.
15. See C. James, *An Universal Military Dictionary in English and French*, pp. 727–28.
16. The rank-and-file strength of each troop was fifty-six privates. W.O. 4/161, Lewis to

Skerrett, 3 October 1795; W.O. 4/337, Lewis to Whyte, Myers, Nicolls, Keppel, Howe, and Whitelocke, 4 June 1795; W.O. 4/161, Windham to Portland, 25 September 1795. Ellis's *History of the First West India Regiment*, which is marred by numerous factual errors, mistakenly states this augmentation as one troop for each regiment (see pp. 80–81).

17. W.O. 1/83, Dundas to Vaughan, No. 14, 17 April 1795.

18. Grey's figure of 11,540 included 740 artillerymen. The total infantry sought by Grey numbered 10,800. C.O. 318/13, Grey to Dundas, "Secret," no. 33, 17 July 1794, enclosure no. 1.

19. Those to be recruited from English-speaking blacks were Whyte's, Myers's, Whitelocke's, and Skerrett's Regiments; those to be raised from among French blacks of St. Domingo were Howe's, Nicolls's, Keppel's, and Lewes's Regiments. W.O. 1/83, Dundas to Vaughan, no. 14, 17 April 1795; W.O. 4/337, Lewis to Skerrett, 15 September 1795; W.O. 6/5, Dundas to Williamson, no. 7, 4 June 1795; W.O. 4/337, Lewis to Lewes, 15 September 1795.

20. W.O. 1/31, Vaughan to Portland, 26 January 1795.

21. W.O. 1/83, Dundas to Vaughan, no. 14, 17 April 1795.

22. C.O. 324/103, circular letter from Portland to the governors of Barbados, St. Vincent, Grenada, Dominica, Tobago, and the Leeward Islands, 18 April 1795.

23. W.O. 1/83, Dundas to Vaughan, no. 14, 17 April 1795.

24. Articles IV, VI, and VII in W.O. 1/61, pp. 367–70; see, for example, in A.O. 3/200, voucher no. 6, abstract 20, 4 November to 31 December 1795; voucher no. 6, abstract no. 21, and voucher no. 20, abstract no. 21, 1 January to 29 February 1796.

25. W.O. 1/61, Portland to "the Officer Commanding in Chief in St. Domingo," September 1795.

26. W.O. 1/83, Dundas to Vaughan, no. 14, 17 April 1795.

27. Ibid.

28. W.O. 1/61, "L'Ordonnance de création des corps Nègres du 26 Juin 1795," articles IX and X, respectively, pp. 367–70; see Appendix A.

29. W.O. 6/5, Dundas to Williamson, 6 November and 10 December 1794.

30. W.O. 1/61, Portland to "Officer Commanding St. Domingo," September 1795.

31. W.O. 1/92, Dundas to Balcarres, no. 3, 30 September 1795.

32. W.O. 1/62, Forbes to Dundas, no. 1, 9 December 1795. "I must also beg leave to observe to you, Sir, with respect to the freedom promised to them after five years Service, that our Situation as to the Slaves in the Colony is extremely critical, the Republicans having taken the utmost pains to disperse amongst those who remain faithful to their Master, and attached to us, the Decree of the Convention giving Emancipation to everyone, and which is perfectly well known to Negroes of every description in the Island.

33. It should be added that general service regiments or regular regiments could serve in any part of the world; fencibles were raised for the duration of the war only.

34. First Battalion the Jamaica Regiment, Lathbury Barracks, Up Park Camp, Kingston, Jamaica, "First Report on British Garrison in Jamaica," Jamaica (mimeographed). The Twentieth actually had a predecessor in the Ninety-ninth or Jamaica Foot. This corps, according to the *Journal of the Society for Army Historical Research* 14 (1935): 181, was raised in England early in 1780 by the West Indian merchants for service in Jamaica; it was disbanded in March 1784.

35. W.O. 4/337, Windham to Portland, 15 July 1795.

36. W.O. 1/86, circular letter from Abercromby to the governors of the Windward and Leeward Islands, 3 January 1797.

37. Duke of York to the King, 12 November 1796, in Arthur Aspinall, ed., *The Later Correspondence of George III*, vol. 2, p. 515.

38. J. H. MacKay Scobie, *An Old Highland Fencible Corps*, p. 3, and note 3, pp. 3–4.

39. Fortescue, *A History of the British Army*, vol. 3, pp. 547–48, and vol. 4 (part II), pp. 889–91.

40. "These Corps of Negroes will be attached to the Colony, and will never be allowed to be taken away in order to be employed elsewhere: they will only be allowed, according to our orders, to go to all the parts of the Island where their service is needed." W.O. 1/61, p. 368.

41. W.O. 1/62, Dundas to Forbes, no. 5, 30 September 1795; W.O. 1/92, Dundas to Balcarres, no. 3, 30 September 1795.

42. C.O. 324/103, circular letter from Portland to the governors of Barbados, St. Vincent, Grenada, Dominica, Tobago, and the Leeward Islands, 18 April 1795; W.O. 4/337, Lewis to Skerrett, 15 September 1795.

43. W.O. 1/617, Brownrigg to Huskisson, 18 November 1795.

44. Duke of York to the King, 12 November 1796, in Aspinall, vol. 2, p. 515.

45. W.O. 1/88, Bowyer to the President of the Council and Speaker of the Assembly, Antigua, enclosed in Minutes of the Council and Assembly, Antigua, 31 January 1799, pp. 292–93.

46. For example, W.O. 4/337, Windham to Portland, 15 July 1795; ibid., Lewis to Skerrett, 15 September 1795.

47. Ibid., circular letter from Lewis to Colonels of black corps, 3 October 1795.

48. See, for example, *Army List*, 1799; and Ellis, *History of the First West India Regiment*, p. 82.

49. *Army List*, 1796.

50. See, for the Second, W.O. 25/644; for the Fourth, which had the most complete set of books, W.O. 25/652–53; for the Fifth, W.O. 25/656; for the Sixth, W.O. 25/657–58; and for the Seventh West India Regiment, W.O. 25/660–62. The transport ferrying the Second West India Regiment to Trinidad sank in 1800 in the Gulf of Paria with the loss of all of the regimental books. See James E. Caulfield, *One Hundred Years' History of the Second Battalion, West India Regiment*, p. 20.

51. W.O. 25/653, f. 26.

52. West Indian service took its expected toll of these drafts. Within two years after their enlistment, nearly all these men were either dead or had been discharged from service as unfit. Ibid.

53. W.O. 25/652.

54. W.O. 12/11239, Muster Roll of 25 June to 24 December 1795.

55. Ellis, *History of the First West India Regiment*, pp. 79–81.

56. W.O. 12/11239, Muster Roll of 25 June to 24 December 1795.

57. W.O. 17/251.

58. Oman, *Wellington's Army, 1809–1814*, p. 199.

59. Jeffery, *Dyott's Diary*, vol. 1, p. 94.

60. See, for example, W.O. 17/251, junior officers' attendance records of the Fifth West India Regiment in 1808.

61. W.O. 1/1105, Stevenson to Windham, 5 June 1800.

62. For example, W.O. 1/95, "Remarks on the Establishment of the West India Regiments. Written in the Year 1801," enclosed in Hislop to the Duke of York, 22 July 1804. This invaluable appraisal of these corps by a colonel of a West India Regiment has been

edited by the author for forthcoming publication in the *Journal of the Society for Army Historical Research*.

63. James, p. 636.

64. Pinckard, *Notes on the West Indies*, vol. 3, pp. 194-95.

65. Richard Glover, *Peninsular Preparation: The Reform of the British Army 1795-1809*, p. 168.

66. See relevant returns for both black and European regiments in W.O. 1/96, 625; W.O. 3/152; and W.O. 27/88, 90 (part I), 92 (part II), 101, 113, 135. Also, see Ellis, *The History of the First West India Regiment*, p. 99. The stigma associated with these corps became self-perpetuating; even at the end of the nineteenth century, cadets who passed lowest out of Sandhurst were posted to the West India Regiments. See Tylden, "The West India Regiments, 1795 to 1927, and from 1958," p. 44.

67. *Army List*, 1799. For a description of Moore's services in the West Indies, see Carola Oman, *Sir John Moore*, pp. 132-60.

68. London, British Museum, Moore MSS, no. 57327.

69. Ibid., nos. 57321, 57320.

70. Ibid., no. 57326, letter book entry of 8 July 1796, Fort Charlotte, St. Lucia; and no. 57320, letter book entry of 18 January 1797, St. Lucia.

71. Ibid., no. 57321, Moore to Brownrigg, 4 September 1796.

72. W.O. 1/83, Vaughan to Dundas, 16 June 1795.

73. Ellis, *History of the First West India Regiment*, pp. 82, 97-99; *Army List*, 1799; P.M.G. 14/75, p. 237. The strength of Malcolm's Rangers in April 1795 was 233 (Ellis, pp. 64-65); that for Soter's Regiment was about 350 (P.M.G. 14/74, p. 278).

74. W.O. 1/31, Milnes to Portland, no. 6, "Private," September 1795.

75. Ibid., Portland to Milnes, no. 2, November 1795, and enclosures.

76. The drafting of the St. Vincent Rangers into the Second West India Regiment in 1795 and 1796 under restrictive conditions of service enabled the colony, for a while at least, to determine the deployment of the unit. See W.O. 1/84, Leigh to Dundas, 8 October 1795, and enclosures.

77. The strength of the First in 1797-1798 was just under 350 (Ellis, p. 103). The Second returned a strength of about 200 in January 1796 (Caulfield, p. 10).

78. These recruiting results do not include the Ninth, Tenth, Eleventh, and Twelfth West India Regiments. Their establishment is discussed below.

79. Ellis, p. 98.

80. W.O. 25/656, folios 1-27.

81. W.O. 25/662, folios 1-39. Apparently, a single corps could be recruited on more than one island because the Seventh was originally ordered to be raised at St. Domingo.

82. Cabinet Minute, 14 August 1795, enclosed in Dundas to the King, 15 August 1795, in Aspinall, vol. 2, pp. 380-81; The King to Dundas, 16 August 1795, ibid., pp. 381, 384.

83. W.O. 1/85, Leigh to Dundas, 5 December 1795. Leigh wrote this report just prior to the induction of several hundred slaves at Barbados on 25 December.

84. C.O. 152/77, Stanley to Portland, no. 61, 15 July 1795; C.O. 285/3, Lindsay to Portland, no. 9, 3 August 1795.

85. W.O. 1/86, Bowyer to Dundas, 8 September 1798; Ibid., Dundas to Bowyer, "Private," 14 November 1798.

86. Goveia, *Slave Society*, p. 149.

87. C.O. 28/65, Ricketts to Portland, 28 June 1795 and enclosure, and C.O. 285/3, Mackenzie to Portland, no. 12, 3 September 1795, respectively.

88. C.O. 318/16, Milne to King, 6 November 1798.

89. C.O. 318/19, Abercromby to Hislop, 20 May 1796, enclosure in Trigge to Hobart, no. 30, 22 January 1802.

90. See, for example, William A. Young, *The West India Common-Place Book*, p. 214. Young, among other things, was a plantation owner and governor of Tobago from 1807 to 1815.

91. W.O. 1/95, "Remarks . . . ," enclosed in Hislop to the Duke of York, 22 July 1804. As discussed above, every British island embodied units of slaves.

92. C.O. 152/78, Thomson to Portland, no. 11, 19 February 1798 and enclosures no. 3 and no. 5; ibid., no. 26, 10 August 1798. The total adult white population on the island at this time was about 1,200.

93. In December 1795, Jamaica claimed that about 2,000 of its slaves were employed daily as pioneers. At the same time the governor of Dominica declared that 2 percent of the island's slave population was employed as imperial pioneers. By September 1797, the army reported it had raised a pioneer corps of 3,509 slaves provided by the Windward and Leeward Islands. See C.O. 140/85, *Votes of the Assembly* (Jamaica), minutes of 14 December 1795, p. 67; W.O. 1/82, Johnstone to Abercromby, 14 April 1796; W.O. 1/86, Jones to Cuyler, 20 September 1797.

94. For the economic argument, see Douglas Hall, "Incalculability as a Feature of Sugar Production during the Eighteenth Century," pp. 340–52.

95. C.O. 285/3, Lindsay to Portland, "Private," 6 September 1795. Only three months later, in December, Tobago furnished the army with 395 slaves. This was the large body of blacks enlisted into the Seventh West India Regiment at Barbados. They were provided by private contractors, a method of procurement unsuccessfully exploited by the British government; see C.O. 285/4, Portland, no. 8, 7 February 1796. Jamaicans cited harvest time as the reason for refusing to cooperate in raising the Sixth West India Regiment.

96. C.O. 285/3, Lindsay to Portland, "Private," 6 September 1795.

97. Moore MSS, no. 57327.

98. D. J. Murray, *The West Indies and the Development of Colonial Government, 1801–1834*, pp. xii–xiv, 1–31.

99. Mutiny Act of 1807. The question of the legal status of the West India soldier, culminating in this act, will be discussed in chapter 4.

100. C.O. 324/65, Perceval and Law to Hobart, 14 December 1801.

CHAPTER 3

1. A. P. Kup, "Alexander Lindsay, 6th Earl of Balcarres, Lieutenant Governor of Jamaica, 1794–1801," p. 333; H.O. 30/1, Balcarres to Dundas, no. 4, 29 November 1795.

2. C.O. 140/85, Minutes of the Assembly, 14 December 1795, Votes of the Assembly, p. 67. However, on the same day the Assembly was also busy with a plan to raise two ranger companies in the parish of St. Elizabeth. The cost amounted to £2,000 local currency every two months, of which £1,200 had already been raised (ibid., pp. 69–70).

3. W.O. 1/767, Williamson to Portland, no. 2, 12 July 1795. The number of free blacks and free coloreds in Jamaica's militia had increased in the three years since the beginning of the war and certainly accounts for some part of the failure to enlist them in any large numbers into the West India Regiments. The following comparison also illustrates the significant decline in the number of white militiamen.

	March 1793	March 1796	Change
White cavalry	1,079	1,259	+ 180 ⎫ −1,339
White infantry	5,725	4,206	−1,519 ⎭
Colored infantry	1,384	1,567	+ 183 ⎫ + 363
Black infantry	584	764	+ 180 ⎭
Total	8,772	7,796	

C.O. 137/107, Abstract of Jamaica's Defence Arrangement, 1790–1802, enclosed in Hobart to Nugent, no. 4, 4 February 1802.

4. W.O. 6/5, Balcarres to Portland, 21 July 1795, enclosed in Dundas to Forbes, no. 5, 30 September 1795; and W.O. 1/92, Dundas to Balcarres, no. 3, 30 September 1795.

5. W.O. 17/1988. According to the Jamaica monthly returns for 1796, these two regiments, or rather their cadres, arrived from St. Domingo in May 1796. They remained at least until October.

6. W.O. 40/9, Duke of York to Abercromby, 5 December 1796; C.O. 137/98, Portland to Balcarres, 10 January 1797.

7. C.O. 137/98, Balcarres to Portland, 7 April 1797. According to the enclosed "General Statement of His Majesty's Forces in Jamaica, 1 April 1797," the total strength of the Sixth was then twenty-seven.

8. Ibid., Whitelocke to King, 23 April 1797.

9. Ibid., Balcarres to Portland, 23 May 1797.

10. According to Curtin, "the tensions between the colored and white members of the European society were by far the most serious." On the status of free coloreds in Jamaica before 1830, see Curtin, *Two Jamaicas*, pp. 42–46.

11. Goveia, *Slave Society*, p. 222.

12. Balcarres even recommended the recruitment of colored slaves as an alternative to free coloreds since recruiting the former would not sap the strength of the militia; he also thought that arming colored slaves would not disturb the lines of distinction and subordination between the races. C.O. 137/98, Balcarres to Portland, 23 May, 6 June, and 9 June 1797.

13. Report of a committee of inquiry enclosed in ibid., Balcarres to King, "Secret and Confidential," 30 July 1797.

14. Ibid., Whitelocke to King, 23 April 1797. Musquito coast Indians had previously been employed on several occasions as auxiliaries against Jamaica's truculent Maroons and also against Spain in 1742 and in 1747.

15. C.O. 137/98, Minutes of the Council, 23 May 1797, enclosed in Balcarres to Portland, 25 May 1797.

16. Jamaica Act 30 George III C 9, entitled: "An Act to secure to His Majesty's Troops, that now are, or hereafter may be quartered in this Island, for the protection thereof to the number for which the Faith of the Country stands pledged, the subsistence they now receive on certain conditions."

17. C.O. 137/98, Minutes of the Council, 23 May 1797, enclosed in Balcarres to Portland, 25 May 1797.

18. Ibid., Portland to Balcarres, [n.d.], August 1797.

19. Resolutions of the meeting of the freeholders of St. John's Parish, Point Hill Barracks, in *The Royal Gazette* of [n.d.] June 1797; Remonstrance of the Grand Jury of the County of Middlesex, 1 June 1797, enclosed in ibid., Balcarres to Portland, 9 June 1797.

20. Ibid., Balcarres to Portland, 20 June 1797. Total British rank-and-file in June, including artillery, was 1,021.

21. W.O. 17/251, 1 July, monthly return of Sixth West India Regiment; C.O. 137/98, Balcarres to Portland, 4 July 1797. Although the colonists were unanimous in their hostility to the raising of a West India Regiment on the island, they were not averse to using black troops in an emergency. In March of the following year, when the controversy was still raging, several companies of the Sixth were purposely retained on the island for use against runaway slaves. W.O. 1/769, extract of a letter from Balcarres to Portland, 2 March 1798, p. 443.

22. The committee's report is enclosed in C.O. 137/98, Balcarres to King, "Secret and Confidential," 30 July 1797. A copy of "An Act To regulate the Sale of Gunpowder, And to prevent selling Fire-Arms to Maroons and Slaves" is enclosed in ibid., Balcarres to Portland, 19 August 1797. When Balcarres inspected the Sixth on August 18, it had a total rank-and-file of 130, of which 120 were free blacks and 10 only were slaves. Ibid., Balcarres to Portland, 19 August 1797.

23. Ibid., Balcarres to King, "Secret and Confidential," 30 July 1797, and Portland to Balcarres, "Most Secret and Confidential," October 1797.

24. Ibid., Ricketts to Balcarres, 7 August 1797, enclosed in Balcarres to Portland, 19 August 1797.

25. Ibid., Balcarres to Portland, 19 August 1797.

26. Kup, "Balcarres," p. 328. "An Act for Regulating the Manumission of Negro Mulatto and other Slaves, and to Oblige the owners to make a provision for them during their lives," enclosed in ibid.

27. Ibid., Balcarres to Portland, 6 June 1797.

28. C.O. 137/99, enclosure no. 2 in Balcarres to Portland, no. 3, 10 December 1797.

29. A large number of German soldiers were then in British pay and serving in the West Indies. Among these corps were the Lowenstein Chasseurs and Fusiliers, Waldstein's Regiment, the Royal Etrangers, and the Hompesch Hussars and Fusiliers. All of these corps were later incorporated into the various battalions of the Sixtieth Regiment. The Sixtieth, then, had a decidedly German character. See Cecil C. P. Lawson, *A History of the Uniforms of the British Army*, vol. 4, pp. 139–49.

30. C.O. 137/99, enclosure no. 2 in Balcarres to Portland, no. 3, 10 December 1797.

31. W.O. 40/10, Duke of York to Portland, 8 May 1798, and Portland to the Duke of York, 10 May 1798; W.O. 17/1990.

32. C.O. 137/98, Portland to Balcarres [n.d.] August 1797.

33. Ibid., 12 September 1797.

34. W.O. 40/10, Duke of York to Portland, 8 May 1798, and Portland to the Duke of York, 10 May 1798; C.O. 137/99, Portland to Balcarres, 10 May 1798.

35. According to Portland, the principle of a racially mixed force was to be "religiously" adhered to in all the other islands. C.O. 137/98, Portland to Balcarres, 12 September 1797.

36. Helen Taft Manning, *British Colonial Government After the American Revolution: 1782–1820*, p. 241.

37. C.O. 137/103, enclosure in Balcarres to Portland, 30 October 1799.

38. Anticipating a hostile reception should these troops be permitted to remain for any length of time, Balcarres drafted the privates, about 120 men, into the Sixth and shipped them to Honduras. C.O. 137/100, Balcarres to Portland, 29 October 1798.

39. W.O. 17/1991.

40. C.O. 137/107, Abstract of Jamaica's Defence Arrangements 1790–1802, enclosure in Hobart to Nugent, no. 4, 4 February 1802; W.O. 1/405, Portland to Balcarres, "Secret," 7 April 1799.

41. W.O. 1/771, Portland to Dundas, 10 March 1800.

42. See, for example, the resolutions of the merchants and planters of 6 May 1800 in C.O. 137/107, Abstract of Jamaica's Defence Arrangements, 1790–1802, enclosure in Hobart to Nugent, no. 4, 4 February 1802.

43. W.O. 1/771, Balcarres to Portland, 15 September 1800.

44. C.O. 137/99, enclosure no. 1 in Balcarres to Portland, 3 March 1798; W.O. 17/1990.

45. C.O. 137/107, Hobart to Nugent, no. 6, 2 April 1802.

46. For all this, see random pages in W.O. 25/644, 656, 657, 662; W.O. 6/131, Huskisson to Brownrigg, 18 September 1797.

47. Compare H.O. 30/1, Knox Memorandum, 25 August 1795, enclosed in Dundas to Portland, 26 August 1795 with W.O. 1/85, "Preparations made by the Quarter Master General for the Army to Serve under the Orders of His Excellency Sir Ralph Abercromby, K.B., " enclosed in Abercromby to Dundas, 9 April 1796. Abercromby was the Commander in Chief, West Indies, for one year, from about November 1795 to November 1796.

48. W.O. 1/85, Dundas to Abercromby, no. 3, 28 October 1796. The commander at Jamaica was similarly instructed.

49. Fortescue, *History of the British Army*, vol. 4 (part I), p. 325.

50. According to Peter Gay, toward the end of the eighteenth century antislavery sentiment had swelled into the torrent of abolitionism. Roger Anstey, *The Atlantic Slave Trade and British Abolition, 1760–1810*, p. 125.

51. C.O. 153/31, Dundas to Cuyler, "Secret," no. 9, 18 January 1798.

52. Most recruits, perhaps in jest, were named after contemporary British politicians, generals, and notables from history and literature. Thus *Description and Succession Books* abound with such names as "Private William Windham," "Corporal Pitt," "Corporal Duke Portland," and Privates "Hannibal," "Achilles," and "Othello." Others were given hybridized names like "Corporal Quashey Jeremiah" and "Private Congo Jack." None were allowed to keep their African names. See, among other sources, W.O. 25/644, 652–53, 656, 2246. For a brief eyewitness account of recently landed slaves being processed into British military service, see Jerome S. Handler, ed., "Memoirs of An Old Army Officer."

53. For references to contractual arrangements between the Army and merchants, see W. O. 1/86, James Bontein contract, enclosure no. 5, and enclosures nos. 3, 6, Abercromby to Dundas, 26 January 1797; ibid., the Chollet, Campbell, and McNully contracts, enclosures in Cuyler to Dundas, 23, 29 March and 9 May 1798. Another, the Charles Rance contract, appears in its entirety as Appendix B.

54. Total purchases was arrived at by combining those for the Jamaica Command, which recruited separately and consistently about half the number recruited by the Windward and Leeward Islands Command. (See Table 1.) For Jamaica, see pertinent returns in W.O. 25/644; W.O. 40/20; W.O. 17/251; and W.O. 1/630. The total cost was determined by multiplying total purchases by the average price per slave paid by the Windward and Leeward Island Command. It must be noted that the number 13,400 does not include an indefinite—but probably considerable—number of additional slaves bought by the British government to perform other military related functions, particularly those carried out by the quartermaster general's department. It also does not include slaves purchased privately to replace worn-out blacks, several thousand of whom had been hired out to the army, nor slaves purchased simultaneously in Portuguese East Africa as recruits for Britain's Ceylon Regiments. See C.O. 285/4, Minutes of the Tobago Assembly, 19 June 1795, enclosure in Hobart to Nugent, no. 6, 2 April 1802; (Ceylon): C.O. 318/25, Myers to Hobart, no. 10, 6 June 1804, enclosure no. 5; ibid., Myers to Camden, no. 13, 31 August 1804; G. Tylden, "The Ceylon

Regiments, 1796 to 1874," pp. 124–28; Geoffrey Powell, *The Kandyan Wars*, pp. 147–48.

55. Curtin, *The Atlantic Slave Trade*, Table 65, p. 216.

56. See Seymour Drescher, *Econocide: British Slavery in the Era of Abolition*, pp. 25–32, 205–13.

57. Wilberforce to Pitt, 14 September 1804, in Robert and Samuel Wilberforce, eds., *The Correspondence of William Wilberforce*, vol. 1, pp. 239–40.

58. "Lord Camden has mentioned to me another part of the scheme, that of buying slaves for recruiting our black regiments" (ibid).

59. The alleged and actual mutinies, along with the legal battle, are discussed below.

60. John Fuller, M.P., Sussex: "How can this [action] be reconciled with the conduct of the right hon. the chancellor of the exchequer on the present occasion, I am utterly at a loss to conceive. This is supporting a measure in one way, and opposing it in another." *Hansard's Parliamentary Debates*, First Series, vol. 3, Debate in Commons on the Slave Trade Abolition Bill, 28 February 1805. Fuller's speech, col. 656. Pitt's answer to this and similar charges, on this occasion, was evasive and confusing. He denied the existence of a specific plan of government to buy slaves. Then he suggested the validity of the charges by Fuller and others; however, he drew a rather fine distinction between purchasing slaves and buying their redemption from a state of slavery (Pitt's speech, col. 668, in ibid). Fox and Wilberforce spoke, but both chose to direct their comments to other matters (Fox's and Wilberforce's speeches, cols. 660–62 and 668–73, respectively). Pitt's use of the word *redemption* to rebuke critics on this occasion is worthy of special note. Since redemption was a central concept in the evangelical denunciation of slavery and the trade, was its use by Pitt a cagey effort to justify his recruitment policy to Evangelicals? On the importance of this concept in evangelicalism, Professor Anstey says: "Evangelicals . . . apprehended salvation primarily through the concept of redemption; when they related the idea of redemption, in its existential, individual application, to God's great redemptive purpose . . . they saw that, historically, redemption was not least a redemption from physical bondage . . . ." (*The Atlantic Slave Trade*, p. 189).

61. Professor Anstey's brilliant analysis of Britain's slave trade and efforts to end it offers a case in point. Despite the general certainty and clarity that pervades the book, Anstey retreats before the enigmatic Pitt and is forced to presume the reasons for Pitt's perplexing actions. See *Atlantic Slave Trade*, pp. 346, 348, 358.

62. For instance, Ragatz, *The Fall of the Planter Class*, p. 253; Frank Klingberg, *The Anti-Slavery Movement in England*, pp. 93–94; Reginald Coupland, *The British Anti-Slavery Movement*, pp. 95–99; and William Law Mathieson, *British Slavery and its Abolition, 1823–1838*, pp. 8–9, 20; Eric Williams, *From Columbus to Castro*, pp. 261–62; and Eric Williams, *Capitalism and Slavery*, pp. 148–49.

63. Anstey, *Atlantic Slave Trade*, pp. 276–78.

64. R. R. Palmer, *The Age of the Democratic Revolution*, vol. 2, pp. 569–75; Mathieson, *British Slavery*, p. 20.

65. The Danish slave trade was abolished on 1 January 1803. Dale Porter, *The Abolition of the Slave Trade in England, 1784-1807*, p. 120.

66. W.O. 1/86, Dundas to Cuyler, no. 18, 17 January 1798.

67. The destruction of St. Domingo did open for the moment, however, the way for a world sugar boom and a concomitant increased demand for slaves which was being satisfied, even in the Spanish islands, by British ships. Moreover, Britain's retention of Trinidad in 1802, with its huge expanses of uncleared land, and planter designs on St. Vincent, which was opened up as a result of the wholesale deportation of dissident groups, certainly titilated

British investors. The political consequences of all of this, plus the subsequent British reconquest of the rich lands of the Dutch Guianan colonies soon after the rupture of the Amiens Peace in 1803, helped materially to delay the death of the British slave trade. See David B. Davis, *The Problem of Slavery*, pp. 437–42.

68. Anstey, *Atlantic Slave Trade*, pp. 286–409; also Patrick Lipscomb, "William Pitt and the Abolition Question: A Review of an Historical Controversy," pp. 97–127.

69. It could also have been a decision reached outside the cabinet by the principal parties. According to Professor J. Steven Watson, "Pitt often enough decided policy outside the cabinet with Dundas or his cousin Grenville. In cabinet he would then listen and reveal decisions" (*The Reign of George III, 1760–1815*, p. 301). The fact that the decision may have been arrived at in this manner does not detract from the line of argument, since the effect would be the same.

70. During the second period of Pitt's first administration, 1794–1801, Windham served as secretary at war, Portland as home secretary, and Dundas as secretary of war; Grenville was foreign secretary. The author is unaware of the position of Cornwallis vis-à-vis the trade. The Marquis, in February 1795, became the Master General of the Ordnance. In 1798 this post ceased having cabinet rank; it was restored in 1804. In 1795 the post of Commander in Chief of the British army was excluded from cabinet. See Watson, *The Reign of George III*, pp. 580–81.

71. See, for example, Wylie Sypher, *Guinea's Captive Kings: British Anti-Slavery Literature of the XVIIIth Century*, p. 17; Anstey, *Atlantic Slave Trade*, p. 282.

72. Klingberg, *Anti-Slavery Movement in England*, states that Windham's first publicly hostile stand on abolition occurred in April 1798 (p. 112). This appears to be somewhat late. In any event, he doubtless evidenced his private hostility to the measure much sooner.

73. On Britain's manpower crisis during the war, see Correlli Barnett, *Britain and Her Army, 1509–1970: A Military, Political and Social Survey*, pp. 234, 254–58.

74. W.O. 1/632, York to Windham, 18 March 1806.

75. See ibid., Gordon to Shee, 10 June 1806.

76. See Anstey, *Atlantic Slave Trade*, p. 6, and the footnote.

77. W.O. 1/634, Gordon Memorandum, 8 April 1807 and enclosure Dawson to Gordon, 9 November 1806. See Appendix C. I have estimated that about 1,000 slaves were obtained by the British army in the West Indies between April 1807 and 1 March 1808, the final date by which slavers cleared from Britain on or before 1 May 1807 had to reach their Caribbean destination. Assuming that a contract was entered into by the British government and Dawson, these slaves could have been part of the Dawson consignment. See Table 1.

78. *Statutes of the United Kingdom of Great Britain and Ireland*, 47 George III, Session I, c. 32, Article 103. For this development, see *Parliamentary Debates*, vol. 7, Debate in Commons on the Mutiny Bill, 6 June 1806, George Canning's speech, cols. 543–58; ibid., Debate in House of Lords on Mutiny Bill, 13 June 1806, Earl of Westmoreland's speech, cols. 648–50; Fortescue, *A History of the British Army*, vol. 5, pp. 301–303. Under the same Act, Europeans enlisted as infantrymen served for seven years.

79. *Statutes of the U.K.*, 47 George III, Session I, c. 36, Articles 4 and 7, respectively. Article 17, as in the Mutiny Act, stipulated that Africans only be enlisted for unlimited service. For this development, see Young, *West India Common-Place Book*, pp. 241–42; *Parliamentary Debates*, vol. 9, Debate in Commons on Slave Trade Abolition Bill, 9 March 1807, Lord Howick's speech, col. 66.

80. For instance, Lipscomb, "William Pitt," pp. 118–19; Anstey, *Atlantic Slave Trade*, p. 412.

81. By March 1793, eighty-seven blacks had been purchased. See C.O. 137/88, Grenville to Effingham, "Secret," 6 October 1790; ibid., "Secret," 23 October 1790; ibid., no. 7, 6 November 1790; C.O. 137/107, Abstract of Jamaica's Defence Arrangement, 1790-1802, in Hobart to Nugent, no. 4, 4 February 1802.

82. For example, Anstey, *Atlantic Slave Trade*, passim.

83. Orde Coombs, ed., *Is Massa Day Dead? Black Moods in the Caribbean*, p. 93.

84. Klingberg, *Anti-Slavery Movement*, p. 129; Anstey, *Atlantic Slave Trade*, pp. 398-400.

85. For instance, W.O. 1/902, extract of the Sullivan Memorandum, c. December 1804; Castlereagh to Wellesley, 21 and 25 August 1804 in Duke of Wellinton, ed., *Supplementary Dispatches, Correspondence and Memoranda of Field Marshall Arthur Duke of Wellington*, vol. 4, pp. 520-24. Earlier proposals to raise corps of free coloreds, free blacks, and East Indians for service in the West Indies can be found in W.O. 1/88, 617, 1105-6, 1109; W.O. 4/280; and W.O. 6/131.

86. Excerpts of the Order in Council are quoted in Robert Kuczynski, *Demographic Survey of the British Colonial Empire*, vol. 1, pp. 112-13. Instructions to commanders of Royal Navy ships and privateers are in W.O. 1/742, pp. 65-74.

CHAPTER 4

1. Great Britain, War Office, *Manual of Military Law*, p. 85.

2. W.O. 1/95, "Remarks . . . ," enclosed in Hislop to the Duke of York, 22 July 1804.

3. Elsa Goveia, "The West Indian Slave Laws," p. 24. According to Fortescue, if West India soldiers were made subject to local slave laws, one magistrate could order a black soldier to be whipped publicly and two magistrates could order him hanged. Fortescue, *History of the British Army*, vol. 4 (part I), p. 543.

4. W.O. 1/623, Trigge to Brownrigg, 21 September 1801, enclosure no. 3.

5. Ibid., Trigge to Brownrigg, 21 September 1801; W.O. 1/86, Bowyer to Dundas, 6 September 1798; C.O. 318/33, Bowyer to Castlereagh, 10 February 1808.

6. See Pinckard, *Notes on the West Indies*, vol. 3, p. 197.

7. C.O. 137/123, Carmichael to Castlereagh, 27 July 1808; see also ibid., General Orders, 12 August 1808, enclosed in Carmichael to Castlereagh, 12 August 1808.

8. Once a worn-out slave left to die along the roadside was found by a detachment of West India soldiers. Their efforts to save him failed. See Handler, "Memoirs of an Old Soldier."

9. C.O. 318/28, Castlereagh to Bowyer, 26 December 1805. Compare this treatment with the shameful way the Union government generally treated its black troops during the American Civil War. See Genovese, *Roll, Jordan, Roll*, pp. 152-58, 706-07.

10. Captain Holwell to Magistrates, 14 January 1805, in John Burdon, ed., *Archives of British Honduras*, vol. 2, p. 77.

11. *Manual of Military Law*, pp. 11-14, 85.

12. W.O. 1/623, Trigge to Brownrigg, 21 September 1801.

13. 5 and 6 William and Mary, c. 15, sec. 2, referred to in Charles M. Clode, *The Military Forces of the Crown: Their Administration and Government*, vol. 2, p. 7.

14. Robert B. Scott, *The Military Law of England*, pp. 187-88. Copies of the oaths are found in this reference as well as in the back of the *Description and Succession Book* of the Seventh West India Regiment, W.O. 25/661, folios 112-13.

15. 8 George III, c. 2, referred to in Clode, *Military Forces*, vol. 2, p. 8.

16. W.O. 25/653, folios 28–36.

17. For the Seventh West India Regiment, for example, see W.O. 25/662.

18. W.O. 27/90, part 2, "Inspecting Officer's Report. Detachment Sixth West India Regiment. On the 24th day of July 1806"; ibid., part 1, "Major General W. Archer's Inspection Report of the Fourth West India Regiment. Surinam, Fort New Amsterdam, 10 January 1806"; and C.O. 137/123, Villettes to Castlereagh, 15 June 1808.

19. W.O. 1/88, Minutes of the Council and Assembly (Antigua), 20, 31 December 1798 and 31 January 1799, pp. 272–73, 284.

20. W.O. 1/86, Bowyer to Dundas, 6 September 1798.

21. Eventually Private Miller was tried before a garrison court martial. W.O. 1/771, King to Huskisson, 4 July 1800, and enclosures. It is interesting to note that by the end of the eighteenth century, the Dutch Army in the West Indies apparently had avoided this problem by recruiting only free blacks. See W.O. 1/149, Spiering to Hughes, 11 July 1805; and W.O. 1/150, Report of the Committee of the Court of Policy, no. 2 enclosure in Hughes to Windham, 28 May 1806.

22. W.O. 1/624, Grinfield to Brownrigg, no. 45, 2 November 1802. A "bitt" was equivalent to six pence sterling.

23. W.O. 1/95, "Remarks on the Establishment of the West India Regiments . . . 1801," enclosed in Hislop to the Duke of York, 22 July 1804.

24. A copy of the discharge certificate is in W.O. 25/661, folios 113–14.

25. While the issue was being debated throughout the British West Indies, there were some indications of colonial acceptance of the West India Regiments. In 1803, Trinidad was reported to have been "quietly conciliated" to the presence of black soldiers in its garrisons. The good conduct of these troops was cited as the reason for acceptance. C.O. 318/21, Grinfield to Hobart, no. 51, 25 February 1803. By August 1804, London was being told that the colonies no longer questioned the utility of black regiments and that colonial opposition to these corps "decreases daily." C.O. 318/25, Myers to Camden, no. 15, 28 August 1804.

26. Nonetheless, in some garrisons, blacks actually outnumbered white regulars.

27. See C.O. 137/106 and 108 for correspondence dealing with Jamaica's continued efforts in 1801 and 1802 to remove the Second Regiment and substitute an all-white garrison.

28. W.O. 1/771, Portland to Hobart, 8 July 1801 and enclosure.

29. W.O. 1/96, Beckwith to Gordon, no. 46, 10 December 1805 and enclosure.

30. W.O. 1/619, Brownrigg to Huskisson, 9 November 1798 and enclosure; W.O. 6/131, Huskisson to Brownrigg, 29 November 1798; W.O. 1/769, Portland to Balcarres, 9 August 1797, enclosed in King to Huskisson, 19 August 1797.

31. W.O. 1/619, enclosure in Brownrigg to Huskisson, 9 November 1798; C.O. 153/31, Portland to the Attorney and Solicitor Generals, 12 November 1798.

32. W.O. 1/770, Portland to Bentinck, 10 March 1799, enclosed in King to Huskisson, 25 March 1799.

33. W.O. 1/88, Gloster to Bentinck, 10 January 1799, enclosed in Attorney General (Gloster) to Dundas, 25 January 1799; W.O. 1/87, Bowyer to Dundas, 31 January 1799.

34. C.O. 153/31, Portland to Attorney and Solicitors General, 12 November 1798, pp. 266–67.

35. W.O. 1/88, Attorney and Solicitors General's Report to Portland, 11 March 1799, enclosed in King to Huskisson, 11 March 1799.

36. C.O. 324/65, Scott and Mitford to Portland, 11 March 1801.

37. Ibid., Law and Percival to Hobart, 14 December 1801.

38. *Manual of Military Law*, p. 190.

39. This case is briefly discussed in W.O. 1/632, Trigge to Brownrigg, 21 September 1801, enclosure no. 3.

40. Scott, *Military Law of England*, p. 185.

41. Ibid., p. 183.

42. Goveia, "The West Indian Slave Laws," p. 21.

43. C.O. 324/65, Law and Percival to Hobart, 14 December 1801.

44. Ibid.

45. C.O. 137/108, Nugent to Hobart, "Private," 28 June 1802.

46. W.O. 1/632, Trigge to Brownrigg, 21 September 1801, enclosure no. 3.

47. *Parliamentary Debates*, vol. 8, Debate in the House of Lords on the Slave Trade Abolition Bill, 6 February 1807, Lord Hardwiche's speech, col. 678; speech of Lord Grenville, col. 678.

48. C.O. 318/30, Bowyer to Windham, no. 18, 31 October 1806.

49. C.O. 318/31, Bowyer to Windham, no. 25, 10 January 1807.

50. W.O. 1/96, Beckwith to Gordon, no. 46, 10 December 1805 and enclosure; C.O. 318/30, Bowyer to Windham, no. 18, 31 October 1806.

51. C.O. 318/31, Bowyer to Windham, no. 25, 10 January 1807. By mentioning that the testimony of West India soldiers was admitted as evidence in courts-martial, Bowyer had drawn attention to a secondary legal battle between the colonies and the army over the question of admissibility of slaves' testimony in military courts. According to colonial law, the evidence of slaves could be presented only in slave courts; as the West India soldiers had been declared slaves under the operation of colonial police regulations, this law would also apply to them. The question of the admissibility of the testimony of slaves in military courts apparently was first raised in Surinam in 1801 after its conquest by Britain. The question was finally resolved in 1809, when the law officers of the Crown ruled that the evidence of slaves at military proceedings was admissible. See W.O. 81/27, Morgan to Trigge, "Private," 5 February 1801; W.O. 72/30, Carmichael to Judge Advocate General, 30 April 1809; ibid., Opinions of the Attorney and Solicitors General, 26 June 1809; W.O. 81/40, Ryder to Gordon, 17 June 1809 and Ryder to Carmichael, 15 July 1809; W.O. 81/44, Sutton to Beckwith, 4 May 1811.

52. Disbandment became an issue because of the peace preliminaries of 1 October 1801, and the signing of a definite, although fragile, peace between Britain and France at Amiens on 27 March 1802. Peace had seemed practically assured since Addington took over from Pitt in February 1801; the new prime minister sought public support through economy. See Watson, pp. 409, 412.

Disbandment posed some fundamental questions. Where, for instance, could blacks be discharged? And how, if discharged, were they to support themselves? Lord Hobart, who termed it "so delicate a measure," well understood the serious consequences of disbanding West Indian soldiers before it had been determined if they were to enter West Indian society as freedmen or slaves. See C.O. 318/19, Hobart to Trigge, no. 15, 6 May 1802.

53. On the mutiny, see Stephen G. P. Ward, *Faithful: The Story of the Durham Light Infantry*, pp. 84–85; anon., "The Mutiny of the 8th West India Regiment From the Papers of a Veteran Officer"; anon., "A Further Account of the Mutiny of the 8th West India Regiment"; W.O. 1/90, 95, 96; C.O. 318/19, 20; and C.O. 71/30, 34, 109.

54. C.O. 71/34, Johnstone to Hobart, no. 16, 1 May 1802, enclosure no. 5.

55. C.O. 318/20, Grinfield to Hobart, no. 5, 17 September 1802 and enclosure no. 4.

56. C.O. 318/19, enclosure in Trigge to Hobart, no. 44, 4 May 1802.

57. Ibid. The Proceedings also reveal that fraudulent transactions had resulted in irregular pay for the troops used to clear the land. Responsibility for these activities were found to rest with Andrew Cochrane Johnstone, Colonel of the Eighth and Governor of Dominica. He was promptly removed from his government posts; but at his court-martial in 1805, he was shamefully acquitted of several counts of fraudulent practices. Later he was involved in other disreputable transactions but, again, appears to have evaded punishment. See W.O. 71/109, folios 2–4, 501; Alan C. Burns, *History of the British West Indies*, note on p. 544; *Dictionary of National Biography*, p. 83; and Johnstone's own *Correspondence*.

58. For the raising and disbandment record of the West India Regiments, see Appendix D. With the renewal of the war in 1803, the establishment of the West India Regiments was augmented from a rank-and-file strength of 600 to 1000.

59. W.O. 1/96, Beckwith to Gordon, no. 46, 10 December 1805 and enclosure.

60. C.O. 318/28, Beckwith to Castlereagh, no. 23, 10 December 1805; C.O. 318/29, Beckwith to Castlereagh, no. 41, 2 March 1806; W.O. 1/632, Beckwith to Gordon, 27 March 1806, enclosed in Gordon to Shee, 8 May 1806.

61. *Parliamentary Debates*, vol. 8, Debate in the House of Lords on the Slave Trade Abolition Bill, 6 February 1807, Lord Grenville's speech, col. 678; ibid., vol. 9, Debate in Commons on Mutiny Bill, 9 March 1807, Secretary at War's speech, col. 63.

62. No doubt this notice appeared simultaneously in other West Indian newspapers.

63. This figure is compiled chiefly from the December return of 1807, which shows the effective strength of these corps. It also includes discharged blacks and those doing garrison duties. The total number enfranchised would be substantially higher if an indeterminate number of blacks in the Royal Navy and in white regiments were included.

64. W.O. 4/729, Howick to Glenelg, 18 January 1836.

65. W.O. 4/342, Bragge to Somerset, 17 January 1804; James E. Caulfield, *One Hundred Years' History of the Second Battalion, West India Regiment*, p. 27.

66. *History of the British Army*, vol. 7, p. 26.

67. 6 George III, c. 12.

68. Quoted in D. J. Murray, *The West Indies and the Development of Colonial Government, 1801–1834*, pp. 1–2, 4.

CHAPTER 5

1. Guerrilla-style warfare in fact preceded Britain's entry into the conflict. The struggle in St. Domingo, which began in 1791 as a consequence of the slave insurrection, was a guerrilla war. There was some element of irregular warfare in most, if not all, West Indian conflicts, including secondary operations that were part of larger and more formally conducted campaigns and the various wars against the Maroons. These operations, however, were on comparatively small scales, and were mostly limited, for logistical reasons, to coastal areas; they were also very much the exception rather than the rule. For a glimpse of all this see Thomas O. Ott, *The Haitian Revolution, 1789–1804*, p. 50; Marshall Smelser, *The Campaigns for the Sugar Islands*, pp. 39–59; R. C. Dallas, *The History of the Maroons*, passim; S. A. G. Taylor, *The Western Design*, pp. 98–110; J. C. Stedman, *Narrative of Five Years' Expedition against the Revolted Negroes of Surinam*, passim; and Richard Pares, *War and Trade in the West Indies, 1739–1763*, pp. 227–64.

2. The latter category included Drualt's Guadeloupe Rangers, Gaudin de Soter's Royal Island Rangers, the South American Rangers, and O'Meara's Rangers. These corps were

taken on the British Establishment in December 1798 as the Ninth, Tenth, Eleventh and Twelfth West India Regiments, respectively (see Appendix D). Each corps had eight companies and a rank-and-file strength of 456. The officers were mostly Frenchmen who held only temporary commissions. See W.O. 4/339, Windham to Fawquier, 6 December 1798; ibid., Windham to Maitland, 18 October 1798; W.O. 1/1109, Hislop to Hobart, 21 May 1803; W.O. 1/95, Hislop to Trigge, 4 January 1802, enclosed in Trigge to Brownrigg, no. 9, 22 January 1802; *Army List 1799*.

3. See frontispiece. This photograph is a copy of a print in Milne, *The Standards and Colours of the Army*, plate XVI. The uniform is described by Cecil C. P. Lawson, et. al., in "Military Dress: West India Regiments, 1800-1810," p. 119. The uniform described is the dress uniform and certainly not that worn on active service.

4. R. Money Barnes, *Military Uniforms of Britain and the Empire*, p. 60.

5. Even Fortescue fails to mention the West India Regiments and West Indian service in his discussion of the evolution of the light infantry. See *History of the British Army*, vol. 4 (part II), pp. 916-21.

6. Moore's operations against the brigands at St. Lucia are described later in this chapter. For Manningham, see Fortescue, *History of the British Army*, vol. 4 (part II), p. 918.

7. W.O. 17/1988; A.O. 3/265, unnumbered papers, "District of Port au Prince; Supplementary Account of Money Disbursed by John Wigglesworth Esquire, Commissary General of Saint Domingo from 1st March 1796 to 24th February 1797," Abstract no. 5, "Subsistence & Allowance to Colonial Corps."

8. W.O. 25/653, folios 25-28.

9. C.O. 140/85, Minutes of the Assembly, 14 December 1795, *Votes of the Assembly*, p. 68.

10. W.O. 1/62, Dundas to Forbes, no. 2, "Most Secret," 30 September 1795, and Forbes to Dundas, no. 2, "Most Secret," 9 December 1795.

11. Ibid., Forbes to Dundas, no. 1, 9 December 1795.

12. C.O. 140/85, Letter from Sonothonax to General Beauvais, enclosed in Simcoe to Balcarres, 1 June 1797, read into the Minutes of the Jamaica Council, 31 July 1797, *Journal of the Council*.

13. Edwards, *Historical Survey . . . of San Domingo*, p. 392.

14. Klingberg is incorrect in stating that Britain withdrew from the island on 1 January 1798 (see his *Anti-Slavery Movement*, p. 104). Maitland had not decided on evacuation until July 1798. C.O. 137/100, Mailtand's first letter of 31 July 1798 to Balcarres.

15. C.O. 137/106, Portland to Nugent, "Private and Confidential," 18 November 1801. A French army under le Clerc began its invasion of St. Domingo in December 1801.

16. W.O. 1/68, Maitland to Dundas, 6 July 1798, enclosure no. 8.

17. Edwards, *Historical Survey*, p. 391; W.O. 1/68, Maitland to Dundas, 6 July 1798, enclosure no. 5.

18. A.O. 3/265, unnumbered papers, "Account B, No. 2, District of Mole St. Nicolas. An Account of Money Disbursed . . . between the 25th of June 1796 and 24th of April 1797," Abstract no. 3, "Subsistence & Allowance to Colonial Corps."

19. C.O. 153/31, Dundas to Bowyer, 22 August 1798; C.O. 137/100, Maitland's first letter of 31 July 1798 to Balcarres.

20. W.O. 1/68, Maitland to Dundas, 6 July 1798, enclosure no. 5.

21. C.O. 137/100, Balcarres to Portland, 26 July 1798.

22. Edwards, *Historical Survey*, p. 399.

23. The Eighth West India Regiment, raised in 1795 as Skerrett's Foot, was disbanded

in 1796, then reraised in June 1798 when the Loyal Dominica Rangers was taken on the British Establishment. Official correspondence dealing with the reraising of the Eighth is found principally in W.O. 1/82, 86, 88; W.O. 4/339.

24. Pinckard, *Notes on the West Indies*, vol. 1, pp. 382–83. According to General Leigh (W.O. 1/85, "Return of a Brigade of Black Troops, Barbados, 10 March 1796," enclosure in Leigh to Dundas, 10 March 1796), Pinckard's estimate is high by about 400 men.

25. For a summary of the services of the First West India Regiment during the St. Lucia campaign, see Ellis, *History of the First West India Regiment*, pp. 85–92; see also W.O. 1/85, "Return of Killed, Wounded and Missing in the Island of St. Lucia from 28 April to 24 May 1796 inclusive," enclosure no. 2 in Abercromby to Dundas, no. 16, 31 May 1796.

26. Bryan Edwards quoted in Ellis, *History of the First West India Regiment*, pp. 85, 92.

27. Moore MSS, no. 57320, Moore to his father, 20 August 1796, 11 October 1796, and 18 January 1797; no. 57321, Moore to Brownrigg, 4 September 1796; no. 57326, letter book entry of 8 July 1796; no. 57327, Moore to Abercromby, 2 September 1796.

28. The total force under Moore's command at this time was 3,260; see W.O. 1/86, "distribution of the Forces in the Windward & Leeward Charibee Islands with the Corps doing duty in each taken from the latest Returns. St. Pierre, Martinico, 13 November 1796," enclosure in Graham to Dundas, 15 November 1796, pp. 35–38.

29. Moore MSS, no. 57320, Moore to his father, 18 January 1797.

30. Ibid., no. 57327, Moore to Abercromby, 2 September 1796; and no. 57321, Moore to Brownrigg, 4 September 1796.

31. C.O. 101/34, Mackensie to Portland, 6 July 1795; ibid., 16 May 1795.

32. Ibid., 11 August 1795, enclosure no. 4.

33. W.O. 1/767, extract of a letter from President Mackensie to the Duke of Portland, 15 September 1795.

34. Brigadier General A. Campbell to Lord Cathcart, 19 April 1795, quoted in H. Everard, *History of Tho⁵ Farrington's Regiment*, p. 195.

35. C.O. 137/123, Carmichael to Castlereagh, 27 July 1808, and no. 2 enclosure.

36. Notable exceptions of white troops adept at irregular warfare were various German Jaeger (light infantry) regiments in British service in the West Indies and the battalions of the Sixtieth Regiment, several of which also served in the West Indies. These troops were, however, comparatively few in number.

For black corps casualty information, see, for Grenada, Jeffery, *Dyott's Diary*, vol. 1, p. 99; for St. Vincent, casualty returns of the Second West Regiment from January to October 1796 in W.O. 1/85 and W.O. 1/86; and for Dominica, W.O. 1/82, Johnstone to Dundas, 6 November 1797, enclosure no. 5.

37. Quoted in Caulfield, *One Hundred Years' History . . . West India Regiment*, pp. 13–14. The action described occurred at St. Vincent.

38. W.O. 1/86, Dundas to Cuyler, no. 8, 17 January 1798; ibid., Cuyler to Dundas, 3 April 1798; ibid., Bowyer to Dundas, 13 July 1798; and C.O. 152/79, Bowyer to Dundas, 19 January 1799. With the possible exception of the Puerto Rico expedition of 1797, West India Regiments participated in all campaigns during the insurgent phase of the war.

39. W.O. 1/82, "Notes from Sir Ralph Abercromby about the West Indies. London 10 November 97," pp. 626–27.

40. Fortescue, *History of the British Army*, vol. 4 (part II), p. 918.

41. W.O. 1/88, Johnstone to Dundas, "Private," 7 June 1798; W.O. 1/95, Colonel Hislop's Memorandum, "Remarks . . . ," enclosure in Hislop to the Duke of York, 22 July 1804. See also the proposal to train 200 Africans of the Eleventh Regiment as riflemen, W.O. 6/131, Huskisson to Brownrigg, 7 January 1800.

42. In July 1809, no fewer than five battalions of the Sixtieth were in garrisons in the West Indies. See Charles Oman, *Wellington's Army, 1809–1814*, pp. 333–37.

43. W.O. 40/9, Abercromby's circular to West Indian governors, 3 January 1797.

44. C.O. 318/32, "Abstract In which the Casualties of the European Troops are discriminated from those of the African, & a comprehensive view of the whole afforded," enclosed in "General Return of the Sick and Wounded in . . . the Windward and Leeward Colonies . . . from December 1799 to January 1803. . . . " See also C.O. 318/20, Grinfield to Hobart, "Private and Confidential," no. 23, 5 December 1802, enclosures no. 1 and no. 2; and C.O. 318/21, Grinfield to Hobart, no. 42, 31 January 1803, enclosures nos. 1 and 2.

45. C.O. 153/31, Dundas to Cuyler, "Secret," no. 9, 18 January 1798.

46. W.O. 1/90, Trigge to Dundas, no. 8, 14 March, no. 10, 22 March and no. 11, 27 March 1801.

47. The honors were "Dominica," 1805 (First West India Regiment); "Martinique," 1809 (First and Fourth West India Regiments); and "Guadeloupe," 1810 (First and Fourth West India Regiments). See W.O. 3/47, "W.W." [William Windham] to Somerset; W.O. 3/195, W. W. to Fanquier, 26 November 1808; W.O. 3/580, W.W. to Beckwith, 26 November 1808; W.O. 3/381, Calvert to Officer Commanding Fourth West India Regiment, 11 November 1817; W.O. 3/383, Calvert to Officer Commanding First West India Regiment, 6 May 1818; W.O. 3/222, Calvert to Secretary to the Clothing Board, 11 November 1817; W.O. 3/68, Calvert to Somerset, 6 May 1818; and W.O. 3/163, "Memorandum for the War Office," 7 May 1818.

48. The First and Fifth West India Regiments took part in the New Orleans operation. Both British Honduras (Belize) and the Guianas, areas where West Indian Regiments had served, are considered part of the West Indies or, more appropriately, part of the West Indian region; there are numerous historical, economic, military, and administrative links between these areas and the Caribbean islands.

49. Abercromby to Dundas, "Private," 20 November 1799, Melville Papers, William L. Clements Library, University of Michigan; and Duke of Wellington, ed., *Supplementary Despatches, Correspondence and Memoranda*, vol. 6, pp. 35–82.

50. W.O. 1/352, Thornton to Hobart, 6 October 1802.

51. According to a return entitled "Statement of Reductions," which was prepared in 1817, a detachment of 200 men belonging to the Fourth West India Regiment was included among the Gibraltar garrison. See W.O. 4/719, p. 207. For this development, see also C.O. 318/20, Hobart to Grinfield, no. 1, 4 September 1802; ibid., Grinfield to Hobart, no. 14, 22 October 1802; W.O. 1/630, Foxe to Gordon, "Private," 16 January 1805; C.O. 318/31, Bowyer to Windham, no. 28, 8 February 1807.

52. Barnes, *Military Uniforms of Britain and the Empire*, p. 120; C.O. 318/25, Myers to Hobart, no. 10, 6 June 1804, enclosure no. 5; ibid., Myers to Camden, no. 13, 31 August 1804.

53. Castlereagh to Wellesley, 21 and 25 August 1804, in Wellington, *Supplementary Despatches*, vol. 4, pp. 520–24.

54. For British interests in western Africa, see W.O. 1/92, extract of the Sullivan Memorandum, written around December 1804, pp. 153–70.

55. W.O. 1/352, Thornton to Hobart, 6 October 1802. The Maroons in question were the Trelawny Maroons of Jamaica who had rebelled in 1795; upon their surrender in 1796, they were transported to Halifax, Nova Scotia, and subsequently, in 1800, to Freetown, Sierra Leone.

56. See Wellesley's "Memorandum on the Plan Proposed of an Interchange of Native

Troops of India and the Negro Corps of the West Indies," in Wellington, *Supplementary Despatches*, vol. 4, pp. 520–31.

57. Caulfield, *One Hundred Years' History*, pp. 36–37; and Christopher Fyfe, *A History of Sierra Leone*, p. 135.

58. Shiva Tosh Das, *Indian Military: Its History and Development*, p. 83.

59. *Manual of Military Law* (1899 edition), p. 247. During World War I, for example, West India soldiers served in the Middle East.

60. In 1858, however, there was a complete change in the uniform worn by West India soldiers; at the express request of Queen Victoria, these troops were issued an adaptation of the uniform worn by the Zouaves of the French army. The uniform, unlike any worn in the British army before or since, is still worn today by the Jamaica Military Band. G. Tylden, "The West India Regiments," plates facing pp. 46 and 47, and p. 47.

61. The print appearing in this study is a photocopy of Smith's watercolor. For additional information on the uniform, see Barnes, *Military Uniforms of Britain and the Empire*, p. 96 and plate facing p. 96. See also Robert and Christopher Wilkinson-Latham, *Infantry Uniforms . . . of Britain and the Commonwealth, 1742–1855*, p. 152.

62. C.O. 318/32, "Abstract. In which the Casualties of the European Troops are discriminated from those of the African, & a comprehensive view of the whole afforded," enclosed in "General Return of the Sick and Wounded in . . . the Windward and Leeward Colonies . . . from December 1799 to January 1803. . . . " These and subsequent casualties were not battlefield related.

It should be kept in mind that West India soldiers at this time constituted only about one-third of the total British garrison. There were occasions, however, when returns showed an unusually high sickness rate among black troops. On one such occasion Dundas demanded an explanation since, as he pointed out, one of the reasons for raising black regiments was the belief that they were better able to withstand the rigors of West Indian service. Dundas was promptly informed that the high illness rate had occurred among "new Negroes." It was necessary to inoculate them against smallpox, and their subsequent reaction to the vaccine was the major reason for the large number of disabled blacks. In addition to the afteraffects of the vaccine, the seasoning process of these newcomers to the West Indies and the fact that they did not wear shoes—which frequently resulted in accidents and chigoe infections—contributed to the disproportionate number of indisposed West India soldiers.

Nor were officers of West India Regiments spared the ravages of the climate. From April 1796 to February 1802, the enormous number of 590 officers succumbed to illness. For all this, see W.O. 1/96, Grinfield to Brownrigg, no. 18, 5 October 1802; W.O. 1/89, Dundas to Trigge, no. 20, 24 September 1800; W.O. 1/90, Trigge to Dundas, 20 November 1800; ibid., Dundas to Trigge, no. 5, 14 March 1801; Barnes p. 96; and Young, p. 218.

63. Neil Cantlie, *A History of the Army Medical Department*, vol. 1, p. 240.

64. Pinckard, *Notes on the West Indies*, vol. 1, p. 201.

65. Correlli Barnett, *Britain and Her Army, 1509–1970*, p. 144.

66. "Regulations to be observed by Troops embarked in Transports for Service Abroad, particularly by those destined for the West Indies," in [Henry Dundas], *Facts Relative to the Conduct of the War in the West Indies*, pp. 181–85; W.O. 1/769, Loftus to Pelham, 5 October 1797; and W.O. 1/96, Grinfield to Brownrigg, No. 27, 13 October 1802.

67. C.O. 137/123, Carmichael to Castlereagh, 28 July 1808.

68. W.O. 1/95, enclosure in Coote to Gordon, 22 March 1806.

69. John Davy, *The West Indies Before and Since Slave Emancipation*, p. 464.

70. C.O. 318/32, Dr. Theodore Gordon's "Observations" enclosed in "General Return of the Sick and Wounded . . . from December 1799 to January 1803 . . ."

71. Cantlie, *History of the Army Medical Department*, vol. 1, p. 232, 253; C.O. 318/32, Dr. Gordon's "Observations"; ibid., 137/123, Carmichael to Castelreagh, 10 September 1808.

72. Goveia, *Slave Society*, p. 132; St. Julien Childs, "Sir George Baker and the Dry Belly-Ache," pp. 213–40. Childs' article contains an excellent account of the gradual linking of colic, dry bellyache, with lead poisoning and lead-contaminated rum. Sir Gilbert Blane, in the third edition (1799) of his *Observations on the Diseases of Seamen*, p. 298, noted that the "flux," a disease prevalent among sailors, was caused by the presence of lead in rum and originated from the receptacles employed in the distillation process. See also McLeod Patterson and William Jernigan, "Lead Intoxication from 'Moonshine'," pp. 126–30.

73. Pinckard, *Notes on the West Indies*, vol. 2, p. 254; and C.O. 318/25, Myers to Camden, 2 July 1804, enclosure no. 2.

74. W.O. 1/82, pp. 677–91; Cantlie, *History of the Army Medical Department*, vol. 1, pp. 241–42; W.O. 1/95, "Report of a Board of Inspection . . . at Up Park Camp. 6 March 1806," enclosed in Coote to Gordon, 22 March 1806; C.O. 137/123, Carmichael to Castelreagh, 10 September 1808.

75. Dundas, *Facts Relative to the Conduct of the War*, pp. 192–93; C.O. 318/21, Grinfield to Hobart, no. 70, 24 May 1803; C.O. 318/30, Morrison to Shee, 23 December 1806; C.O. 318/31, Bowyer to Windham, no. 30, 17 April 1807 and enclosure; C.O. 318/34, enclosure in Wellesley to Cooke, 2 January 1808; and C.O. 137/123, Carmichael to Castlereagh, 10 September 1808.

76. C.O. 28/65, Portland to Ricketts and Milne, [n.d.] January 1796; W.O. 1/624, Brownrigg to Sullivan, 4 May 1802; C.O. 137/123, Carmichael to Castlereagh, 10 September 1808; Dundas, *Facts Relative to the Conduct of the War*, pp. 182, 188; C.O. 137/123, Carmichael to Castlereagh, 10 September 1808; and C.O. 137/126, Carmichael to Castlereagh, 26 January 1809.

77. A typical treatment for yellow fever, according to one authority, involved bleeding of twenty to thirty ounces, repeated doses of tartar emetic to induce vomiting, purgation by calomel and salts, and frequent doses of antimoneal powder followed by blistering and further bleedings. In desperate cases, the soldier was given a large glass of gin with "20 grains of salt of hartshorn, a drachm of bark, 10 grams of snakeroot, and 1 grain of opium; and all repeated every two hours!" See Cantlie, *History of the Army Medical Department*, vol. 1, pp. 253–54.

78. In October 1808, the entire Royal Marine garrison at Marie Galante was incapacitated by the excessive consumption of rum and was replaced by captured French slaves. C.O. 318/34, Cochrane to Pole, 10 October 1808; see also C.O. 318/21, enclosures nos. 1 and 4 in Grinfield to Hobart, no. 70, 24 May 1803.

79. C.O. 318/31, Bowyer to Windham, no. 30, 17 April 1807, and enclosures; and C.O. 318/30, Morrison to Shee, 23 December 1806. It is quite possible that Chollet benefitted personally from the army's policy of providing locally purchased rum. Moreover, while serving as the head of the commissariat, Chollet was also a supplier of slaves, a clear conflict of interest (see n. 55, chapter 3). Perhaps for this reason, he refused to relinquish the records of slave purchases he possessed as commissary general. Local rum producers probably lobbied strenuously against the introduction of Azores wine.

80. W.O. 4/729, Howick to Baring, 20 June and 30 September 1836; ibid., Howick to Hill and Spearman, 15 February 1837; W.O. 4/730, Sullivan to Spearman, 21 September 1837; ibid., Howick to Baring, 31 May 1838; ibid., Macaulay to Trevelyan, 19 February 1840; ibid., Macaulay to Gordon, 12 February 1840; and C.O. 318/34, enclosure in Wellesley to Cooke, 2 January 1808.

81. C.O. 318/33, Bowyer to Castlereagh, no. 57, 8 February 1808.

82. W.O. 27/88, Maitland to Myers, 16 July 1804; ibid., "Inspecting Officer's Report, 6th West India Regiment. Post New Amsterdam, 17 August 1804"; W.O. 27/89, Maitland to Myers, 19 July 1805; W.O. 27/90 (part I), Brigadier General Hislop's Report, 12 March 1806; C.O. 318/34, enclosure in Wellesley to Cooke, 2 January 1808; and W.O. 27/101 (part I), Maitland to Beckwith, 12 October 1810.

Pinckard tells us that the daily diet of white troops at Guiana in 1796 included salted beef, salted pork, and salted meat soup. Some "slave food," yams and plantains, supplemented this menu. See *Notes on the West Indies*, vol. 2, p. 254. One of the best descriptions of the diet of black soldiers is supplied by the Confidential Report of the Seventh West India Regiment at Curaçao in 1815. Each soldier reportedly received weekly supplies of seven pounds of flour (which was converted into nine pounds of bread), five ounces of coffee, and nine ounces of sugar. He received daily one pound of fresh or salted beef or nine ounces of salted pork, together with a "gill" of rum and three farthings compensation money for rice and peas. For all this, each soldier's pay was stopped 6 p. each day. Fresh beef was supplied by special contract, while salted provisions and flour were supplied by the commissariat. Given the extent to which the white soldier was defrauded in the eighteenth century, it seems very unlikely that the black soldier often received these allotments. See W.O. 27/135, Major General Le Conteur's Confidential and Inspection Report of the Seventh, 30 September 1815.

83. For example, W.O. 4/729, Howick to Glenelg, 18 January 1836.

84. Ibid.

CHAPTER 6

1. See, for example, W.O. 27/88, "Inspecting Officer's Report, 6th West India Regiment, Fort New Amsterdam, 17 August 1804" and "Inspecting Officer's Report, Detachment of the 3rd West India Regiment . . . 10 July 1804"; W.O. 27/90, part 2, "Inspecting Officer's Report. Detachment 4th W.I. Regiment. On the 5 August and 6th September 1806 . . . in the Colonies of Demerary and Berbice respectively. . . . "

2. The paymaster, adjutant, quartermaster, chaplain, and the surgeon and his assistant.

3. For the particulars surrounding a detachment of the Sixth West India Regiment, see W.O. 27/97, part I, Inspecting Officer's Report to Beckwith, 31 October 1809.

4. W.O. 27/90, part I.

5. W.O. 27/90, part I, "General Half Yearly Inspection Report of the Army in the Windward and Leeward Islands etc. for the 24th December 1805. Head Quarters, Barbados, May 1806." The Second was then at Jamaica and the Bahamas, and the Fifth was at the Honduras Settlement.

6. Ibid., Inspecting Officer's Report to Beckwith, 31 October 1809.

7. W.O. 27/97, "1st West India Regiment, Return of Regiment Courts Martial From 29 December 1808 to 3 October 1809."

8. C.O. 137/123, Carmichael to Castlereagh, 10 September 1808.

9. W.O. 27/108, Hull to Morrison, 30 June 1812 (Inspection Report Fifth West India Regiment, Jamaica, 30 June 1812). Black holes were probably small cell-like structures built either below or just above the ground surface. Punishment resulted from the cramped quarters and the isolation, in addition to the hot and dark interiors.

10. See, for example, W.O. 25/653, for the records of those slaves recruited from January 1796 to December 1798. Desertion records compiled in W.O. 25/2907 are of no value. The most complete records are to be found in the periodic returns.

11. *Dominica Journal or Weekly Intelligencer*, 19 March 1814. A copy of this newspaper is found in C.O. 71/49, "Miscellaneous Section."

12. W.O. 27/88, "Inspecting Officer's Report. Detachment . . . 1st West India Regiment. On the 22 of July 1804 . . . " W.O. 27/90, part I, "Inspecting Officer's Report. A Detachment . . . 6th West India Regiment. On the 11th day of January", 1806.

13. W.O. 27/88, Hislop to Myers, 20 July 1804; W.O. 27/89, "Inspecting Officer's Report of a Detachment of the First West India Regiment. On the 17th of July 1805 . . . "

14. Belize Manuscript Records, Magistrate Letters, Series A, Barrow to the Magistrates, 27 February 1798, referred to in John Burdon, ed., *Archives of British Honduras*, vol. 1, p. 244.

15. C.O. 137/121, Hamilton to Coote, 19 January 1808; see also W.O. 1/95, Confidential Inspection Report, Fifth West India Regiment, Belize, 21 November 1808, pp. 274–77. The Fifth's long confinement and neglect at Belize under deplorable circumstances had long-term adverse effects on discipline, interior economy and field exercises. See W.O. 27/105, part I, Hull to Morrison, 26 January 1812; and W.O. 27/108, Hull to Morrison, 30 June 1812 and enclosures.

16. W.O. 27/97, part I, Inspecting Officer's Report to Beckwith, 31 October 1809.

17. W.O. 27/113, Wood to Beckwith, 1 November 1812. Contrast the dispersal policy, and its attendant evils, with the cantonment system in use in India. Royal as well as East India Company regiments were provided, under the system of cantonment, with quarters designed and located for permanent housing. Cantonments were also located close to one another, for strategic reasons, and near towns and villages. This system, which resulted from the Company's centralization of the responsibility for troop accommodation and deployment, was vastly superior to the unworkable situation in the Caribbean where responsibility was divided between the government and the many local assemblies. See H. H. Dodwell, ed., *The Cambridge History of India*, vol. 6, p. 161. For the continuation of the policy of dispersal of West India Regiments, see relevant returns in W.O. 27/108, 133; and Ellis, *History of the First West India Regiment*, pp. 347–59.

18. In the British army, particularly in the infantry, just after the Crimean War, the percentage of illiterates was 60 percent. See H. de Watteville, *The British Soldier*, p. 148.

19. W.O. 1/769, Evidence relating to the conspiracy is contained in the minutes of the Privy Council, St. Christopher, 20 August 1797, enclosed in King to Huskisson, 11 December 1797; see also W.O. 25/643, folios 25–28; and W.O. 1/86, Bowyer to Dundas, 8 September 1798.

20. W.O. 27/108, Hull to Morrison, 30 June 1812; W. O. 27/90, part I, "Major General W. Archer's Inspection Report of the 4th West India Regiment. Surinam, Fort New Amsterdam, 10 January 1806."

21. Ibid., "Brigadier General Hughes' Inspection Report of the Right Wing of the 4th West India Regiment, Post Brandwaght, Surinam, 26 August 1806."

22. C.O. 137/123, Villettes to Castlereagh, 15 June 1808, and Carmichael to Castlereagh, 27 July 1808.

23. W.O. 27/90, part II, "Inspecting Officer's Report Detachment 6th West India Regiment. On the 24th day of July 1806."

24. W.O. 27/101, part I, Wale to Beckwith, 5 November 1810.

25. See, for example, W.O. 1/634, the Gordon Memorandum of 8 April 1807, pp. 317–20. Among the least desired as recruits were men from Angola; see W.O. 1/88, Johnstone to Dundas, "Private," 7 June 1798. See table 4, compiled from the *Description and Succession Book* of the Fifth West India Regiment.

26. Ellis is quoted in Henry Chichester and George Burges-Short, *Records and Badges*, p. 878; Philip D. Curtin, *The Atlantic Slave Trade*, p. 184.

27. Ibid., pp. 184–90.

28. Curtin, *The Atlantic Slave Trade*, passim; Orlando Patterson, *The Sociology of Slavery*, pp. 113–44; and Anstey, *Atlantic Slave Trade*, pp. 58–88.

29. W.O. 25/656, folios 1–2. The *Description and Succession Books* of the West India Regiments, with their, literally, thousands of entries, contain considerable data on the ethnic origins of the New World African slave. These often diligently prepared recruiting records have yet to attract proper scholarly attention.

30. W.O. 25/644, folios 7, 14.

31. C. K. Meek, *The Northern Tribes of Nigeria*, vol. 1, pp. 44–45; Curtin, ed., *Africa Remembered*, pp. 257–58.

32. For instance, W.O. 25/644, 656, passim.

33. The newspaper and its date are unknown; only the advertisement, which is dated "Fort Augusta, July 13, 1801," was attached to General Sir George Nugent's dispatch to Lord Hobart of 21 December 1801, in C.O. 137/106.

34. For instance, W.O. 25/656, folios, 2, 4, 6.

35. W.O. 25/656.

36. *Sociology of Slavery*, pp. 145–54.

37. Tylden, "West India Regiments," p. 43.

38. W.O. 1/95, enclosed in Hislop to the Duke of York, 22 July 1804.

39. W.O. 1/647, Duke of York to Liverpool, 15 August 1811.

40. Ibid.

41. W.O. 1/647, Duke of York to Liverpool, 15 August 1811.

42. W.O. 4/425, Palmerston to Harrison, 23 December 1811.

43. W.O. 4/308, 23 January 1812; ibid., Palmerston to Beckwith, same date.

44. W.O. 4/311, 9 May 1814.

45. W.O. 27/108, Hull to Morrison, 30 June 1812.

46. Ibid., W.O. 27/113, Gifton to Munro, 14 October 1812; ibid., "Half Yearly Confidential Report . . . Seventh West India Regiment . . . 5th day of October 1812," enclosed in Hodgson to Morrison, "Confidential," 21 November 1812.

47. W.O. 27/135.

48. W.O. 27/133, "Half Yearly Confidential Report of His Majesty's 4th West India Regiment. Inspected by Lieut.-Colonel J. Lyons Nixon," Antigua, 15 May 1815.

49. Ibid., O'Meara to Fuller, 22 June 1815.

50. John Davy, *West Indies Before and Since Slave Emancipation*, pp. 537, 539.

51. Fortescue, *History of the British Army*, vol. 4 (part II), pp. 898–903.

52. See J. Steven Watson, *The Reign of George III, 1760-1815*, pp. 28–30, 508–14. The immense increase of manufacturing power in Britain did not prevent France from producing more muskets during the war. See Richard Glover, *Peninsular Preparation*, p. 47n.

53. Fortescue, *History of the British Army*, vol. 4 (part II), Appendix C, p. 938.

54. W.O. 27/90, part I, "Inspection . . . 1st West India Regiment. On the 25 of February 1806"; ibid., "First West India Regiment. Clothing Return . . . 20 January 1806"; ibid., " . . . Clothing Return of a Detachment . . . 6 March 1806." See also ibid., "General Half Yearly Inspection Report of the Army in the Windward and Leeward Islands . . . for the 24th December 1806."

55. Ibid., "Brigadier General Hughes' Inspection Report . . . 26 August 1806."

56. Ibid., part II, Maitland to Bowyer, 17 July 1806.

57. W.O. 27/108, Beckwith to C-in-C, Horse Guards, "Confidential," 18 July 1812. The absence of reports of clothing shortages for the West India Regiments for the years prior to and even immediately following 1800 is an indication not that the corps were adequately clothed during this period but that inspection of the regiments did not commence until 1799. If the plight of Britain's European regiments from 1793 to 1799 is a reliable indicator of the chaos in the clothing system, then West India soldiers must have suffered equally, if not more; they were new corps and dependent on a long and vulnerable supply route.

58. Windham to Campbell, 14 March 1800 and enclosure, "Public Office Letters 1800," NRA [SCOT] 0473, Scottish Record Office, Edinburgh.

59. Ibid. Mismanagement was to hound the Seventh almost to the end of the war. See W.O. 27/90, part I, "General Half Yearly Inspection Report of the Army in the Windward and Leeward Islands . . . 24 December 1805 . . . "; ibid., "Inspection Officer's Report . . . 20th day of May 1806"; W.O. 27/108, part I, Garrison Orders, Headquarters, Pieter Maay (Curacao), 30 May 1812; W.O. 27/113, Hodgson to Morrison, "Confidential," 21 November 1812 and enclosures; W.O. 27/135, "Confidential Report on the Inspection of the 7th . . . Curaçao, 30 September 1815."

60. Ibid., Taylor to Campbell, 9 April, 25 July, 27 August, 1 and 3 September 1800.

61. Ibid., Calvert to Campbell, 16 June 1800 and enclosures, and 25 November 1800 and enclosures.

62. Ibid., 9 December 1800.

63. These recommendations and the reasons for their rejection are discussed in Fortescue, *History of the British Army*, vol. 4 (part II), pp. 900–03.

64. See chapter 5, note 4.

65. W.O. 3/152, Crewe to Moore, 17 October 1803.

66. Information, including a sketch by Cecil C. P. Lawson of the West India Regiments for the period 1800–1810 is in Lawson, et al, *History of the Uniforms of the British Army*, pp. 119–20. Of much greater value is Carman's "Infantry Clothing Regulations, 1802."

67. Lawson, et al, p. 119; Carman, p. 220.

68. Glover, *Peninsular Preparation*, pp. 46–62.

69. W.O. 27/90, part I, "Inspecting Officer's Report 1st West India Regiment . . . 22nd of January 1806 . . . at Prince Rupert's . . . "; ibid., Brig.-General Hislop's Inspection Report of the Eighth West India Regiment, 12 March 1806; ibid., "Inspection Officer's Report . . . 7th West India Regt. . . . 20th day of May 1806"; W.O. 27/135, "Confidential Report . . . 7th West India Regiment . . . Curaçao, 30 September 1815."

70. W.O. 27/88, Maitland to Myers, 16 July 1804.

71. For the location of military posts in proximity to estates, see, for example, the juxta-position of Monk's Hill, a military station at Falmouth, Antigua, and the Bodkin Plantation in the view "Planting the Sugar-Cane" in William Clark's *Ten Views in the Island of Antigua*, 1823. Copies of this view appear in Eric Williams, *From Columbus to Castro*, facing p. 400; and Gregson Davis, *Antigua Black: Portrait of an Island People*, p. 51. Also see C.O. 137/126, Carmichael to Castlereagh, 26 January 1809.

72. C.O. 137/123, Carmichael to Castlereagh, 28 July 1808.

73. W.O. 1/95/27, Proceedings of the Court of Inquiry, Martinique, 28 April 1802, enclosed in Trigge to Brownrigg, no. 61, 4 May 1802.

74. Ragatz, p. 32; Pinckard, 1: 268–69; and Brathwaite, p. 300.

75. W.O. 1/95/27, Proceedings of the Court of Inquiry, Martinique, 28 April 1802, enclosed in Trigge to Brownrigg, no. 61, 4 May 1802.

76. W.O. 1/769, Evidence relative to the conspiracy of the Fourth West India Regiment,

minutes of the Privy Council, St. Kitts, 20 August 1797, enclosed in King to Huskisson, 11 December 1797.

77. W.O. 1/95, Hislop's "Remarks . . . " enclosed in Hislop to the Duke of York, 22 July 1804.

78. C.O. 318/19, Trigge to Hobart, no. 39, 2 April 1802.

79. C.O. 137/123, Carmichael to Castlereagh, 27 July 1808.

80. General Orders, 29 October 1800, enclosed in Calvert to Campbell, 29 October 1800, "Public Office Letters 1800," NRA [SCOT] 0473, Scottish Record Office, Edinburgh.

81. Young, *West India Common-Place Book*, p. 214.

82. W.O. 1/770, Ottley to Portland, 17 May 1799, enclosed in King to Huskisson, 4 July 1799; and Brathwaite, *Development of Creole Society*, p. 160.

83. Marriage was one of several reforms of 1823 aimed at ameliorating the condition of the slave, but little or no success was achieved until some years later.

84. W.O. 1/95, Hislop's "Remarks . . . ," enclosed in Hislop to the Duke of York, 22 July 1804. At the time Hislop wrote, West India soldiers were still considered slaves, and hence their children would be "the property of the government."

85. C.O. 318/25, Myers to Camden, 2 July 1804, enclosure no. 2.

86. W.O. 17/251, "Half Yearly Return of Women legally Married & Children belonging to the 5th (or Duke of York's) West India Regiment . . . 24 December 1807"; W.O. 27/135, "General Return . . . 1st West India Regiment," 30 October 1815; and C.O. 295/48, Woodford to Bathurst, no. 351, 12 December 1819.

87. Belize Manuscript Records, Magistrates Meetings, Series A. 3, Slave Court, 13 July 1807, in Burdon, *Archives of British Honduras*, vol. 2, p. 105.

88. W.O. 127/113, "Half Yearly Confidential Report . . . Seventh West India Regiment . . . 5th day of October 1812," enclosed in Hodgson to Morrison, "Confidential," 21 November 1812; and W.O. 27/108, Hull to Morrison, 30 June 1812.

89. Patterson, *The Sociology of Slavery*, pp. 207-08. The salaries quoted were probably in local currency.

90. W.O. 1/95, Trigge to Brownrigg, no. 56, 23 April 1802; Great Britain, War Office, *General Regulations and Orders for the Army*, (1816), p. 121.

91. See Joseph, "The British West Indies Regiment, 1914-1918," pp. 94-124; and Elkins, "A Source of Black Nationalsim in the Caribbean," pp. 99-103. The political awakening of Cipriani, the revered Trinidadian nationalist, was occasioned by his experiences with the British West Indies Regiment during World War I. See C.L.R. James, *The Life of Captain Cipriani*.

92. C.O. 318/20, Hobart to Grinfield, 7 October 1802; ibid., Grinfield to Hobart, 20 December 1802, enclosure no. 1.

93. C.O. 318/21, Grinfield to Hobart, no. 56, 3 March 1803.

94. Belize Manuscript Records, Magistrates Meetings, Series B, Magistrates Meeting, 19 March 1810, in Burdon, *Archives of British Honduras*, vol. 2, p. 136.

95. The total annual cost to the British government at this time to hire slaves for pioneer service was reported as £16,000 sterling. This sum is unusually small and probably reflects the curtailment of military activity in the West Indies during the four years prior to the Peace of Amiens in 1802. The resumption of the war in 1803 resulted in higher costs. See C.O. 318/19, Trigge to Hobart, no. 41, 23 April 1802.

96. For all this, see C.O. 318/27, "Comparative State of Expence between the Work of the Black Soldiers and of hired Negroes on a Average, through the West India Colonies. Barba-

dos, May 1805," enclosure in/and Myers to Camden, no. 70, 8 May 1805. According to this study, the cost per diem to hire a slave had risen to 3s. 4d. The daily ration reportedly issued to each hired slave, which cost one shilling, was comprised of one pound of flour and one pound of salted beef or twelve ounces of pork. See also, Barnett, *Britain and Her Army, 1509-1970*, p. 241; and C.O. 318/19, Trigge to Hobart, no. 41, 23 April 1802.

CHAPTER 7

1. W.O. 1/96, Bowyer to Gordon, no. 190, 6 February 1808, and enclosure.

2. The reasons given for retaining the life-time enlistment for black recruits were economic burden that would accrue to the West Indian colonies from the shorter enlistments, and the fear of discharging into the colonial slave society an increasing number of blacks who had had military training. See Hansard's *Parliamentary Debates*, First Series, vol. 7, Debate in Commons on the Clause in the Mutiny Bill calling for limited service, 6 June 1806, Canning's speech, cols. 547-48; ibid., Debate in the House of Lords on the same measure, 13 June 1806, Earl of Westmoreland's speech, p. 650. (It should also be kept in mind that in 1806 the West India soldier was still regarded as a slave.) Ibid., vol. 9, Debate in Commons on the Slave Trade Abolition Bill, 9 March 1807, Lord Howick's speech, p. 66. See also Young, *West India Common-Place Book*, pp. 241-42; and Fortescue, *History of the British Army*, vol. 5, pp. 301-03.

3. Excerpts of the Order in Council of 16 March 1808 are quoted in Robert Kuczynski, *Demographic Survey of the British Colonial Empire*, vol. 1, pp. 112-13. For instructions to commanders of Royal Navy ships and privateers, see W.O. 1/742, pp. 65-74.

4. The same was also done in order to recruit foreigners in British pay. *Manual of Military Law*, pp. 191-92.

5. W.O. 1/645, return, p. 477 and "Abstract," p. 469.

6. W.O. 27/92, part II, "General Return . . . 1st West India Regiment . . . 6th Day of May 1808; and W.O. 27/135, "General Return . . . 1st West India Regiment."

7. Kuczynski, *Demographic Survey*, vol. 1, pp. 114-19; Asiegbu, *Slavery and the Politics of Liberation, 1787-1861*, pp. 24, 27-28.

8. The monthly returns of the African Recruiting Establishment are in W.O. 17/1164. See also C.O. 318/46, Beckwith to Liverpool, no. 150, "Military," 18 May 1812; and W.O. 25/658, folios 31-34.

9. C.O. 137/123, Castlereagh to Villettes, 11 April 1808; C.O. 318/44, Beckwith to Liverpool, no. 101, 7 May 1811; C.O. 318/33, Bowyer to Castlereagh, no. 65, 28 May 1808, and enclosure; and C.O. 137/134, Morrison to Liverpool, no. 53, 30 April 1812.

10. C.O. 318/46, Beckwith to Liverpool, no. 135, 14 February 1812.

11. C.O. 137/131, Morrison to Liverpool, no. 35, 22 December 1811; ibid., Liverpool to Morrison, no. 7, "Civil," 8 February 1812; C.O. 137/134, Liverpool to Morrison, no. 9, "Civil," 29 February 1812; ibid., Morrison to Liverpool, no. 52, 30 April 1812; ibid., Torrens to Peel, 13 June 1812; and C.O. 318/46, Beckwith to Liverpool, no. 144, "Military," 17 April 1812.

12. W.O. 25/662, folios 1-103.

13. W.O. 1/92, Whitelock Memorandum, 26 November 1796, pp. 501-02; W.O. 1/351, Fraser to Dundas, no. 3, 23 January 1801; W.O. 1/95, Hislop's "Remarks," enclosed in Hislop to the Duke of York, 22 July 1804; C.O. 318/30, Bowyer to Windham, no. 21, 21 November 1806, and enclosure; W.O. 1/96, Myers to Clinton, no. 11, 13 May 1804; ibid.,

Bowyer to Gordon, no. 190, 6 February 1808; W.O. 6/152, Bunbury to Barrow, 20 September 1811; W.O. 1/648, Duke of York to Liverpool, 4 October 1811; and W.O. 1/649, Torrens to Tash, 19 November 1811.

14. W.O. 1/351, Dundas to Fraser, 15 November 1800; W.O. 1/628, Duke of York to Camden, 13 June 1804; W.O. 1/638, Duke of York to Castlereagh, 3 May 1808; C.O. 318/39, David Dundas to Liverpool, 6 December 1809, and enclosures; and Great Britain, Parliament, *Parlimentary Papers* (Commons), 1812, vol. 10, no. 370, "Papers relating to Recruiting Depot on the Coast of Africa," p. 301.

15. J. J. Crooks, *A History of the Colony of Sierra Leone*, pp. 73–75.

16. Ibid., p. 81.

17. W.O. 1/648, Duke of York to Liverpool, 4 October 1811.

18. Robert Thorpe, *A Reply . . .*, p. 84; Ellis, p. 16.

19. *Slavery and the Politics of Liberation*, p. 33.

20. W.O. 17/1164. An island was sought as the site for the recruiting depot because recruits could be confined during training preparatory to being shipped to the West Indies. See Crooks, *History of the Colony of Sierra Leone*, p. 88.

21. W.O. 4/414, Merry to Torrens, 11 July 1810.

22. Cited in Butt-Thompson, *Sierra Leone in History and Tradition*, p. 160–63.

23. Kuczynski, p. 116.

24. W.O. 4/730, Sullivan to Somerset, 5 April 1838. The author has not been able to determine when this recruiting depot was established.

25. Asiegbu, *Slavery and the Politics of Liberation*, p. 31. African troops had been used by the Dutch in South Africa as early as the seventeenth century. John B. Wright, *Bushman Raiders of the Drakensberg, 1840–1870*, pp. 25–26; see also George McCall Theal, *History and Ethnography of Africa South of the Zambesi*, vol. 3, p. 187.

26. W.O. 4/718, Palmerston to Hislop and Gascoyne, 3 May 1816; C.O. 318/53, Ramsey to Torrens, 17 November 1816, pp. 225–26; C.O. 318/52, York to Fuller, 21 January 1816; C.O. 137/142, Manchester to Bathurst, 4 May 1816; W.O. 4/719, Palmerston to O'Meara, 4 November 1816; and Kuczynski, *Demographic Survey*, p. 119.

27. C.O. 318/53, York to Bathurst, 16 January 1817; W.O. 4/719, Circular to Colonels and Officers commanding West India Regiments, and the Paymaster General, 5 February 1817.

28. C.O. 318/53, York to Bathurst, 16 January 1817.

29. Ibid.

30. Ibid., Torrens to Goulburn, 14 March 1817; ibid., Robinson to Leith, 4 May 1817; W.O. 3/163, Calvert to the Secretary at War, 3 November 1817; W.O. 4/719, Circular to Agents, Colonels and Officers Commanding the Third and Fourth West India Regiments; ibid., Palmerston to Officer Commanding the Third West India Regiment; C.O. 318/54, Torrens to Combermere, 30 November 1818; and C.O. 295/63, Woodford to Bathurst, no. 584, "Military," 6 December 1824.

31. C.O. 318/54, Torrens to Combermere, 30 November 1818.

32. C.O. 318/53, Torrens to Goulburn, 24 July 1817.

33. C.O. 137/119, Castlereagh to Coote, no. 8, 6 August 1807; C.O. 137/31, Morrison to Liverpool, no. 35, 22 December 1811; C.O. 318/46, Beckwith to Liverpool, no. 130, "Military," 28 January 1812; C.O. 137/134, Lyon to Liverpool, 3 March 1812; C.O. 137/142, Manchester to Bathurst, 4 May 1816; C.O. 318/53, Torrens to Goulburn, 24 July 1817; C.O. 318/54, Combermere to Bathurst, no. 16, "Military," 24 January 1818; and

C.O. 295/46, Woodford to Bathurst, no. 274, 29 January 1818. See also, Young, *West India Common-Place Book*, pp. 213–16.

34. C.O. 318/53, Torrens to Goulburn, 24 July 1817; C.O. 318/55, Combermere to Bathurst, no. 22, "Military," 8 January 1819; ibid., Young to Kempt, 13 January 1819, pp. 249–50; and ibid., Bathurst's note on the bottom of the last page of this dispatch.

35. C.O. 318/55, Treasury to Goulburn, 23 March 1819, pp. 191–92. This was the policy established for the Third Regiment. It is assumed that troops of the other disbanded West India Regiments were disposed of on the same basis.

36. C.O. 295/48, Woodford to Bathurst, no. 351, 12 December 1819; and C.O. 318/55, Combermere to Bathurst, no. 24, "Military," 1 May 1819, and enclosures.

37. C.O. 295/48, Woodford to Bathurst, no. 351, 12 December 1819; and C.O. 318/55, Lord Commissioners of the Treasury to Goulburn, July 1819, pp. 209–13; ibid., Combermere to Bathurst, no. 24, "Military," 1 May 1819, and enclosures.

38. Ibid., Lord Commissioners of the Treasury to Goulburn, July 1819, pp. 209–13.

39. Michael Horowitz, ed., *Peoples and Cultures of the Caribbean*, p. 532.

40. W.O. 25/656, folios 1–27; Belize Manuscript Records, Despatches Inward, Record 1, Bathurst to Arthur, 12 March 1817, in Burdon, *Archives of British Honduras*, vol. 2, p. 199.

41. *The Port of Spain Gazette*, 14 October 1842. A copy of this edition appears in C.O. 300/4. W.O. 3/225, Despatch to the Director General of the Army Medical Department, 31 October 1818. See also Crooks, *A History . . . Sierra Leone*, p. 96; and Fyfe, *History of Sierra Leone*, p. 136.

42. Claude George, *The Rise of British West Africa*, pp. 223–24.

43. C.O. 318/33, Bowyer to Castlereagh, no. 57, 10 February 1808.

44. *History of the British Army*, vol. 4 (part II), p. 891. By referring to the extension of the principle of raising African corps for service in British tropical garrisons, Fortescue had in mind several such units as: the Gold Coast Constabulary, which was raised in 1844 and renamed the Gold Coast Regiment in 1901; the King's African Rifles, formed in 1902 from an amalgamation of the Central African Rifles, the Uganda Rifles, and the East Africa Rifles; the Nigeria Regiment, which was formed in 1899; the Sierra Leone Battalion; and the Gambia Company. In British southern Africa, Hottentot regiments had been raised as early as 1796. *Askari* corps, or African regiments, were also raised in Ceylon, as noted earlier, and in India were used in the private service of local rulers.

Local white resistance to arming blacks was manifested during the British government's successful efforts to raise the Rhodesian African Rifles from 1939 to 1940; it was very similar to the white opposition in the West Indies almost 150 years earlier. Rhodesian newspapers were filled with letters asserting that the inevitable result of arming and training large numbers of blacks would be the extinction of whites. They reminded the populace, in gruesome detail, of the Matabele and Mashona rebellions that had occurred just before the turn of the century. As in the case of the West India Regiments, however, the anticipated bloodbath did not occur. Instead, Matabele and Mashone recruits proved loyal troops and distinguished themselves in bitter fighting in malaria-infested Burmese jungles. Gloomy predictions of serious agricultural losses should blacks be lured away from the farm labor gangs were also disproven when it was noted that less than 1 percent of the male farm labor force would be affected by military recruitment. For all this, see Barnes, *Military Uniforms of Britain and the Empire*, pp. 176, 266, 276; Tylden, "The Ceylon Regiments, 1796 to 1874," pp. 124–28; and Christopher Owen, *The Rhodesian African Rifles*, passim.

45. *Royal Gazette* of 13–20 March 1819, quoted in Brathwaite, *Development of Creole*

Society, p. 36. See also anon., "Mr. Urban, April 10," *The Gentleman's Magazine* 85 (January to June 1815):295-96.

CHAPTER 8

1. For all of this, see Davis, *Problem of Slavery*, p. 80; Roy Lewis and Yvonne Foy, *The British in Africa*, p. 184; Christopher Owen, *The Rhodesian African Rifles*, pp. 1-4; and Harry Rudin, *Germans in the Cameroons, 1884-1914*, p. 197.

2. Ernest W. Lefever, *Spear and Scepter*, p. 18. Of course, between the period of decolonization and 1970, the nonpolitical stance of African armies changed. By 1970 there had been more than thirty coups, in which former British colonial armies in tropical Africa had played decisive roles.

3. Ragatz came to this conclusion because of his own stereotyped view of the slave, a view that would have been roundly endorsed by the planter class—from whence it came: "The West Indian negro had all the characteristics of his race. He stole, he lied, he was simple, suspicious, inefficient, irresponsible, lazy, superstitious, and loose in his sexual relations." See *Fall of the Planter Class*, pp. 27, 32-33.

4. The most hideous of these was the butchering of 206 helpless women and children by sepoy mutineers at Cawnpore. See Richard Collier, *The Great Indian Mutiny*, pp. 139-50, 170-72, 181-83. A distorted view of history still prompts Britishers to regard the old Indian Army as the jewel of the colonial armies, even though, unlike the African Army, it had a long, mutinous tradition capped by the massive rebellion of the Bengal Army in 1857.

5. See Murray, *West Indies and Development of Colonial Government*, p. 43. Official records are found chiefly in C.O. 137/123, 126.

6. An insight into the socializing effect of the British army in the West Indies is provided by Brathwaite, *Development of Creole Society*, pp. 106, 160, 300-01. On the subject of attitudes of whites to blacks, see also pp. 176-92.

7. For this development in British tropical Africa, see, for example, Samson C. Ukpabi, "Military Recruitment and Social Mobility in Nineteenth Century British West Africa," pp. 87-107. The King's African Rifles had a training school where discharged soldiers could learn to become craftsmen and welfare officers. See Brian Bond and Ian Roy, *War and Society*, vol. 2, p. 33.

8. The evidence on detribalization is not conclusive. For example, when questioned recently about tribal loyalties and how these might conflict with white rule, blacks of the Rhodesian African Rifles were quoted as saying "The army is my tribe." However, as Robin Luckham has shown, tribal identity was an important issue in, for instance, the behavior of the Nigerian Army during the Biafran civil war. For all of this, see Allan C. Fisher, "Rhodesia, A House Divided," p. 654; and Luckham, *The Nigerian Military*, pp. 177-97.

9. As mentioned in Chapter 7, one authority estimates that discharged African soldiers constituted one-eighth the total population of Trinidad in 1862. British Honduras, now Belize, also had a large military population, which was replenished with mutinous sepoy troops after the abortive insurrection of the Bengal Army in 1857. See Gordon Lewis, *The Growth of the Modern West Indies*, p. 290.

10. For the origin of this concept, see Lefever, *Spear and Scepter*, pp. 18-21.

11. Selwyn D. Ryan, *Race and Nationalism in Trinidad and Tobago*, p. 28.

BIBLIOGRAPHY

Even the least assiduous reader of notes cannot have failed to notice that the essential manuscript materials for this study were the original correspondence between British army commanders, West Indian governors, committees of correspondence, and other colonial officials in the Caribbean, and Government ministers, members of Parliament, colonial agents, and absentee planters in Britain. The most complete collection of these vital documents is to be found at the Public Record Office, London, although some duplicate copies of correspondence, as well as private papers, are located in public archives in the West Indies and North America. The most important of these records are the numerous volumes of War Office and Colonial Office papers. The relevant correspondence contained within the various classes of these two groups for the period under study is enormous, and until now many of these papers have remained virtually untouched, particularly the War Office records.

BIBLIOGRAPHIES AND GUIDES TO SOURCES

An Alphabetical Guide to Certain War Office and Other Military Records Preserved in the Public Record Office. No. 53. New York: Kraus Reprint Corp., 1963.

Guide to the Contents of the Public Record Office. 3 vols. London: Her Majesty's Stationery Office, 1963.

Higham, Robin, ed. *A Guide to the Sources of British Military History.* Berkeley and Los Angeles: University of California Press, 1971.

Index to British Military Costume Prints, 1500–1914. London: Army Museum's Ogilby Trust, 1972.

List of Colonial Office Records Preserved in the Public Record Office. No. 36. New York: Kraus Reprint Corp., 1963.

List of the Records in Treasury, the Paymaster General's Office, the Exchequer and Audit Departments and the Board of Trade, to 1837, Preserved in the Public Record Office. No. 46. New York: Kraus Reprint Corp., 1963.

List of War Office Records Preserved in the Public Record Office. No. 28. New York: Kraus Reprint Corp., 1963.

Ragatz, L. J. *A Guide for the Study of British Caribbean History, 1763–1834:*

Including the Abolition and Emancipation Movements. New York: DaCapo Press, 1970.

White, Arthur S. *Bibliography of Regimental Histories of the British Army.* London: Society for Army Historical Research, 1965.

ARCHIVES

Public Record Office, London.

War Office Papers

W.O. 1/ Correspondence: In-letters, Secretary at War and Secretary for War
/31, 51–52, 55, 58, 60–62, 65, 68, 82–90, 92, 95–96, 135–36, 141–42, 149–51, 251, 351–52, 405, 617, 619, 623–26, 628–30, 632, 634–35, 638, 645, 647–49, 742, 767, 769–71, 839, 902, 1105–06, 1109.

W.O. 3/ Correspondence: Out-letters, Commander in Chief
/17, 22, 34, 36, 47, 68, 152, 163, 195, 222, 225, 381, 383, 580, 582.

W.O. 4/ Correspondence: Out-letters, Secretary at War
/149, 158, 160–61, 167, 173, 203, 206, 280, 308, 311, 337–39, 341–42, 414, 425, 718–19, 729–30.

W.O. 6/ Correspondence: Out-letters, Secretary of State
/5, 131, 133, 152, 184.

W.O. 7/ Correspondence: Out-letters, Departmental
/101.

W.O. 12/ Returns: General
/11239–40.

W.O. 17/ Returns: Monthly
/251, 1164–67, 1988–92, 2000.

W.O. 24/ Returns: Establishments
/591, 594, 596, 602–21.

W.O. 25/ Returns: Registers, Various
/644, 652–53, 656–58, 660–62, 1077, 2246, 2907.

W.O. 26/ Miscellanea: Miscellany Books
/37.

W.O. 27/ Returns: Inspection
/85, 88–90, 92, 97, 99, 101, 103, 105, 108, 113, 133, 135.

W.O. 40/ Correspondence: Selected Unnumbered Papers
/9–10, 15, 20, 22.

W.O. 47/ Ordnance Office: Minutes
/2384.

W.O. 71/ Judge Advocate General's Office: Courts-Martial, Proceedings
/109.

W.O. 72/ Judge Advocate General's Office: Courts-Martial, Letters and Miscellaneous Documents
/30.

W.O. 81/ Judge Advocate General's Office: Letter Books
/27, 40, 44.

Colonial Office Papers

C.O. 5/ America and West Indies: Original Correspondence, etc.
/267.
C.O. 28/ Barbados: Original Correspondence
/65, 69.
C.O. 71/ Dominica: Original Correspondence
/30, 34, 38, 46, 49, 109.
C.O. 101/ Grenada: Original Correspondence
/34-35.
C.O. 137/ Jamaica: Original Correspondence
/25, 61, 75, 88-90, 99-101, 103, 106-08, 119, 121-23, 126, 129, 131, 134, 142.
C.O. 138/ Jamaica: Entry Books
/39.
C.O. 140/ Jamaica: Sessional Papers
/84-85.
C.O. 152/ Leeward Islands: Original Correspondence
/60, 77-79, 87.
C.O. 153/ Leeward Islands: Entry Books
/28, 30-31.
C.O. 267/ Sierra Leone: Original Correspondence
/127.
C.O. 285/ Tobago: Original Correspondence
/3-4.
C.O. 295/ Trinidad: Original Correspondence
/37, 46, 48, 63.
C.O. 300/ Trinidad: Miscellanea
/4.
C.O. 318/ West Indies: Original Correspondence
/12-13, 15-16, 19-22, 24-25, 27-35, 38-40, 44, 46, 51-55.
C.O. 324/ Colonies, General: Entry Books, Series I
/65, 103, 116.

Home Office Papers

H.O. 30/ Various: Correspondence and Papers, Departmental: War and Colonial Office
/1.
H.O. 50/ Various: Correspondence and Papers, Military: Correspondence, etc.
/386.
H.O. 51/ Various: Correspondence and Papers, Military: Entry Books
/147.

Paymaster General's Office Papers

P.M.G. 2/ Ledgers
  /47.
P.M.G. 14/ Miscellaneous Books
  /74–75.

Treasury Papers

T. 81/ Expired Commissions, etc: Santo Domingo Claims Committee
  /21.

Exchequer and Audit Department Papers

A.O. 3/ Accounts, Various
  /200, 265.

Other Manuscript Sources

Ann Arbor, Michigan. University of Michigan. William L. Clements Library. Melville (Henry Dundas) Papers.

Edinburgh. Scottish Record Office. "Public Office Letters 1800", NRA [SCOT] 0473.

Kingston, Jamaica. Lathbury Barracks, Up Park Camp. "First Report on British Garrison in Jamaica"; "Second Report on British Garrison in Jamaica"; "Report on Troops Stationed at Jamaica."

London. British Museum. Add. MSS. 28062, "A Proposal to raise a Corps of Foot in less than Three Months in the West Indies, to consist of Free Mulattoes and Blacks."

London. British Museum. Moore Papers, Nos. 57320–1; 57326–7.

London. West India Committee. *Minutes of the Meetings of the West India Planters and Merchants*, vol. II, meetings from February 1793 to April 1801.

PRINTED MATERIALS

Books

Anstey, Roger. *The Atlantic Slave Trade and British Abolition, 1760–1810.* Atlantic Highlands, N.J.: Humanities Press, 1975.

Asiegbu, Johnson. *Slavery and the Politics of Liberation, 1787–1861.* London: Longman, Green & Co., Ltd., 1969.

Aspinall, Arthur, ed. *The Later Correspondence of George III.* 5 vols. Cambridge: Cambridge University Press, 1962–1970.

Barnes, R. Money. *A History of the Regiments & Uniforms of the British Army.* London: Seeley Service & Co., Ltd., 1957.

———. *Military Uniforms of Britain and the Empire.* London: Seeley Service & Co., Ltd., 1957.

Barnett, Correlli. *Britain and Her Army, 1509–1970: A Military, Political and Social Survey.* London: Penguin Press, 1970.

Bell, Wendell, ed. *The Democratic Revolution in the West Indies: Studies in Nationalism, Leadership and the Belief in Progress.* Cambridge, Mass.: Schenkman Pub. Co., Inc., 1967.

Blane, Gilbert. *Observations on the Diseases of Seaman.* 3rd ed. London: Murray and Highley, 1799.

Bond, Brian, and Ian Roy, eds. *War and Society: A Yearbook of Military History.* 2 vols. New York: Holmes and Meier, 1977.

Boxer, C. R. *The Dutch in Brazil, 1624-1654.* Oxford: Clarendon Press, 1957.

Brathwaite, Edward. *The Development of Creole Society in Jamaica, 1770-1820.* Oxford: Clarendon Press, 1971.

Bryant, Arthur. *The Years of Endurance, 1793-1802.* London: Collins, 1942.

———. *Years of Victory, 1802-1812.* London: Collins, 1944.

Burdon, John, ed. *Archives of British Honduras.* 3 vols. London: Sifton Praed & Co., Ltd., 1931-1935.

Burns, Alan C. *History of the British West Indies.* London: Allen and Unwin Ltd., 1954.

Butler, Lewis; William George; and Steuart Hare. *The Annals of the King's Royal Rifle Corps.* 5 vols. London: Smith, Elder & Co., and John Murray, 1913-1932.

Butt-Thompson, Frederick W. *Sierra Leone in History and Tradition.* London: Witherby, 1936.

Caldecott, Alfred. *The Church in the West Indies.* London: 1898; reprint ed., London: Frank Cass & Co., Ltd., 1971.

Cantlie, Neil. *A History of the Army Medical Department.* 2 vols. Edinburgh and London: Churchill Livingston, 1974.

Carter, Henry R. *Yellow Fever: An Epidemiological and Historical Study of Its Place of Origin.* Baltimore: Williams & Wilkins Co., 1931.

Caulfield, James E. *One Hundred Years' History of the Second Battalion, West India Regiment, from date of raising, 1795-1895.* London: Foster Groom & Co., 1899.

Chichester, Henry, and George Burges-Short. *The Records and Badges of Every Regiment and Corps in the British Army.* London: Gale and Polden, Ltd., 1902.

Clode, Charles M. *The Military Forces of the Crown: Their Administration and Government.* 2 vols. London: John Murray, 1869.

Cobbett, W. *The Parliamentary History of England.* vols. 31-35.

Coke, Thomas. *A History of the West Indies.* 3 vols. London: 1808-1811; reprint ed., London: Cass & Co., Ltd., 1971.

———. *An Account of the Rise, Progress and Present State of the Methodist Missions.* London: George Story, 1804.

Collier, Richard. *The Great Indian Mutiny: A Dramatic Account of the Sepoy Rebellion.* New York: E. P. Dutton & Co., Inc., 1964.

Coombs, Orde, ed. *Is Massa Day Dead? Black Moods in the Caribbean.* Garden City, N.Y.: Anchor/Doubleday, 1974.

Coupland, Reginald. *The British Anti-Slavery Movement.* Oxford: Oxford University Press, 1933; reprint ed., London: Frank Cass & Co., Ltd., 1964.

Crooks, J. J. *A History of the Colony of Sierra Leone, Western Africa.* Dublin: Brown and Nolan, Ltd., 1903.

Cundall, Frank. *The Governors of Jamaica in the Seventeenth Century.* London: The West India Committee, 1936.

Curtin, Philip D. *Africa Remembered: Narratives by West Africans from the Era of the Slave Trade.* Madison: University of Wisconsin Press, 1967.

———. *The Atlantic Slave Trade: A Census.* Madison: University of Wisconsin Press, 1969.

———. *Two Jamaicas: The Role of Ideas in a Tropical Colony, 1830–1865.* New York: Atheneum, 1970.

Curtis, Edward. *The Organization of the British Army in the American Revolution.* New Haven: Yale University Press, 1926.

Dallas, R. C. *The History of the Maroons.* 2 vols. London: A. Straham, 1803.

Das, Shiva Tosh. *Indian Military: Its History and Development.* New Delhi: Sagar Publications, 1969.

Davis, David B. *The Problem of Slavery in the Age of Revolution, 1770–1823.* Ithaca: Cornell University Press, 1975.

Davis, Gregson. *Antigua Black: Portrait of an Island People.* San Francisco: Scrimshaw Press, 1973.

Davy, John. *West Indies Before and Since Slave Emancipation.* London: W. and F. G. Cash, 1854.

Dodwell, H. H., ed. *The Cambridge History of India.* 6 vols. Cambridge: Cambridge University Press, 1932.

[Dundas, Henry]. *Facts Relative to the Conduct of the War in the West Indies.* London: J. Owen, 1796.

Edwards, Bryan. *An Historical Survey of the Island of Saint Domingo.* London: John Stockdale, 1801.

Ellis, Alfred B. *The History of the First West India Regiment.* London: Chapman and Hall Ltd., 1885.

Everard, H. *History of Thoˢ Farrington's Regiment Subsequently Designated the 29th (Worcestershire) Foot, 1694–1891.* Worcester: Littlebury & Co., 1891.

Fortescue, John W. *A History of the British Army.* 13 vols. London: Macmillan & Co., Ltd., 1899–1930.

———. *The British Army, 1783–1802.* London: Macmillan & Co., Ltd., 1905.

———, ed. *Calendar of State Papers, Colonial Series, America and West Indies.* London: Mackie & Co., Ltd., 1903.

Fyfe, Christopher. *History of Sierra Leone.* Oxford: Clarendon Press, 1962.

Gardner, William. *A History of Jamaica.* London: T. Fisher Unwin, 1909.

Genovese, Eugene D. *Roll, Jordan, Roll: The World the Slaves Made.* New York: Random House, 1972.

George, Claude. *The Rise of British West Africa.* London: 1904; reprint ed., London: Frank Cass & Co., Ltd., 1968.

Glover, Richard. *Peninsular Preparation: The Reform of the British Army, 1795-1809.* Cambridge: Cambridge University Press, 1963.

Goveia, Elsa. *Chapters in Caribbean History.* Barbados: Caribbean University Press, 1970.

———. *Slave Society in the British Leeward Islands at the End of the Eighteenth Century.* New Haven: Yale University Press, 1965.

Great Britain, *Parliamentary Papers* (Commons), vol. 10. "Papers relating to Recruiting Depot on the Coast of Africa" (no. 370), 1812.

Great Britain, *Parliamentary Papers* (Commons), vol. 12. "Papers relating to Captured Negroes enlisted, and recruiting of Negroe Soldiers in Africa, for the West India Regiments" (no. 345), 1813-1814.

Great Britain, *Sessional Papers* (Commons), vol. 19. "Order sent to the Colonies for emancipating the Slaves belonging to the Crown" (no. 305), 1831.

Great Britain, War Office. *Army Lists, 1795-1816.*

Great Britain, War Office. *General Regulations and Orders for the Army,* 1816, 1822.

Great Britain, War Office. *Manual of Military Law,* 1914.

Great Britain, War Office. *Regulations for the use of His Majesty's Troops upon their arrival in the West Indies,* 1795.

Hansard, T. C. *The Parliamentary Debates.* First Series, vols. 3, 7, 8.

Harlow, Vincent, and Frederick Madden, eds. *British Colonial Developments, 1774-1834: Select Documents.* Oxford: Clarendon Press, 1953.

Hazard, Samuel. *Santo Domingo: Past and Present.* London and New York: 1873.

Horowitz, Michael, ed. *Peoples and Cultures of the Caribbean: An Anthropological Reader.* Garden City, New York: The Natural History Press, 1971.

Jackson, Robert. *A Treatise on the Fevers of Jamaica.* London: 1791.

James, Charles. *An Universal Military Dictionary in English and French.* 4th ed. London: T. Egerton, 1816.

James, C. L. R. *The Black Jacobins: Toussaint L'Ouverture and the San Domingo Revolution,* rev. 2nd ed. New York: Vintage Books, Alfred Knopf, Inc., 1963.

Jeffery, Reginald W., ed. *Dyott's Diary, 1781-1845: A Selection From the Journal of William Dyott, Sometime General in the British Army and Aide-de-Camp to His Majesty King George III.* 2 vols. London: A. Constable & Co., Ltd., 1971.

Johnson, John J., ed. *The Role of the Military in Underdeveloped Countries.* Princeton: Princeton University Press, 1962.

[Johnstone, Andrew Cochrane]. *Correspondence between the Hon. Col. Cochrane Johnstone and the Departments of the Commander in Chief and Judge Advocate General.* London: J. Barfield, 1805.

———. *Defence of the Honourable Andrew Cochrane Johnstone.* London: J. Barfield, 1805.

Leach, J. *Rough Sketches of the Life of an Old Soldier.* London: Longman, Rees, Orme, Brown and Green, 1831.

Jourdan, Winthrop. *White Over Black: American Attitudes Towards the Negro, 1550-1812.* Baltimore: Penguin Books Inc., 1969.

Keen, Benjamin, ed. *Readings in Latin-American Civilization: 1492 to the Present.* Boston: Houghton Mifflin Co., 1955.

Klein, Herbert S. *Slavery in the Americas: A Comparative Study of Virginia and Cuba.* Chicago: Quadrangle Books, 1971.

Klingberg, Frank. *The Anti-Slavery Movement in England: A Study in English Humanitarianism.* New Haven: Yale University Press, 1926; reprint ed., New York: Archon Books, 1968.

Knight, Franklin W. *Slave Society in Cuba During the Nineteenth Century.* Madison: University of Wisconsin Press, 1974.

Kuczynski, Robert. *Demographic Survey of the British Colonial Empire.* 3 vols. London: Oxford University Press, 1948-1953.

Lawson, Cecil C. P. *A History of the Uniforms of the British Army.* 4 vols. New York: A. S. Barnes & Co., 1970.

Leith, Andrew Hay, ed. *Memoirs of the Late Lt.-General Sir James Leith.* London: William Stockdale, 1818.

Lefever, Ernest W. *Spear and Scepter: Army, Police and Politics in Tropical Africa.* Washington, D.C.: The Brookings Institution, 1970.

Lewis, Gordon. *The Growth of the Modern West Indies.* New York: Monthly Review Press, 1968.

Lewis, Roy, and Foy, Yvonne. *The British in Africa.* London: Weidenfeld and Nicolson, 1971.

Little, Kenneth. *Negroes in Britain: A Study of Racial Relations in English Society.* London: Keegan, Paul, Trench, Trubner & Co., Ltd., 1947.

Luckham, Robin. *The Nigerian Military: A Sociological Analysis of Authority and Revolt, 1960-1967.* Cambridge: Cambridge University Press, 1971.

Mackesy, Piers. *The War for America, 1775-1783.* Cambridge, Mass.: Harvard University Press, 1965.

Manning, Helen Taft. *British Colonial Government After the American Revolution: 1782-1820.* New Haven: Yale University Press, 1933.

Mathieson, William Law. *British Slavery and its Abolition, 1823-1838.* London: Longman, Green & Co., Ltd., 1926; reprint ed., New York: Octagon Books, Inc., 1967.

Meek, C. K. *The Northern Tribes of Nigeria.* 2 vols. London: Oxford University Press, 1925; reprint ed., New York: Negro Universities Press, 1969.

Milne, Samuel M. *The Standards and Colours of the Army from the Restoration, 1661, to the Introduction of the Territorial System, 1881.* Leeds: Goodall and Suddeck, 1893.

Murray, D. J. *The West Indies and the Development of Colonial Government, 1801-1834.* Oxford: Clarendon Press, 1965.

Newbolt, Henry. *The Story of the Oxfordshire and Buckinghamshire Light Infantry.* London: Country Life and George Newnes, Ltd., 1915.

Oman, Carola. *Sir John Moore.* London: Hodder & Stoughton, 1953.

Oman, Charles. *Wellington's Army, 1809–1814*. London: Edward Arnold, 1913.

Ott, Thomas O. *The Haitian Revolution, 1789–1804*. Knoxville: University of Tennessee Press, 1973.

Owen, Christopher. *The Rhodesian African Rifles*. London: Leo Cooper, Ltd., 1970.

Palmer, R. R. *The Age of the Democratic Revolutions*. 2 vols. Princeton: Princeton University Press, 1959–1964.

Pares, Richard. *War and Trade in the West Indies, 1739–1763*. Oxford: Oxford University Press, 1936; reprint ed., London: Frank Cass & Co., Ltd., 1963.

Patterson, Orlando. *The Sociology of Slavery: An Analysis of the Origins, Development and Structure of Negro Slave Society in Jamaica*. Rutherford, N.J.: Fairleigh Dickinson University Press, 1969.

Pinckard, George. *Notes on the West Indies: Written during the Expeditions under the Command of the late General Sir Ralph Abercromby*. 3 vols. London: Longman, Hurst, Rees and Orme, 1806.

Pipes, Daniel, "The Origins of Islamic Military Slavery." Unpubl. Ph.D. diss., Harvard University, 1978.

Porter, Dale. *The Abolition of the Slave Trade in England, 1784–1807*. Hamden, Conn.: Archon Books, 1970.

Powell, Geoffrey. *The Kandyan Wars*. London: Leo Cooper, 1973.

Poyer, John. *The History of Barbados*. London: Mawman, 1808; reprint ed., London: Frank Cass & Co., Ltd., 1971.

Price, Richard, ed. *Maroon Societies: Rebel Slave Communities in the Americas*. Garden City, N.Y.: Anchor-Doubleday, 1973.

Ragatz, Lowell J. *The Fall of the Planter Class in the British Caribbean, 1763–1833: A Study in Social and Economic History*. New York: Appleton-Century-Crofts, 1928; reprint ed., New York: Octagon Books, 1971.

Rose, J. Holland. *William Pitt and the Great War*. London: G. Bell & Sons, Ltd., 1912.

Rudin, Harry. *Germans in the Cameroons, 1884–1914: A Case Study in Modern Imperialism*. New York: Archon Books, 1968.

Ryan, Selwyn D. *Race and Nationalism in Trinidad and Tobago: A Study in Decolonization in a Multiracial Society*. Toronto: University of Toronto Press, 1972.

Sanderlin, George, ed. and trans. *Bartolmé de Las Casas: A Selection of His Writings*. New York: Alfred A. Knopf, 1971.

Schomburgh, Robert H. *The History of Barbados*. London: Longman, Brown and Green, 1848; reprint ed., London: Frank Cass & Co., Ltd., 1971.

Scobie, I. H. Mackay. *An Old Highland Fencible Corps*. London: William Blackwood & Sons, 1914.

Scott, Robert B. *The Military Law of England*. London: T. Goddard, 1810.

Smelser, Marshall. *The Campaign for the Sugar Islands, 1759: A Study in Amphibious Warfare*. Chapel Hill: University of North Carolina Press, 1955.

[Smith, Hamilton]. *Costume of the Army of the British Empire*. London: W. Bulmer, 1815.

Smith, Robert A. *Eighteenth Century English Politics.* New York: Holt, Rinehart and Winston, Inc., 1972.

Stedman, J. C. *Narrative of a Five Years' Expedition Against the Revolted Negroes of Surinam, 1772-1777.* London: 1796.

Stephens, Leslie, and Sidney Lee, eds. *Dictionary of National Biography.* 28 vols. London, 1921-1959.

Stewart, J. *A View of the Past and Present State of the Island of Jamaica.* Edinburgh: Oliver and Boyd, 1823.

Swift, Jonathan. *The Conduct of the Allies.* London: John Morphew, 1711.

Sypher, Wylie. *Guinea's Captive Kings: British Anti-Slavery Literature of the XVIIIth Century.* University of North Carolina Press, 1942; reprint ed., New York: Octagon Books, 1969.

Taylor, S. A. G. *The Western Design: An Account of Cromwell's Expedition to the Caribbean.* Kingston, Jamaica: The Institute of Jamaica and the Jamaica Historical Society, 1965.

Theal, George McCall. *History and Ethnography of Africa South of the Zambesi.* 3 vols. London: Allen & Unwin, Ltd., 1922.

Thorpe, Robert. *A Reply 'Point by Point' to the Special Report of the Directors of the African Institution.* London, 1815.

Ward, Stephen G. P. *Faithful: The Story of the Durham Light Infantry.* London: Thomas Nelson, 1963.

Watson, J. Steven. *The Reign of George III, 1760-1815.* Oxford: Oxford University Press, 1960.

Watteville, H. de. *The British Soldier: His Daily Life from Tudor to Modern Times.* London: J. M. Dent & Sons Ltd., 1954.

Wellington, Duke of, ed. *Supplementary Despatches, Correspondence and Memoranda of Field Marshall Arthur Duke of Wellington, K.G.* 15 vols. London: John Murray, 1858-1872.

Western, J. R. *The English Militia in the Eighteenth Century.* Toronto: University of Toronto Press, 1965.

Wilberforce, Robert and Samuel, eds. *The Correspondence of William Wilberforce.* 2 vols. Philadelphia: Henry Perkins, 1841.

Wilkinson-Latham, Robert and Christopher. *Infantry Uniforms: Including Artillery and other Supporting Troops of Britain and the Commonwealth, 1742-1855.* London: Blandford Press, 1969.

Williams, Eric. *Capitalism and Slavery.* New York: Capricorn Books, 1966.

————. *From Columbus to Castro: The History of the Caribbean, 1492-1969.* New York: Harper & Row, 1970.

————, ed. *Documents on British West Indian History, 1807-1833.* Port-of-Spain: Trinidad Publishing Co., Ltd., 1952.

Winks, Robin. *The Blacks in Canada: A History.* New Haven: Yale University Press, 1971.

Wright, John B. *Bushman Raiders of the Drakensberg, 1840-1870.* Pietermaritzburg: University of Natal Press, 1971.

Young, William A. *The West India Common-Place Book.* London: Mcmillan, 1807.

Articles

Anon. "Mr. Urban, April 10." *The Gentleman's Magazine.* 85 (January to June 1815):295–96.

———. "The Mutiny of the 8th West India Regiment from the Papers of a Veteran Officer." *United Service Magazine.* (October 1851), no. 275, pp. 207–09.

———. "A Further Account of the Mutiny of the 8th West India Regiment." *United Service Magazine.* (November 1851), no. 276, pp. 399–401.

Buckley, Roger N. "The Destruction of the British Army in the West Indies, 1793–1815: A Medical History." *Journal of the Society for Army Historical Research,* forthcoming.

———, ed. "Brigadier General Thomas Hislop's Remarks on the Establishment of the West India Regiments—1801." *Journal of the Society for Army Historical Research,* forthcoming.

Carman, W. Y. "Infantry Clothing Regulations, 1802." *Journal of the Society for Army Historical Research* 19 (1940):200–35.

Childs, St. Julien. "Sir George Baker and the Dry Belly-Ache." *Bulletin of the History of Medicine* 44 (1970):213–40.

Elkins, W. F. "A Source of Black Nationalism in the Caribbean: The Revolt of the British West Indies Regiment at Taranto, Italy." *Science and Society* 34, no. 9 (Spring 1970):99–103.

Fisher, Allan C. "Rhodesia, A House Divided." *National Geographic* 147 (May 1975):640–71.

Gilbert, Arthur N. "An Analysis of Some Eighteenth Century Army Recruiting Records." *Journal of the Society for Army Historical Research* 54, no. 217 (Spring 1976):38–47.

Hall, Douglas. "Incalculability as a Feature of Sugar Production during the Eighteenth Century." *Social and Economic Studies* 10 (1961):340–52.

Handler, Jerome S., ed. "'Memoirs of An Old Army Officer'—Richard A. Wyvill's Visits to Barbados in 1796 and 1806–7." *Journal of the Barbados Museum and Historical Society* 35 (March 1975).

Joseph, C. L. "The British West Indies Regiment, 1914–1918." *Journal of Caribbean History* 2 (May 1971):94–124.

Kup, A. P. "Alexander Lindsay, 6th Earl of Balcarres, Lieutenant Governor of Jamaica, 1794–1801." *Bulletin of the John Rylands University Library* 57 (1974–75):327–65.

Lawson, Cecil C. P., et al. "Military Dress: West India Regiments, 1800–1810." *Military Collector and Historian* 20, no. 4:119–20.

Lipscomb, Patrick. "William Pitt and the Abolition Question: A Review of an Historical Controversy." *Proceedings of the Leeds Philosophical and Literary Society* 12 (June 1966-April 1968):87–127.

Orr, G. M. "The Origin of the West India Regiment." *Journal of the Royal United Service Institution* (February 1927):129–36.

Patterson, McLeod, and William Jernigan. "Lead Intoxication from 'Moonshine.'" *GP* 40 (October 1969):126–30.

Tylden, G. "The Ceylon Regiments, 1796 to 1874." *Journal of the Society for Army Historical Research* 30 (1952):124–28.

——. "The West India Regiments, 1795 to 1927, and from 1958." *Journal of the Society for Army Historical Research* 40 (March, 1962):42–49.

Ukpabi, Samson C. "Military Recruitment and Social Mobility in Nineteenth Century British West Africa." *Journal of African Studies* 2 (Spring, 1975): 87–107.

Newspapers

Cornwall Chronicle (Jamaica)
The Dairy and Kingston (Jamaica) *Daily Advertiser*
Dominica Journal or *Weekly Intelligencer*
London Gazette
The Port-of-Spain (Trinidad) *Gazette*
The Royal Gazette (Jamaica)
St. Jago Gazette (Jamaica)
The Tobago Gazette

INDEX

Abercromby, Sir Ralph, 34, 92; use of slave ranger corps, 14–15; authorized to purchase slaves, 53; manumission, 70; military operations, 88–92; permanency of West India Regiments, 94; strategic role for West India Regiments, 95

Abolition, British: political significance, 41; reasons for delay of, 57–62, 171–72*n*67; suddenness, 62; effect on recruitment in Africa, 130–34

Abolition Act, *1807*, 60, 62, 78, 130, 152

Adams, Private James, 116

Addington, H., 72, 77–78

African Recruiting Establishment, 131, 132–33, 135

Alcoholism, 100–02, 103–04, 181*n*78

Alderly, Private Samuel, 116

American Revolution, 3, 4, 12, 22, 43, 99, 101; impact on metropolitan-colonial relations, 40, 80

Angola, 154

Angus's Black Rangers, 90

Anstey, Roger, 56, 171*n*60

Antigua, 4, 14, 108

Arcahaye, St. Domingo, 86

Arima, Trinidad, 136

Army, British: problems of white recruitment, 2–4; periodic strength, 3, 9, 121, 168*n*20; clothing shortage, 3, 121–23; criminals, 3, 136; casualties/health, 3–4, 11, 97, 99–105, 121, 160*n*22; slave pioneers, 4, 10, 126, 135, 167*n*93; British Establishment, 20, 93, 94, 114; cost of commissions, 22; ratio of black to white troops, 30, 69; officer absenteeism, 32–34; officers, 34–35, 132; foreigners,

49, 50–51, 87, 121, 135–36, 169*n*29; Army Extraordinaries, 55; troop augmentations and reductions, 60, 79–80; governance, 63–81 passim; uniform, 83–84, 93, 97, 98, 122–23; Light Brigade, 92–93; impact of insurgent war on, 92–94; police function, 100; dispersion of regiments, 108, 183*n*17; illiteracy, 111, 119; mutinies, 117, 141, 142; relations with slaves, 124; white civilian labor, 127; regiments as labor corps, 127–28; pay, 128, 163*n*12, 182*n*82; hired slaves, 128–29, 53–62, 150–55, 187*n*96; African colonial forces, 131, 132 (table), 140–41, 143, 144, 189*n*44; agent of reform, 142, 190*n*6; plans to raise corps of non-whites, 173*n*85; cantonment system, 183*n*17. *See also* Fencibles; Militia, metropolitan; Ranger (Jaeger) Corps; Regiments, European; West India Regiments

Army, Dutch, 174*n*21

Army, French, 10, 11–12, 38, 159*n*11

Army, United States, 94

Army List, 15, 19, 30–31; *1796*, 21, 30–31; *1797*, 30; *1798*, 30; *1799*, 30; *1807*, 153

Ashanti (ethnic group), 96

Ashanti War (*1823*), 96

Asiegbu, Johnson, 131, 133–34

Askaris, 141, 142, 144, 189*n*44

Bahama Garrison Company, 137

Bahamas, 9, 69, 153

Baillie, Private Charles, 116

Balcarres, Earl, 29, 87; recruiting the Sixth West India Regiment, 43–52 passim